LEADERSHIP REPORT

1998

KEY ISSUES SHAPING THE FUTURE OF HEALTH CARE

Alden Solovy, Editor

press

AMERICAN HOSPITAL PUBLISHING, INC.
An American Hospital Association Company
CHICAGO

This publication is designed to provide accurate and authoritative information in regard to the subject matter covered. It is sold with the understanding that neither the author nor the publisher is engaged in rendering legal, accounting, or other professional service. If legal advice or other expert assistance is required, the services of a competent professional should be sought.

The views expressed in this publication are strictly those of the authors and do not necessarily represent official positions of the American Hospital Association.

Cover design by Andrea Federle-Bucsi

Library of Congress Cataloging-in-Publication Data
The hospitals & health networks leadership report : key issues shaping
   the future of health care / edited by Alden Solovy
        p.   cm.
   Includes bibliographical references and index.
   1. Health services administration—United States. 2. Health
services administration—United States—Statistics. I. Solovy,
Alden T.
   [DNLM: 1. Health Facilities—organization & administration.
   2. Partnership Practice—organization & administration. 3. Delivery
of Health Care, Integrated—organization & administration.
   4. Interprofessional Relations. WX 150 H834 1998]
RA971.H582 1988
362. 1'1'068—dc21
DNLM/DLC
for Library of Congress   97-46585
                                                                          CIP

ISBN: 1-55648-216-7   Item Number: 108100

For Ami

CONTENTS

ABOUT THE EDITOR

Alden Solovy is executive editor of *Hospitals & Health Networks,* a widely published author, and a frequent speaker on the evolution of the health care economy. He has written three books, and edited another, on health care finance and strategy. Prior to joining the magazine, Solovy served as director of market and business analysis for Premier, Inc., and as a consultant in capital finance for Health Facilities Corp., where he specialized in capital planning and debt transactions. He has assisted in more than $500 million in hospital financings. Solovy holds two master's degrees: an MBA from the University of Chicago, where he specialized in economics and finance and conducted research into hospital closure; and a master's in public affairs journalism from the University of Illinois at Springfield, where he specialized in state education funding policy. His writing and reporting have been recognized by the Illinois Press Association, the Chicago Headline Club, and the American Society of Business Press Editors. Solovy has overall responsibility for the content and quality of *Hospitals & Health Networks.*

CONTRIBUTORS

Jon Asplund is a staff writer for *AHA News,* where he covers health care finance, business issues, insurance, stocks, and information technology. Prior to joining *AHA News,* Asplund was a managing editor of three community newspapers at Pioneer Press in the suburban Chicago area. He earned his bachelor's degree in journalism from the University of Illinois in 1988.

Jan Greene is a contributing writer for *Hospitals & Health Networks.* Prior to joining the magazine, Greene covered health and medicine for the Las Vegas (Nev.) *Review-Journal* and was a reporter covering politics and environment for the San Luis Obispo (Calif.) *Telegram-Tribune.* She has also reported from Washington, D.C., on environmental issues for the Bureau of National Affairs, Inc., and Fairchild Publications. Greene has written a book on the politics and science of pesticide regulation and coauthored two others on environmental issues.

Kevin Lumsdon is managing editor of *Hospitals & Health Networks.* Lumsdon joined the magazine in 1991 and has held various writing and editing posts. He has written extensively about operations improvement and management issues. Prior to joining the magazine, Lumsdon was editor of *Healthcare Financial Management.* He received his master's degree in magazine journalism from Syracuse University in 1988. Lumsdon has more than 15 years of experience as a writer and editor in health care and education.

Harris Meyer is a senior writer at *Hospitals & Health Networks.* A health care reporter since 1983, Meyer has received numerous journalism awards for his work, including both the first prize in 1996 and second prize in 1997 from the National Institute for Health Care Management. He previously served as national reporter at *American Medical News.* Meyer has also reported for United Press International and NBC-TV. His articles have appeared in the *Boston Globe, Los Angeles Times,* and *Chicago Tribune.*

Christopher Serb is a staff writer for *Hospitals & Health Networks,* where he covers information technology, business issues, and other topics. Prior to joining the staff, Serb worked at *North Shore* magazine, Winnetka, Ill., and the *American Banker* in Washington, D.C. He earned a bachelor's degree in English from the College of the Holy Cross in 1992, and a master's degree in journalism from Northwestern University in 1995. Prior to graduate school, Serb worked for two years as an employment counselor for homeless Atlantans.

Margaret F. Schulte, DBA, FACHE, is vice president for research and development with American Hospital Publishing, Inc., Chicago, and adjunct professor with the Health Care Management program of the Keller Graduate School of Management, Chicago, where she teaches policy and ethics. She previously served as director of education with the Health Care Financial Management Association, Westchester, Ill. Schulte cofounded and served on the faculty of Mercer University's Graduate Program in Health Care Policy and Administration, Atlanta, where she taught ethics for four years and served as consultant to the Mercer University School of Medicine Faculty Practice Plan. During and prior to this time, Schulte worked as a consultant to hospitals and physician practices for more than 10 years. Earlier in her career, she served as director of development for Health Group, Inc., an Atlanta-based for-profit hospital company; as Director of Certificate of Need for the state of West Virginia; and as associate administrator of Our Lady of the Way Hospital in Martin, Ky. She earned her DBA from Nova Southeastern University, Fort Lauderdale, where her research focused on management ethics in health care.

Reid Sunseri is the research director at American Hospital Publishing, Inc., where he performs health care research for *Hospitals & Health Networks* and other AHPI publications. He has previous research experience at the Illinois Hospital & HealthSystems Association, the University of Illinois Institute of Government and Policy Analysis, and the American Medical Association. He earned his master's degree in economics from the University of Illinois at Chicago in 1995.

FOREWORD

The art of progress is to preserve order amid change and to preserve change amid order.
—Alfred North Whitehead

The way of progress is neither swift nor easy.
—Marie Curie

The notion of progress frightens some people and excites others. For me, it's a little bit of both. I've found that by getting together and sharing ideas of progress with colleagues I respect and trust, the fears diminish and the excitement builds. This book provides a forum for health care leaders to get together and say what kind of progress they want.

Health care inevitably progresses, but not always in a straight line. Most apparent is the progress we all expect in the tangible business of delivering health care and ensuring that delivery systems are financially viable. More subtle, but possibly more important, is the progress in the more abstract conceptions of health care, such as policy, strategy, and ethics. When it comes time to assess the progress we've made, *The* Hospitals & Health Networks *Leadership Report* will be an invaluable aid for locating ourselves on the serpentine line of progress. It's a road map of progress, really, and if we're all looking at the same map—even if we're in different boardrooms and different offices in different cities—progress will be a *little* swifter, a *little* easier.

If this book represents a form of virtual collaboration for health care leaders across the United States, the process of making the book took collaboration of a more concrete variety. Three AHPI departments—market research, editorial, and the books team—pooled their resources to come up with one unique resource. From drafting survey questions and analyzing data to writing the chapters and typesetting the pages, every step of the way was a collaborative effort. Moreover, all of these various tasks were handled in-house by the talented staff of AHPI. *The* Hospitals & Health Networks *Leadership Report* is a milestone in my tenure as publisher of AHPI, and I am proud of the book for reasons that go beyond its usefulness as a tool for health care leaders. It truly embodies our mission: Improving health through information.

Michael Springer
Publisher and CEO
American Hospital Publishing, Inc.

PREFACE

As the health care field continues to develop in unanticipated directions, the level of anxiety among its business leaders has reached a plateau. The executives steering the course of hospitals, managed care organizations, and medical groups recognize that clinical advances, new payment structures, and policy shifts will continue to proliferate. Some have further recognized that this climate does not reward or even tolerate lone rangers. Instead, collaboration is the skill that gets results.

This book represents an unprecedented industrywide collaboration, a virtual symposium on the state of health care in America. More than 700 executives give their candid, considered opinions on the issues they face every day:
- strategic readiness
- partnerships
- quality
- physician relations
- policy
- information technology
- business ethics

Only *Hospitals & Health Networks,* the flagship publication of the American Hospital Association, a magazine whose history spans more than 75 years, has undertaken a survey so ambitious in concept and comprehensive in scope. This book delivers a package of information invaluable to strategic leaders who base budget, policy, and staff decisions on a realistic appraisal of the environment in which they operate and who themselves shape that environment as their organizations grow and change.

The goal of the *Hospitals & Health Networks* Leadership Survey is to view, examine, and analyze the American health care landscape in all its variety—institutions large and small, for-profits and not-for-profits from every part of the country. Executives cooperated by sharing their experience, their knowledge, and their apprehensions and aspirations; and an expert team of writers has processed the information into a series of thoughtful and reasoned analyses.

The Hospitals & Health Networks *Leadership Report 1998* does not stop with expert analysis. It also presents the data from the survey in a clear format, so that health care executives can make their own analysis and draw their own conclusions. Each health care facility is unique, and while collaboration is essential, uniformity is not a viable mind-set. Executives and decision makers can view the rankings of 21 separate strategic issues, from "commitment to mission" to "competitive pricing," broken down by type of institution, tax status, and region. Survey respondents ranked these issues in two ways, preparedness and importance, on a scale of 1 to 5; and the difference between these numbers is called the "strategic gap."

Interpretation of the *Hospitals & Health Networks* Leadership Survey depends on perspective. Executives from hospitals reveal their anxiety about the future, but also acknowledge that they are key players in current and future collaborations. Executives from managed care organizations feel more confident, but they also bear the responsibility for the rapid pace of change. And executives from physician group practices sometimes feel ill equipped for the financial and managerial tasks they face, yet they know that their medical skills are a permanently valuable resource. The coming years will undoubtedly bring surprises and fluctuations, and the balance of power will undoubtedly shift. As hospitals, managed care organizations, and physician group practices continue to interact not only as competitors but as collaborative partners, solid information on the health care environment will help keep everybody focused and responsible.

ACKNOWLEDGMENTS

Book acknowledgments often seem like a run-on Academy Awards acceptance speech. In the excitement of the moment, the recipient babbles on about colleagues, friends, and family. "Just get on with it," the audience thinks. But the recipient knows the depth of gratitude owed to others and, in joy and respect for their contributions, forces a few moments of homage on the assembled crowd.

This book is a prize of its own variety: a reward for hard work and imagination. My name is on the cover—on the award, if you will—but this project needed the dedication of many people. So, for just a moment, let me play Tom Hanks—or Jodi Foster, if you prefer—and ask you to recognize the efforts of some truly talented people.

Thank you to Mary Grayson for her work on survey conceptualization, development, and interpretation. Thank you to the chapter authors for their work integrating survey results with analysis. Many chapter authors served in multiple roles. Jan Greene wrote the original *Hospitals & Health Networks* cover story. Kevin Lumsdon and Margaret Schulte served on the survey development team. Kevin also assisted in editing several chapters. A special thanks to Reid Sunseri, who was instrumental to this project: He participated in survey conceptualization and development; he was responsible for survey implementation and conducted statistical analyses; he assisted in interpretation; and he reviewed every data table and read each chapter in this book for consistency with the results. Any error or shortcomings with this book are entirely mine.

This volume represents our first opinion-focused data resource, fusing in-house research and analysis with easy-to-read data tables. It took a willingness to experiment with a new production process. For this, thanks to John Ford, Marty Wietzel, and Peggy DuMais.

Thank you to the staff of AHA Press, and especially Mark Swartz, project editor. Mark is a skilled editor and writer, and he shared this talent liberally in this endeavor. Thanks to Jennifer Moorhouse for her dogged determination to keep the project on track.

I owe a special debt of gratitude to Rick Hill, senior editor, for his effort, his faith in the project, and the gentle wisdom he brings to everything he does.

Alden Solovy
Executive Editor
Hospitals & Health Networks

Introduction

Alden Solovy and Reid Sunseri

How many books, articles, and speeches begin something like this: "The U.S. health care system is in a period of tremendous change, and there's no sign of any let-up"? Change is the refrain heard throughout the industry, and the pace of change in health care has yielded a multi-million dollar consulting industry. *Preparing for changing. Leadership during change. Change management.* The forecasters and pundits who talk about change often seem to make the whole thing seem so neat and tidy. So predictable. They say things like "There are five steps in a change process" and "Change begins with leadership."

THE BOILING POINT

In the real world, change is messy. There are unintended consequences of plans and strategies. Competitors and customers react in unpredictable fashion. Then there's that pesky economy, which just seems to go its own way no matter what. Indeed, trying to control change is like trying to control boiling water. At low levels of heat, you can produce a low, relatively steady boil. Turn up the heat and convection kicks in. The boil is wild and erratic, calm in some places and furious in others, with waves and bubbles swinging unpredictably about.[1] In health care, the heat is on high.

Let's be honest. Most of us are sick and tired of thinking about change. We'd like to see the heat turned down so we can get a bit of a break. Fat chance. The pace of change is getting faster and faster. One overarching issue driving change: the high cost of care. Market economics, as well as investors and venture capitalists, are forcing new dynamics into health care financing. Consumers are demanding change as a result of spotty quality and limitations on access. Employers are also concerned about cost, but they, too, are increasingly concerned about quality, access, and coordination in the system. Meanwhile, technological advances are pushing both the limits of our life spans and our comfort with medical ethics. And all this change seems to have left the most vulnerable people behind. In spite of the new economics of health care, the number of uninsured in soaring.[2]

Perhaps it's better that the heat has been turned up. Consider the frog. If you place a frog in boiling water, it'll try to escape. Place the same frog in water at room temperature, and gradually turn up the heat, and it becomes groggy. "The frog's internal apparatus for sensing threats to survival is geared to sudden changes in his environment, not to slow, gradual changes," notes Peter Senge.[3] In fact, the frog becomes so groggy that it allows itself to be boiled to death without a struggle. Well, the rapid boil in the health care industry has certainly gotten our attention. But there are subtler changes, little bubbles forming under the surface as yet undetected, that may one day roar to another unpredictable boil. As Senge suggests, the most obvious forces today may not be the most important ones tomorrow.

THE LEADERSHIP SURVEY

Enter the *Hospitals & Health Networks* Leadership Survey. Our goal: to find out what's bubbling just beneath the surface of health care, to identify the strategic challenges facing the industry. That, in fact, is an enormous task, because you can't successfully examine the undercurrents of change without simultaneously looking at hospitals, managed care organizations (MCOs), and physicians. Yet in spite of all the polling that's done in health care, there seemed to be a huge gap in the executive opinion research. No one, until now, had devised a nationwide survey of senior executives from all three components of integrated delivery. Certainly, there have been many separate opinion surveys, but there was no instrument for comparing how leaders of hospitals, MCOs, and physicians view the same critical issues. Our survey would be the first.

The editors of *Hospitals & Health Networks* and American Hospital Publishing's Market Research team developed a list of key issues facing both individual health care entities and the overall organization and structure of the national health care enterprise. We narrowed the list to eight major topics: finance, information technology, integration and partnerships, medical and business ethics, physician relationships, policy, strategy, and quality. Then we started brainstorming questions. Hundreds and hundreds of questions. It was turning out to be the survey monster that wouldn't die. So, as always in this sort of endeavor, we had to make some choices.

In keeping with the pioneering spirit of the survey, we favored questions that were relatively unexplored in the industry. So we reviewed scores of executive opinion surveys in an attempt to eliminate questions that had more thorough research more readily available. We found that the most interesting and unexplored financing questions were tied to quality. How, for instance, did leaders view the effects of various financing techniques—such as capitation and global case rates—on quality? As a result, we integrated our questions about finance into the other sections of the survey. We also found the questions on strategy asked in previous surveys to be incomplete. Some surveys ask what health care executives think their strategies for the future will be, while other surveys ask executives to identify their key concerns for the future. Until now, no survey has attempted to combine ratings of strategic importance with an executive assessment of how ready their organizations are to handle these changes. It's a concept we call the "strategic gap."

The "Strategic Gap"

Because strategy is key to ensuring survival, the survey asked leaders of hospitals, MCOs, and physician groups to rate the importance of 21 different issues, ranging from strategic issues such as partnering and direct contracting to organizational tactics such as educating the board and finding qualified senior managers. The respondents were asked to rate these issues on a scale of 1 to 5, from extremely unimportant to extremely important. We then asked participants to rate how prepared they feel their institutions are to handle those issues, using the same scale—1 to 5, extremely unprepared to extremely prepared. By using the same scale, we are able to compare their assessments of the importance of a strategy with their readiness to address it. The difference is the strategic gap. Along with the 21 industrywide strategic and tactical issues, we used this technique to examine executive opinions of four specific information technologies and four types of partnership arrangements.

We express this gap as either a positive or a negative number. Negative numbers signify that readiness to address an issue is less than the importance of that issue; in other words, a strategic deficit. For instance, suppose an executive rated information technology "somewhat important" to the success of the organization (a 4 rating), and also pegged the institution at "somewhat unprepared" to deal with it (a 2 rating). Subtracting the two (readiness minus importance) produces a strategic gap of negative 2 (2 - 4 = -2). By combining the results from individual respondents, we get a strong sense of industrywide views of the perceived readiness to address key issues.

In this report, then, a positive gap expresses that the organization believes that its skills meet or exceed the importance of the issue. A negative gap signifies a strategic deficit—that there are potential organizational weaknesses in implementation. For the most part, we found negative gaps. We interpret them to mean that the respondents feel unready, uncertain, or anxious about their ability to handle these challenges. That makes all the more striking those instances where executives indicated positive gaps, or a strongly confident feeling about these challenges.

Methodology and Respondents

Once the initial development process was complete, we had an eight-page questionnaire. AHPI Market Research conducted the 1997 Leadership Survey for *Hospitals & Health Networks* beginning with a pretest of the questionnaire. In April 1997, after revising the survey using results of the pretest, AHPI Market Research mailed the questionnaire and a cover letter to hospital, managed care, and physician group practice executives. A random sample of 2,000 hospital executive titles were pulled from the universe of U.S. general, acute care hospitals. Specialty hospitals were omitted. The 620-name sample of managed care CEOs, presidents, and executive directors were chosen on an nth name basis from the universe of HMOs and PPOs. An nth name random sample was also used to develop the 2,000-name sample of administrators, CEOs, and presidents of physician group practices with four or more physicians. The survey generated 729 responses, for an overall response rate of 15.8 percent. Hospitals represent about 68 percent of the respondents. (See table 1-1.)

Table 1-1. Response Rate				
	Sample size	*Response rate*	*Number of respondents*	*Percent of respondents*
Hospitals	2,000	24.8%	497	68.2%
Managed care organization	620	8.2%	51	7.0%
Physician groups practices	2,000	9.1%	181	24.8%
Total	4,620	15.8%	729	100%

The resulting sample is generally representative geographically with the most notable exceptions as follows: west-north-central states are overrepresented in the pool of hospital respondents, while New England states are underrepresented; Pacific states are overrepresented in the pool of managed care respondents, and east-north-central and Mountain states are underrepresented; New England and Middle Atlantic are overrepresented in the pool of physician group respondents, and Pacific and Mountain states are underrepresented. (See table 1-2.) As a result, opinions from MCOs may reflect a greater knowledge of the effects of managed care than is typical for the nation as a whole. Opinions of physician group executives may reflect less knowledge of the effects of managed care than is typical for the nation as a whole.

Smaller hospitals are overrepresented in the sample; mid-sized hospitals are underrepresented; and the proportion of large hospitals in the pool of respondents parallels that of the United States. (See table 1-3.) Hospitals of 99 beds or fewer make up 44.9 percent of all U.S. general, short-term acute care hospitals but account for 53.5 percent of respondents. Hospitals of 100 to 399 beds make up 46.1 percent of all hospitals and 37.8 of respondents. Hospitals of 400 beds or more make up 8.8 percent of both all U.S. hospitals and Leadership Survey respondents.

More than two-thirds of respondents are from tax-exempt organizations. Nearly 90 percent of hospitals report being tax exempt, while only 22.2 percent of physician group practices are not-for-profit. (See table 1-4.) MCOs are nearly split; 54.9 percent indicate for-profit status.

Respondents' average tenure in health care administration is 18.9 years. Physician group practice executives have the shortest average experience, 16.1 years. Both managed care and hospital executives have been in the field for

Table 1-2. Profiles of Survey Respondents by U.S. Census Divisions						
	Percent of all hospitals[1]	Percent of hospital respondents	Percent of all MCOs[2]	Percent of MCO respondents	Percent of all MD group practices[2]	Percent of MD group respondents
New England	5.4	2.0	6.7	6.0	5.0	8.9
Middle Atlantic	11.6	9.0	10.6	11.8	8.7	12.7
South Atlantic	15.5	14.2	15.8	13.8	18.1	20.6
East-north-central	14.6	14.0	20.4	19.7	14.7	12.7
East-south-central	8.2	8.2	5.1	3.9	5.9	5.1
West-north-central	12.0	17.0	7.2	5.9	9.7	9.6
West-south-central	13.2	14.4	8.7	9.8	8.2	9.5
Mountain	7.0	9.4	9.8	7.8	6.9	3.5
Pacific	11.2	10.2	15.4	21.6	22.6	18.2
Other[3]	1.2	1.0	0	0	.1	0

[1] American Hospital Association.
[2] SKA Research, Inc.
[3] Guam, Puerto Rico, and Virgin Islands.

more than 19 years on average. More than 86 percent of health care leaders answering the survey say they would make management in health care their profession again if they had to do it over. (See table 1-5.) The average age of survey respondents was 47.7 years, with a minimum of 25 years old and a maximum of 75 years.

All findings are presented in terms of valid percents. In other words, we have omitted missing responses before calculating the results. In some cases, the pool of available respondents has been altered due to the use of a "skip pattern" in the survey, a series of related questions in which the respondent skips questions based on answers given above. In these cases, only those with a qualified response on a previous question are counted in the pool of respondents for the related question.

THE *HOSPITALS & HEALTH NETWORKS* LEADERSHIP SURVEY: AN EVOLVING PROCESS

The health care industry will continue to change, and the *Hospitals & Health Networks* Leadership Survey will change with it. We are already preparing the questions for our next effort. We are also working to generate a larger pool of respondents. In the spirit of collaboration we invite the comments and feedback of health care professionals from around the country. Contact us if you have questions or comments on this survey or the next one. We will be happy to learn from your efforts to comprehend the issues and challenges facing health care leaders.

Table 1-3. Profile of Hospital Respondents by Number of Beds

No. of Beds	Percent of U.S. hospitals	Percent of respondents
6–24	5.3	4.7
25–49	17.7	22.8
50–99	21.9	26.0
100–199	25.5	22.3
200–299	13.8	9.8
300–399	6.8	5.7
400–499	3.7	4.5
500+	5.1	4.3

Table 1-4. Profile of Hospital Respondents' Tax Status

Tax status	Percent of U.S. hospitals	Percent of respondents
Investor-owned (For-profit)	14.5	10.2
Tax exempt (Not-for-profit)	85.5	89.8

Table 1-5. Personal Profile of Survey Respondents

	Average age	Average tenure in health administration (years)	Percent of respondents who would repeat career choice
Hospital	48.5	19.9	84.4%
MCO	47.2	19.8	96.1%
Physician group	45.7	16.1	89.1%

Contact: Alden Solovy
Hospitals & Health Networks
American Hospital Publishing, Inc.
737 North Michigan Ave.
Chicago, IL 60611
Phone: 312-440-6800
Fax: 312-951-8491
E-mail: solovy@aha.org
World Wide Web: www.HHNmag.com

References

1. James Gleick, *Chaos: Making a New Science* (New York: Viking, 1987), p. 26.

2. Philip Dunn, "Nearly 45 Million Americans Counted among Uninsured," *AHA News* 33, no. 19 (May 19, 1997): 4.

3. Peter M. Senge, *The Fifth Discipline: The Art and Practice of the Learning Organization* (New York: Doubleday/Currency), pp. 22–23.

2

Strategic Readiness

Jan Greene

Strategy by its very nature is a tricky beast. Take the case of Rick Scott, a man who at one time appeared to be the most cunning strategist in the hospital industry. He brought Columbia/HCA Healthcare Corp. unprecedented earnings and market power using an old Monopoly strategy: buy every property you land on. Scott combined that strategy with two basic principles of management: drive costs down and sales up. And he instituted the strategy at a time when hospitals were considered a terrible investment.[1] What could possibly go wrong?

The Achilles heel turned out to be success itself. As its market clout grew, hard negotiation and market dominance became the corporate ideal. The company's zealousness at driving up revenue finally attracted a federal government crackdown on its Medicare payment strategies. Ironically, it was the phenomenal success of its strategy that catapulted the organization toward corporate crisis. Scott was sacrificed to an unhappy market, and Columbia shifted its tactics, opting for no more physician equity deals, slower growth, and a revamped managerial incentive system.[2]

Strategy is, indeed, a tricky business. The ultimate testament is that in spite of a senior management shake-up and a federal probe, Columbia's core strategy—growth combined with cost and revenue management—remains sound. Strategy is a juggling act between margin and mission, short-run and long-run goals, market forces and community needs—all while trying to predict and adapt to future developments. Keeping one eye on their mission and one eye on a crystal ball, health care leaders prepare for the future by questioning the status quo:

Should I partner with the hospital across town? Or with an HMO? Should that partnership be tight or loose? What computer system should I buy, and if I wait a few months will a better one come along? What's Congress going to do to my Medicare income? Can doctors and hospitals learn to collaborate on common goals? In other words, of all the potential programs, investments, partners and acquisitions—of all the strategic choices—which are best for my organization today and which will take it into the future?

The answers to these questions can change with shocking speed. One day a strategy looks great; the next day it is irrelevant. One example is the physician-hospital organization (PHO). It didn't take long for the strategy of hospitals purchasing physician groups to transform itself from a new, smart way to capture physician loyalty and referrals to a surefire way of losing money. Hospitals that tried it found themselves paying too much for practices and lacking the management expertise to run them.[3] As time goes on, however, the verdict on PHOs may change. Given time to mature, the strategy could take root as hospital leaders learn how to run physician practices and the investment begins to pay off, argues Robert Bohlmann, a senior consultant with the Medical Group Management Association.[4] The rapid change in the health care industry has made the long-term viability of any strategy difficult to predict.

ISSUES FOR HEALTH CARE EXECUTIVES

In an environment of rapid change, strategy can be a daunting endeavor. As a group, executives indicate that they feel at least somewhat prepared to handle most challenges, although there are some key differences in confidence by industry sector. While executives are clearly aware of their predicament, for the most part they see it as interesting and challenging.

Issues for Hospital Executives

The most important issue for hospitals is maintaining a commitment to mission. For not-for-profit hospitals, that mission has long been focused on contributing to the health of the community. But the drive to contain costs and the resulting financial pressure have muddied that focus. In addition, because for-profits have to respond not just to the community but to investors, their missions may include more of an emphasis on the bottom line. But whatever the content of the mission statement, hospital executives clearly see carrying it out as their top priority.

Also on their minds is the difficult issue of information technology. Many hospitals are trying to decide what type of system to invest in, how to manage information in a more cost-effective manner, how to collect quality information for purchasers, and how to improve the organization. The problem becomes thornier when the organization is a system and it wants to share information across sites.

Hospital executives identified Medicare and Medicaid managed care contracting as another top concern. (See figure 2-1.) Clearly, with a large proportion of hospital income coming from these two programs, particularly true for large urban hospitals, the issue of how to ensure a steady stream of Medicare and Medicaid patients is key.[5] It is particularly important as Congress looks to shift more and more seniors into managed care plans as a money-saving device. States are starting to emulate that strategy with the Medicaid program, with varying success. Some of the early versions of Medicaid managed care are deeply troubled; some have found that MCOs are reluctant to bid on contracts to carry out the program. Hospital executives have to keep on top of these

Figure 2-1. Top Five Strategic Goals for Hospitals
1. Commitment to mission
2. Information technology
3. Medicare/Medicaid managed care contracting
4. Educated board
5. Partnering and integration

issues and often get involved with the state legislature to make sure they get a cut of the action.

Another key issue for hospital executives is board education. Board education is the means for having a group of people who can shape long-term strategic decision making through their understanding of the health care system, the changes and challenges in the current environment, and what is likely to be successful in a given market. That kind of intelligence is difficult enough for executives to gather and assimilate; ensuring that lay board members understand the issues can be another daunting challenge.

The hospital executives' responses to the second part of the strategic readiness question—whether they are prepared for these issues—brought some different results. Except for the issue of fulfilling their mission, the other goals executives rank as important did not make it onto the list of those they are ready to address, indicating a disconnection between the issues hospital executives value and those they have mastered. They feel the most comfortable with their ability to recruit and retain qualified senior managers and with their credentialing and liability acumen. Executives have experience with both of these functions, unlike many other aspects of the new health care landscape. Yet this stated comfort could reflect a certain overconfidence. One challenge facing the hospital field is that few managers are developing the kinds of skills that will take the industry into the next century. Recruitment, especially bringing in talent from outside health care, may become more difficult than these executives foresee.

By contrast, the issues the hospital executives feel least prepared to handle are the hallmarks of contemporary health care delivery, including medical savings accounts, physician management companies, and direct contracting with employers. Hospital leaders rank direct contracting among the most important issues they face, but their lack of confidence about it is striking. That is particularly important in light of some hospitals' interest in starting provider-sponsored organizations that would contract directly for either Medicare or commercial business.

Hospital executives feel most anxious about dealing with information technology as measured by the strategic gap. Information technology had the dubious distinction of yielding the largest strategic gap for hospital executives, followed closely by measuring quality of care and outcomes and by partnering and integration. It makes good sense that these three issues would be most vexing to executives: All of them are commonly viewed as important, but none of them have allowed for the type of success expected by hospital executives. Information technology still needs to make vast improvements before it can adequately handle the new integrated health systems. Nor is the science of measuring quality of care as advanced as it needs to be for managing risk, assessing population health status, measuring outcomes, or reporting to customers.

The survey also asked leaders about the issues that are most prominent in their own regions. For hospital executives, 61 percent say indigent care is a problem in their area. This strong response is consistent with the oft-repeated complaint from hospitals that they are losing the funding they need to provide a safety net for the growing population without health insurance.

Meanwhile, 50 percent of the hospital leaders said they have a local problem with the availability of primary care physicians, who are in short supply in some markets because of the historic tendency of medical students to choose a specialty rather than become a generalist. That trend is only slowly changing. The third most-mentioned local problem, hospital overcapacity, was cited by 39 percent of hospital leaders. Also mentioned often, by 38 percent of those running hospitals, was poor community health status.

Some of the most dramatic and emotional confrontations in health care finance occur when hospitals, doctors, and MCOs negotiate with one another over rates. This push-pull dynamic varies by market but there is general agreement that managed care is in the driver's seat. That is particularly true for hospitals. Hospital executives see themselves in a definitely weaker position when negotiating with MCOs. In fact, 69 percent of hospital leaders say their institutions are at a disadvantage in that situation, while just 14 percent think they have the upper hand. Another 17 percent think the match-up is equal. As the American hospital continues to lose power, this imbalance may become even more pronounced.

In contract negotiations between hospitals and doctors, the hospitals again see themselves at a disadvantage, with 41 percent of hospital executives saying that doctors have the upper hand. Another 37 percent think power is balanced equally, while 22 percent of hospital executives give themselves the advantage.

The executives were also asked to look into the future to determine the most likely integration trends of the next decade. In particular, they were asked to identify which of the trends now active in the marketplace would still be around in 10 years. Most hospital leaders say that physicians and hospitals will continue to partner, despite the poor financial results such unions have produced in the recent past. Still, 30 percent of hospital leaders see the trend enduring. Another 18 percent believe provider-sponsored networks or organizations are likely to be viable over the long term.

Issues for Managed Care Organizations

The leaders of MCOs are in an exciting, if risky, position. Theoretically, they have assumed control of much of the health care system, gaining the confidence of employers and government agencies who have turned to them to rein in out-of-control medical spending. At the same time, they face a political backlash fueled by the public's discomfort with the seemingly unbridled power of HMOs and the dominance of for-profit firms with high investor expectations based on the big HMO profit margins achieved in the early 1990s. The past year or two, however, has not been as kind to HMOs, as they hit a point where the easy pickings were gone. They had negotiated provider rates down as much as they could in many high-penetration markets. Now, the challenge for those managed care executives is to answer difficult questions emerging from the endless drive to cut costs and simultaneously maintain quality: How do you change the behavior of physicians who may honestly believe that more medical care is better? How do you alter the expectations of patients who feel the same way? And even thornier is the difficulty of identifying those medical procedures that are the most useful and the most cost-effective when the science of quality measurement is in its infancy.

So while some health care executives may look with envy at their counterparts heading MCOs, running an HMO has its own drawbacks. The good news for these executives is that managed care is an entrenched and accepted way of life in health care, despite the criticism from many doctors and politicians. The bad news is that the changes in managed care continue at a breakneck speed. Just in the past year or two, for instance, it has become clear that consumers–and therefore payers–feel so strongly about choosing their own doctors and specialists that open-access plans without primary care gatekeepers have become big sellers.[6] In light of that trend, executives are asking the question, How do you hold down costs when you start moving back in the direction of fee-for-service? The trend is so new that no one has had a chance to answer that question particularly well. And there are some who question whether HMOs will even exist over the long term once doctors and hospitals learn the basics of bearing risk.

Managed care executives have much to say about the rapid changes in the industry. (See figure 2-2.) They identify information technology as their most important strategic issue. That is consistent with the tremendous importance of information to the future of managed care. To survive and compete, HMOs have to provide concrete evidence that the way they manage care not only maintains or improves quality but that it helps the bottom line as well. HMO executives have traditionally been more adept at building databases to track their members than have their counterparts in hospitals and in physician practices. They must also find the right information technologies with which to manipulate that information. The second strategic issue identified by managed care leaders is commitment to mission. The other top issues are competitive pricing strategies, Medicare/Medicaid managed care contracting, and measuring quality.

Predictably, MCO executives feel most confident of their ability to credential physicians and watch out for liability problems, fairly straightforward business matters. They feel equally adept at direct contracting with employers, which is certainly the HMO's forte. The managed care executives also feel fairly confident about carrying out their mission and devising competitive pricing schemes. Also rated high on the "preparedness" list was expanding physician networks, which make sense, considering how many HMOs are doing just that to offer more choice to members.

The strategic gap analysis offers the most insight into those issues about which managed care leaders feel least secure. Their primary insecurity is information technology. Buying a new information system for all the complex needs in an ever-changing organization is a daunting task. It is an expensive investment that may fail to meet organizational needs or may become obsolete in short order. A related insecurity came in second: measuring quality of care and outcomes. Again, this area is in its infancy. Not until 1997 did the National Committee on Quality Assurance develop the Health Plan Employer Data and Information Set (HEDIS) 3.0, the first set of quality measures for HMOs meant to focus on outcomes and not just on simple preventive measures.[7] Because 1997 was the first year HMOs have had to provide the data, the success of the new program remains undecided, as is the usefulness of the data for employers and consumers.

Unlike the hospital executives, who feel insecure about every topic examined in the survey, the managed care leaders are more likely to have positive feelings about certain issues. In fact, they feel particularly confident about direct contracting with employers and quite confident about dealing with physician management companies and business coalitions. Such dealings are staples of everyday life in managed care.

That confidence in contracting issues became evident again when the managed care executives are asked about who holds the stronger position in

Figure 2-2. Top Five Strategic Goals of Managed Care Organizations
1. Information technology
2. Commitment to mission
3. Competitive pricing strategies
4. Medicare/Medicaid managed care contracting
5. Measuring quality of care/outcomes

contract negotiations. They place themselves at the advantage when it comes to working things out with a hospital (64 percent say the MCO has the upper hand). But another 27 percent of managed care executives think it is more of an even matchup, and 9 percent say the hospital actually has a stronger position.

As for negotiations with physicians, the MCOs again (by 62 percent) see themselves as stronger. Another 22 percent say the matchup is equal and 16 percent say physicians have the upper hand.

When identifying what issues have a high profile in their own communities, the managed care executives named hospital overcapacity by an overwhelming 78 percent. To the person running an HMO, extra, unused space in a hospital is a drag on the economy because the hospital has to keep its rates high enough to support those empty beds. The managed care executives also identify indigent care as an important local issue (65 percent say so); unpaid hospital bills are another drag on the local health care economy. By a smaller proportion (39 percent) managed care executives say the availability of primary care physicians is a local problem.

Issues for Medical Group Practices

Physician group practice respondents identify information technology as the most important strategic issue they face. (See figure 2-3.) For physician groups with multiple sites, being able to share patient records electronically would be a great improvement over the time- and money-wasting practice of sending paper records from one place to another. Also, doctors are beginning to feel the same pressure as other providers to prove their quality. This issue will become especially important as they begin to take on direct contracting. Then physician groups will face the same information technology challenges that health plans endure: compiling and manipulating volumes of data on large groups of people. The problem is complex and expensive.

The doctor groups also focus on the importance of their commitment to mission. Because doctors are trained mainly to be clinical advocates and less to be independent businessmen, one would assume they are referring to the mission of making people well. Another important goal, they say, is measuring quality of care, along with developing the breadth of physician networks and obtaining qualified senior managers.

The issue physician groups feel the most confident of, the survey indicates, is their ability to implement their mission—presumably, caring for patients. They also feel relatively confident about credentialing and expanding physician networks.

On the other hand, the groups feel the least confident about information technology, the issue they consider the most strategically important. Clearly, physician groups are not finding it easy to make the technology choices and big-ticket investments that it takes to prepare for the future. They also report a lack of confidence about measuring quality of care and outcomes. Of all providers, physicians have probably been the least comfortable with the idea of measuring what they do by the numbers. Any system devised to objectively

Figure 2-3. Top Five Strategic Goals of Group Practices
1. Information technology
2. Commitment to mission
3. Measuring quality of care/outcomes
4. Developing breadth of physician networks
5. Availability of qualified senior managers

compare one physician to another is likely to miss the subjective, human side of medicine, some contend. However, the marketplace is forcing such analysis upon doctors, who are already measured in HMOs by the number of patients they see and the amount of time spent with each one.

Physician groups do not identify many areas in which they feel confident, except for dealing with physician management companies, an area in which they are moderately comfortable. They identify indigent care as the most important issue locally (55 percent of respondents); half say hospital overcapacity is a problem; and 28 percent think the availability of primary care physicians is limited in their areas.

As for identifying which party wields the most power in contracting negotiations, physician group managers think MCOs have the upper hand when negotiating with physicians (63 percent of respondents), while 17 percent think the physicians have the upper hand and another 20 percent believe the matchup is equal. In markets where managed care has taken hold, physicians find themselves in competition with other medical groups for contracts, and it does not take long for the bidding process to force payments lower and lower. Unable to say no to large payers, doctors clearly feel at a disadvantage in this situation.

Physician groups see their negotiations with hospitals as a little more balanced. Forty-three percent of the physician group managers say physicians have the upper hand in those situations, while 35 percent say the hospital is more in control. Another 22 percent say the two come to the table with equal amounts of power.

Physician practice managers see pacts among physicians themselves as the top integration trend of the next decade (22 percent of respondents). Another 18 percent think physicians and hospitals will continue to ally, and just 11 percent foresee partnering among doctors, hospitals, and managed care.

COMPARISONS

Hospital executives feel insecure about every issue the survey presented. By contrast, the managed care executives express confidence about a number of issues. And physician group managers, if not overly confident, were at least neutral on many issues. This information implies that hospital executives are the most anxious about their ability to function in the future. They run large, static institutions that could become obsolete in the face of changes in technology and in the health care economy. The move toward outpatient surgery—as well as managed care's ability to get people out of the hospital earlier—have made big acute care hospitals harder to fill.

Another potential reason for the big difference between hospital leaders and managed care executives could be their differing roles in the health care economy. Hospital leaders have had to relinquish much control over the markets they once dominated. By contrast, managed care executives in many markets have been able to walk in and demand price decreases year after year. That difference plays out in their responses to the question about who dominates in managed care negotiations: Everyone agrees that managed care is clearly more in control.

Executives across the board worry about the same issues. (See table 2-1.) In particular, all the health care leaders express similar anxiety about the organization's preparedness for information technology. In a related concern, they all feel uncertain about measuring quality of care. These are clearly issues that are terribly important to an organization's ability to succeed and compete. The institution in a given marketplace that adequately addresses these issues first has a huge advantage over the others. At the same time, these are challenges with no clear answers. And health care executives have to rely on others–namely, quality and information consultants–to come up with solutions.

Improving community health status is a high priority to hospitals, but not particularly high for physician groups, especially those that are for-profit. Similarly, collaborating with community and social organizations is of greatest concern to hospitals and less so for MCOs and group practices. Not-for-profit organizations give those issues greater importance than do for-profits. At the same time, MCOs, particularly for-profit ones, are more interested in competitive pricing strategies than are either hospitals or group practices. These data appear to support the belief that for-profit managed care is more focused on the bottom line than are other organizations in health care.

Differences show up in how health care leaders identify important issues in their geographic region. Managed care executives believe that hospitals are bloated with too many beds; 78 percent of them cite hospital overcapacity as a major problem in their region. Just 38 percent of hospital executives agree. Instead, most name indigent care as the major issue in their community. Many hospitals find themselves with an increasing burden of uncompensated care, especially as the number of uninsured people grows.

Grouping health care executives by their organization's tax status yields some interesting results, especially when it comes to ranking issues for importance to the organization's survival. For instance, not-for-profit hospital leaders rate an educated board much more highly than do the for-profit hospital executives. And the not-for-profit executives are more likely to say that improving community health status is an important goal than are the for-profit leaders.

IMPLICATIONS

The people running hospitals are clearly worried. They are unable to identify a single issue about which they feel particularly confident. One might expect that most of these executives would want to get out of the field altogether, and yet, in a separate area of the survey, the vast majority of leaders, including those running hospitals, say they do not regret going into health care as a career. Many hospital leaders look forward to the challenge of a constantly changing marketplace.

Of course, the price may be some sleepless nights. Respondents consider nearly every one of the 21 issues presented as at least neutral, if not somewhat or extremely important to them. (See table 2-2.) They peg none of the topics as unimportant. Hospital executives identify 10 issues as fairly to extremely important (rated 4 or above), as did those in managed care. Physician practice leaders pinpointed 6 issues as particularly important.

Table 2-1. Three Largest Strategic Gaps by Type of Organization

Hospitals	Managed care organizations	Group practices
1 IInformation technology	Information technology	Information technology
2 Medicare/Medicaid managed care contracting	Measuring quality of care/outcomes	Measuring quality of care/outcomes
3 Measuring quality of care/outcomes	Medicare/Medicaid managed care contracting (tied with) Commitment to mission	Commitment to mission

When those top-priority issues are examined further, we find that the hospital executives feel either somewhat or extremely prepared to address just 1 of their top 10. Those in managed care feel prepared for 4 of their 10 important challenges. Physician practice executives fare even worse, rating their own readiness as below all 6 of their most important issues.

The difference between running a hospital and a health plan becomes even more striking, though, when looking at the number of important strategic gaps each group identified. Hospital executives have significant gaps in eight areas, compared with just two each for managed care and physician practices.

Clearly, the problems keeping most executives up at night are those centering on emerging technology and the new demands of the marketplace. By identifying information technology and measuring quality and outcomes as their top worries, executives of all types send a clear message that they are not getting the information or the products they need to do their job.

Still, the slowing of health care inflation over the past few years has given executives some breathing room. Things could get even more interesting when, inevitably, costs and premiums begin to rise and organizations are prompted to once again wield their budget-cutting shears. At that point,

Table 2-2. Ranking of the Importance of Issues		
Rank	For-Profit Hospitals	Not-for-Profit Hospitals
1	Medicare/Medicaid contracting (4.48)	Mission (4.72)
2	Breadth of physician network (4.38)	Information technology (4.51)
3	Information technology (4.36)	Medicare/Medicaid contracting (4.42)
4	Mission (4.32)	Educated board (4.41)
5	Measuring quality (4.32)	Partnering (4.33)
6	Partnering (4.28)	Measuring quality (4.25)
7	Competitive pricing (4.12)	Breadth of physician network (4.20)
8	State-mandated reform (4.02)	Finding qualified senior managers (4.12)
9	Finding qualified senior managers (3.98)	Community health (4.07)
10	Regulation of PSOs (3.92)	Collaborating with community (4.01)
11	Any willing provider legislation (3.92)	Competitive pricing (3.95)
12	Credentialing (3.90)	Credentialing (3.86)
13	Direct contracting (3.76)	State-mandated reform (3.83)
14	Educated board (3.74)	Regulation of PSOs (3.68)
15	Collaborating with community (3.72)	Direct contracting (3.67)
16	Community health (3.62)	Any willing provider legislation (3.52)
17	Utilization review laws (3.54)	Utilization review laws (3.43)
18	ERISA revision (3.52)	ERISA revision (3.33)
19	MSAs (3.40)	Growth of business coalitions (3.29)
20	Growth of business coalitions (3.40)	MSAs (3.03)
21	Growth of physician management companies (3.28)	Growth of physician management companies (2.92)

Note: Number in parentheses is the mean response based on a scale of 1 to 5, 5 being most important.

long-term, big-picture worries such as computer systems and quality measures could give way to the more immediate issues of restructuring and employee morale.

References

1. Jon Asplund, "Frist's Supporters Expect a Kinder, Gentler Columbia," *AHA News* 33, no. 30 (Aug. 4, 1997): 1.

2. Ibid.

3. *1997 Physician Practice Acquisition Resource Book* (Columbus, Ohio: Center for Healthcare Industry Performance Studies, 1997).

4. Quoted in Jan Greene, "1997 Leadership Survey," *Hospitals & Health Networks* 71, no. 15 (Aug. 5, 1997): 32.

5. *Redesigning Health Care for the New Millennium: An Assessment of the Health Care Environment in the United States* (Irving, Tex.: VHA Inc., 1997), pp. 19–20.

6. Ibid., p. 20.

7. Peter MacPherson, "Measure by Measures," *Hospitals & Health Networks* 70, no. 6 (March 20, 1996): 53–56.

Strategic Readiness   Ranking--All Respondents

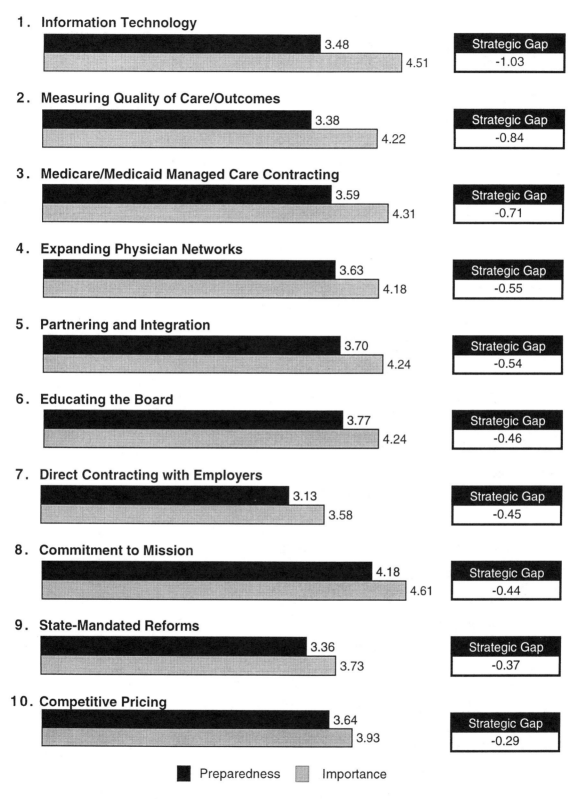

1. Information Technology

3.48
4.51

Strategic Gap
-1.03

2. Measuring Quality of Care/Outcomes

3.38
4.22

Strategic Gap
-0.84

3. Medicare/Medicaid Managed Care Contracting

3.59
4.31

Strategic Gap
-0.71

4. Expanding Physician Networks

3.63
4.18

Strategic Gap
-0.55

5. Partnering and Integration

3.70
4.24

Strategic Gap
-0.54

6. Educating the Board

3.77
4.24

Strategic Gap
-0.46

7. Direct Contracting with Employers

3.13
3.58

Strategic Gap
-0.45

8. Commitment to Mission

4.18
4.61

Strategic Gap
-0.44

9. State-Mandated Reforms

3.36
3.73

Strategic Gap
-0.37

10. Competitive Pricing

3.64
3.93

Strategic Gap
-0.29

■ Preparedness   ▨ Importance

• Combinations are ranked from largest to smallest strategic gap.

• Small discrepancies between the strategic gap and the rankings may occur due to rounding.

Strategic Readiness   Ranking--All Respondents

11. Responding to Community Health Needs

3.63
3.92

Strategic Gap
-0.29

12. Recruiting Qualified Senior Managers

3.83
4.10

Strategic Gap
-0.27

13. Provider-Sponsored Networks

3.45
3.66

Strategic Gap
-0.21

14. Working with Business Coalitions

3.23
3.36

Strategic Gap
-0.14

15. ERISA Revisions

3.17
3.31

Strategic Gap
-0.13

16. New Utilization Review Laws

3.30
3.41

Strategic Gap
-0.11

17. "Any Willing Provider" Legislation

3.43
3.54

Strategic Gap
-0.11

18. Collaborating with Community Health Providers

3.72
3.79

Strategic Gap
-0.07

19. Medical Savings Accounts

3.02
3.03

Strategic Gap
-0.01

20. Credentialing and Liability

3.87
3.85

Strategic Gap
0.02

21. Dealing with Physician Management Companies

3.10
2.95

Strategic Gap
0.15

Strategic Readiness   Ranking--Hospital Executives

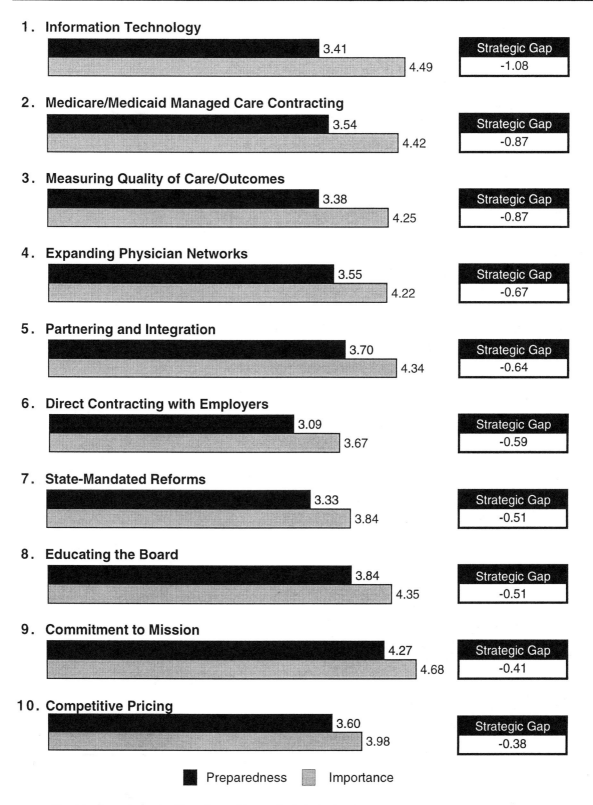

1. **Information Technology**

   Preparedness: 3.41
   Importance: 4.49

   Strategic Gap
   -1.08

2. **Medicare/Medicaid Managed Care Contracting**

   Preparedness: 3.54
   Importance: 4.42

   Strategic Gap
   -0.87

3. **Measuring Quality of Care/Outcomes**

   Preparedness: 3.38
   Importance: 4.25

   Strategic Gap
   -0.87

4. **Expanding Physician Networks**

   Preparedness: 3.55
   Importance: 4.22

   Strategic Gap
   -0.67

5. **Partnering and Integration**

   Preparedness: 3.70
   Importance: 4.34

   Strategic Gap
   -0.64

6. **Direct Contracting with Employers**

   Preparedness: 3.09
   Importance: 3.67

   Strategic Gap
   -0.59

7. **State-Mandated Reforms**

   Preparedness: 3.33
   Importance: 3.84

   Strategic Gap
   -0.51

8. **Educating the Board**

   Preparedness: 3.84
   Importance: 4.35

   Strategic Gap
   -0.51

9. **Commitment to Mission**

   Preparedness: 4.27
   Importance: 4.68

   Strategic Gap
   -0.41

10. **Competitive Pricing**

    Preparedness: 3.60
    Importance: 3.98

    Strategic Gap
    -0.38

■ Preparedness   ▧ Importance

• Combinations are ranked from largest to smallest strategic gap.

• Small discrepancies between the strategic gap and the rankings may occur due to rounding.

Strategic Readiness   Ranking--Hospital Executives

11. Provider-Sponsored Networks

3.37	
3.71	

Strategic Gap
-0.33

12. Responding to Community Health Needs

3.71	
4.02	

Strategic Gap
-0.31

13. Recruiting Qualified Senior Managers

3.87	
4.11	

Strategic Gap
-0.23

14. ERISA Revisions

3.17	
3.35	

Strategic Gap
-0.18

15. Collaborating with Community Health Providers

3.82	
3.99	

Strategic Gap
-0.17

16. "Any Willing Provider" Legislation

3.42	
3.56	

Strategic Gap
-0.14

17. New Utilization Review Laws

3.30	
3.43	

Strategic Gap
-0.14

18. Working with Business Coalitions

3.19	
3.31	

Strategic Gap
-0.12

19. Medical Savings Accounts

2.98	
3.06	

Strategic Gap
-0.08

20. Credentialing and Liability

3.86	
3.87	

Strategic Gap
-0.01

21. Dealing with Physician Management Companies

2.95	
2.96	

Strategic Gap
0.00

Strategic Readiness   Ranking--Managed Care Executives

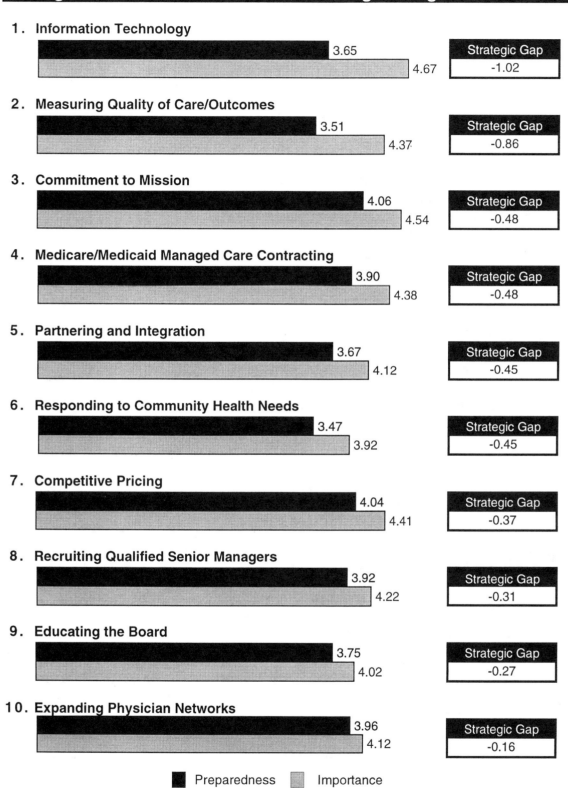

1. **Information Technology**

    3.65
    4.67

    Strategic Gap
    -1.02

2. **Measuring Quality of Care/Outcomes**

    3.51
    4.37

    Strategic Gap
    -0.86

3. **Commitment to Mission**

    4.06
    4.54

    Strategic Gap
    -0.48

4. **Medicare/Medicaid Managed Care Contracting**

    3.90
    4.38

    Strategic Gap
    -0.48

5. **Partnering and Integration**

    3.67
    4.12

    Strategic Gap
    -0.45

6. **Responding to Community Health Needs**

    3.47
    3.92

    Strategic Gap
    -0.45

7. **Competitive Pricing**

    4.04
    4.41

    Strategic Gap
    -0.37

8. **Recruiting Qualified Senior Managers**

    3.92
    4.22

    Strategic Gap
    -0.31

9. **Educating the Board**

    3.75
    4.02

    Strategic Gap
    -0.27

10. **Expanding Physician Networks**

    3.96
    4.12

    Strategic Gap
    -0.16

■ Preparedness   ▨ Importance

- Combinations are ranked from largest to smallest strategic gap.
- Small discrepancies between the strategic gap and the rankings may occur due to rounding.

Strategic Readiness — Ranking--Managed Care Executives

11. ERISA Revisions

3.40
3.48

Strategic Gap
-0.08

12. Provider-Sponsored Networks

3.84
3.84

Strategic Gap
0.00

13. Credentialing and Liability

4.14
4.10

Strategic Gap
0.04

14. "Any Willing Provider" Legislation

3.50
3.42

Strategic Gap
0.08

15. State-Mandated Reforms

3.63
3.55

Strategic Gap
0.08

16. Collaborating with Community Health Providers

3.59
3.49

Strategic Gap
0.10

17. New Utilization Review Laws

3.70
3.44

Strategic Gap
0.26

18. Medical Savings Accounts

3.33
3.02

Strategic Gap
0.31

19. Working with Business Coalitions

3.38
3.00

Strategic Gap
0.38

20. Direct Contracting with Employers

4.14
3.61

Strategic Gap
0.53

21. Dealing with Physician Management Companies

3.35
2.71

Strategic Gap
0.65

Strategic Readiness   Ranking--Physician Group Executives

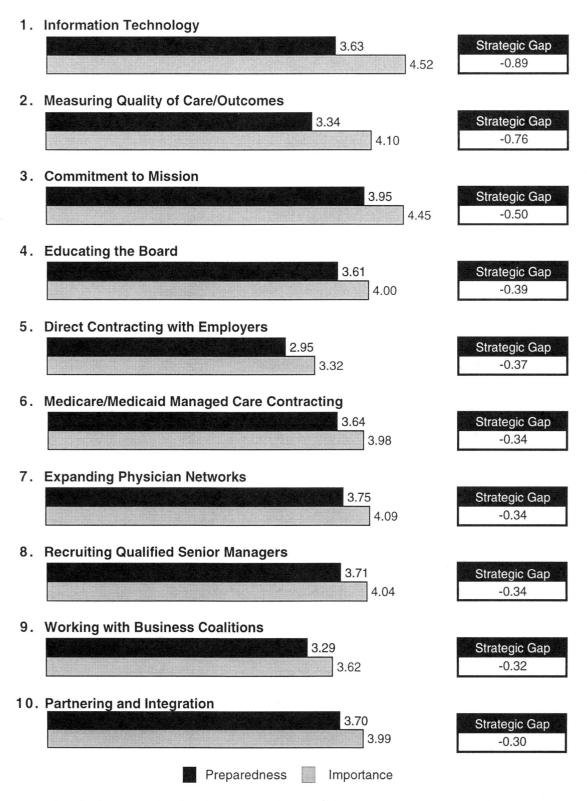

1. Information Technology

3.63

4.52

Strategic Gap
-0.89

2. Measuring Quality of Care/Outcomes

3.34

4.10

Strategic Gap
-0.76

3. Commitment to Mission

3.95

4.45

Strategic Gap
-0.50

4. Educating the Board

3.61

4.00

Strategic Gap
-0.39

5. Direct Contracting with Employers

2.95

3.32

Strategic Gap
-0.37

6. Medicare/Medicaid Managed Care Contracting

3.64

3.98

Strategic Gap
-0.34

7. Expanding Physician Networks

3.75

4.09

Strategic Gap
-0.34

8. Recruiting Qualified Senior Managers

3.71

4.04

Strategic Gap
-0.34

9. Working with Business Coalitions

3.29

3.62

Strategic Gap
-0.32

10. Partnering and Integration

3.70

3.99

Strategic Gap
-0.30

■ Preparedness   ▨ Importance

• Combinations are ranked from largest to smallest strategic gap.

• Small discrepancies between the strategic gap and the rankings may occur due to rounding.

Strategic Readiness   Ranking--Physician Group Executives

11. Responding to Community Health Needs

3.44
3.62

Strategic Gap
-0.18

12. New Utilization Review Laws

3.19
3.33

Strategic Gap
-0.14

13. State-Mandated Reforms

3.37
3.48

Strategic Gap
-0.11

14. "Any Willing Provider" Legislation

3.45
3.51

Strategic Gap
-0.07

15. Competitive Pricing

3.63
3.67

Strategic Gap
-0.04

16. ERISA Revisions

3.13
3.14

Strategic Gap
-0.02

17. Provider-Sponsored Networks

3.55
3.47

Strategic Gap
0.09

18. Medical Savings Accounts

3.05
2.95

Strategic Gap
0.09

19. Credentialing and Liability

3.83
3.73

Strategic Gap
0.10

20. Collaborating with Community Health Providers

3.46
3.31

Strategic Gap
0.17

21. Dealing with Physician Management Companies

3.44
3.01

Strategic Gap
0.42

Strategic Readiness   "Any Willing Provider" Legislation

Overall Results

Importance vs. Preparedness

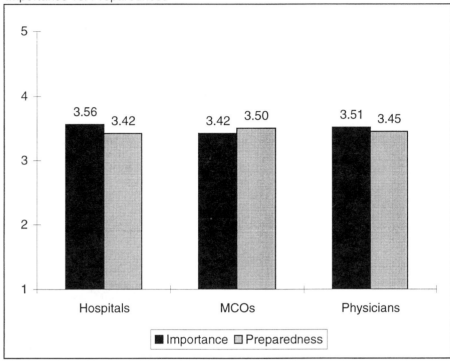

Strategic Gap	
Hospitals	-0.14
MCOs	0.08
Physicians	-0.07

Rank	
Importance	16
Preparedness	13
Strategic Gap	17

- The higher the importance ranking, the more important the issue is to respondents.
- The higher the readiness ranking, the better the respondents view the preparedness of their institutions.
- "Strategic gap" refers to the difference between importance and preparedness.
- The rank refers to the rank of the issues out of the 21 included in the survey. Ranks are given for importance, readiness, and strategic gap. The highest rank is 1; the lowest rank is 21.

Regional Results

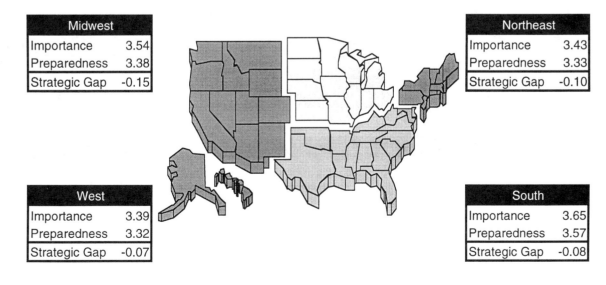

Midwest	
Importance	3.54
Preparedness	3.38
Strategic Gap	-0.15

Northeast	
Importance	3.43
Preparedness	3.33
Strategic Gap	-0.10

West	
Importance	3.39
Preparedness	3.32
Strategic Gap	-0.07

South	
Importance	3.65
Preparedness	3.57
Strategic Gap	-0.08

Hospital Executives
Importance vs. Preparedness

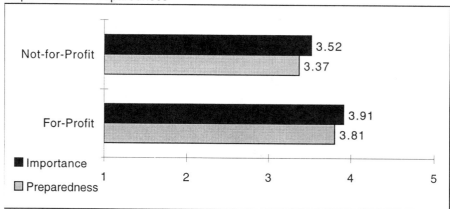

Rank	
Importance	16
Preparedness	11
Strategic Gap	16

Strategic Gap	
Not-for-profit	-0.15
For-profit	-0.11

Managed Care Executives
Importance vs. Preparedness

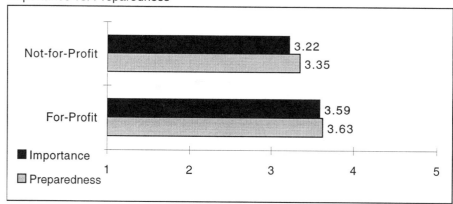

Rank	
Importance	18
Preparedness	16
Strategic Gap	14

Strategic Gap	
Not-for-profit	0.13
For-profit	0.04

Physician Group Practice Executives
Importance vs. Preparedness

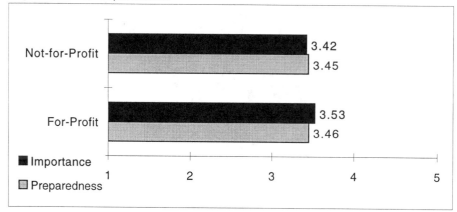

Rank	
Importance	13
Preparedness	12
Strategic Gap	14

Strategic Gap	
Not-for-profit	0.03
For-profit	-0.07

Strategic Readiness   Collaborating with Community Health Providers

Overall Results

Importance vs. Preparedness

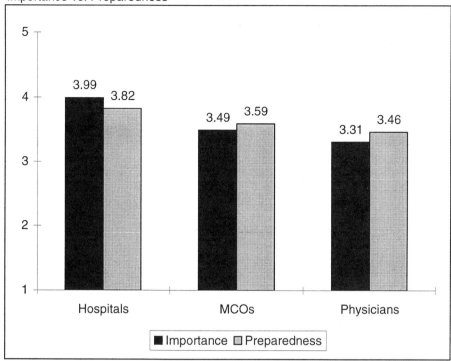

Strategic Gap	
Hospitals	-0.17
MCOs	0.10
Physicians	0.17

Rank	
Importance	12
Preparedness	5
Strategic Gap	18

- The higher the importance ranking, the more important the issue is to respondents.
- The higher the readiness ranking, the better the respondents view the preparedness of their institutions.
- "Strategic gap" refers to the difference between importance and preparedness.
- The rank refers to the rank of the issues out of the 21 included in the survey. Ranks are given for importance, readiness, and strategic gap. The highest rank is 1; the lowest rank is 21.

Regional Results

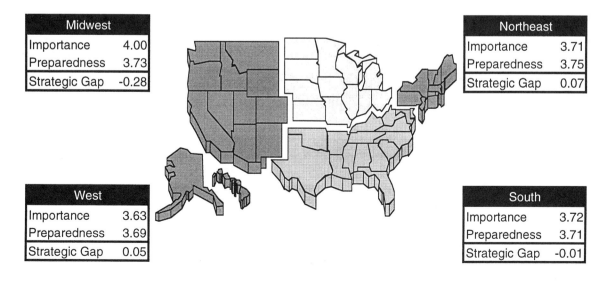

Midwest	
Importance	4.00
Preparedness	3.73
Strategic Gap	-0.28

Northeast	
Importance	3.71
Preparedness	3.75
Strategic Gap	0.07

West	
Importance	3.63
Preparedness	3.69
Strategic Gap	0.05

South	
Importance	3.72
Preparedness	3.71
Strategic Gap	-0.01

Strategic Readiness   Collaborating with Community Health Providers

Hospital Executives
Importance vs. Preparedness

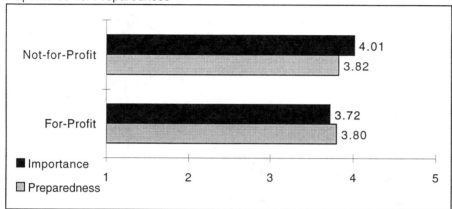

Rank	
Importance	10
Preparedness	5
Strategic Gap	15

Strategic Gap	
Not-for-profit	-0.20
For-profit	0.08

Managed Care Executives
Importance vs. Preparedness

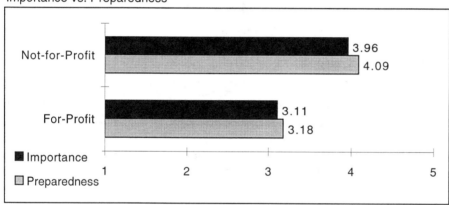

Rank	
Importance	15
Preparedness	14
Strategic Gap	16

Strategic Gap	
Not-for-profit	0.13
For-profit	0.07

Physician Group Practice Executives
Importance vs. Preparedness

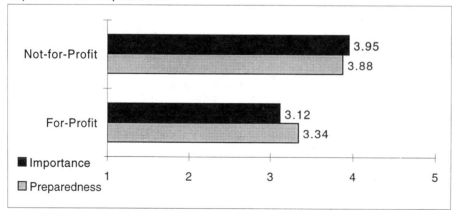

Rank	
Importance	18
Preparedness	11
Strategic Gap	20

Strategic Gap	
Not-for-profit	-0.08
For-profit	0.24

Strategic Readiness   Commitment to Mission

Overall Results

Importance vs. Preparedness

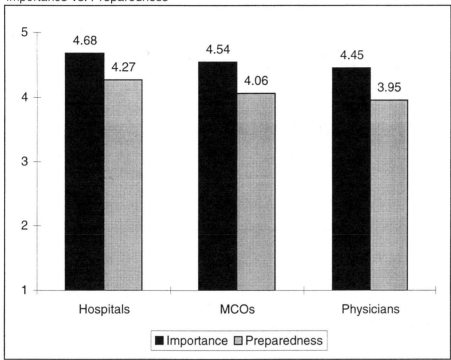

Strategic Gap	
Hospitals	-0.41
MCOs	-0.48
Physicians	-0.50

Rank	
Importance	1
Preparedness	1
Strategic Gap	8

• The higher the importance ranking, the more important the issue is to respondents.
• The higher the readiness ranking, the better the respondents view the preparedness of their institutions.
• "Strategic gap" refers to the difference between importance and preparedness.
• The rank refers to the rank of the issues out of the 21 included in the survey. Ranks are given for importance, readiness, and strategic gap. The highest rank is 1; the lowest rank is 21.

Regional Results

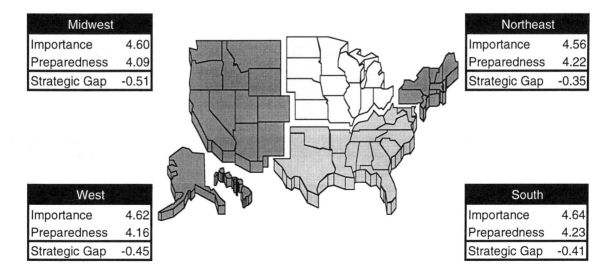

Midwest	
Importance	4.60
Preparedness	4.09
Strategic Gap	-0.51

Northeast	
Importance	4.56
Preparedness	4.22
Strategic Gap	-0.35

West	
Importance	4.62
Preparedness	4.16
Strategic Gap	-0.45

South	
Importance	4.64
Preparedness	4.23
Strategic Gap	-0.41

Hospital Executives

Importance vs. Preparedness

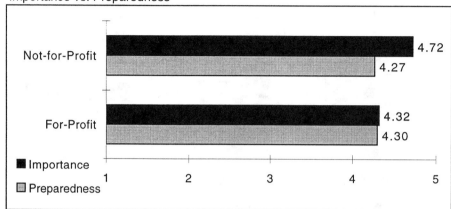

Rank	
Importance	1
Preparedness	1
Strategic Gap	9

Strategic Gap	
Not-for-profit	-0.45
For-profit	-0.02

Managed Care Executives

Importance vs. Preparedness

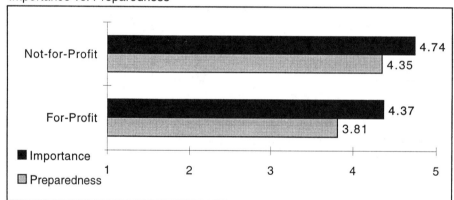

Rank	
Importance	2
Preparedness	3
Strategic Gap	3

Strategic Gap	
Not-for-profit	-0.39
For-profit	-0.56

Physician Group Practice Executives

Importance vs. Preparedness

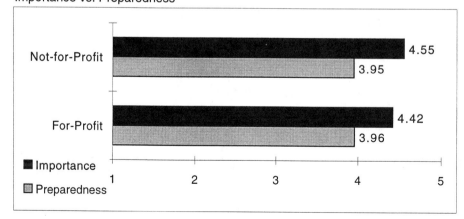

Rank	
Importance	2
Preparedness	1
Strategic Gap	3

Strategic Gap	
Not-for-profit	-0.60
For-profit	-0.46

Strategic Readiness | Competitive Pricing

Overall Results

Importance vs. Preparedness

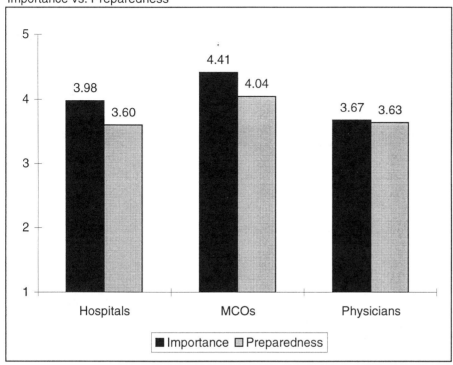

Strategic Gap	
Hospitals	-0.38
MCOs	-0.37
Physicians	-0.04

Rank	
Importance	9
Preparedness	7
Strategic Gap	10

- The higher the importance ranking, the more important the issue is to respondents.
- The higher the readiness ranking, the better the respondents view the preparedness of their institutions.
- "Strategic gap" refers to the difference between importance and preparedness.
- The rank refers to the rank of the issues out of the 21 included in the survey. Ranks are given for importance, readiness, and strategic gap. The highest rank is 1; the lowest rank is 21.

Regional Results

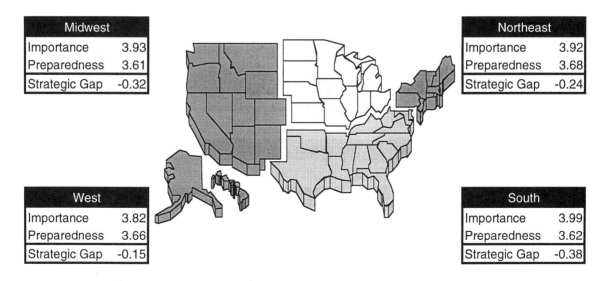

Midwest	
Importance	3.93
Preparedness	3.61
Strategic Gap	-0.32

Northeast	
Importance	3.92
Preparedness	3.68
Strategic Gap	-0.24

West	
Importance	3.82
Preparedness	3.66
Strategic Gap	-0.15

South	
Importance	3.99
Preparedness	3.62
Strategic Gap	-0.38

Strategic Readiness   **Competitive Pricing**

Hospital Executives
Importance vs. Preparedness

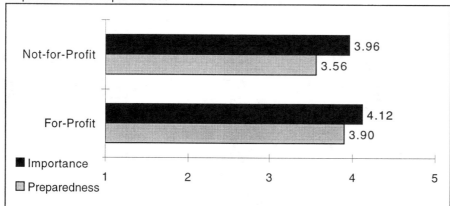

Rank	
Importance	11
Preparedness	8
Strategic Gap	10

Strategic Gap	
Not-for-profit	-0.39
For-profit	-0.22

Managed Care Executives
Importance vs. Preparedness

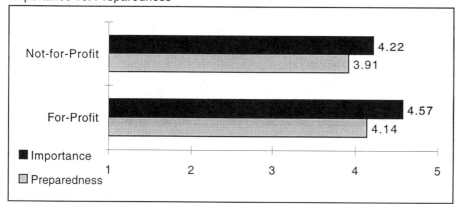

Rank	
Importance	3
Preparedness	4
Strategic Gap	7

Strategic Gap	
Not-for-profit	-0.30
For-profit	-0.43

Physician Group Practice Executives
Importance vs. Preparedness

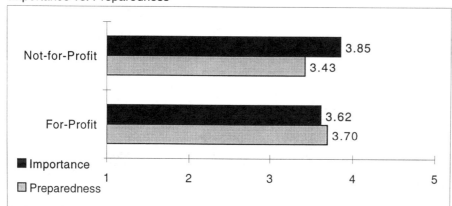

Rank	
Importance	10
Preparedness	7
Strategic Gap	15

Strategic Gap	
Not-for-profit	-0.43
For-profit	0.08

Strategic Readiness   **Credentialing and Liability**

Overall Results

Importance vs. Preparedness

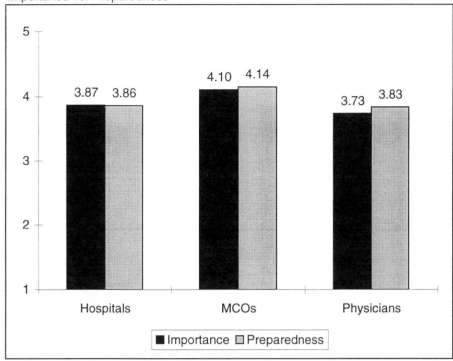

Strategic Gap	
Hospitals	-0.01
MCOs	0.04
Physicians	0.10

Rank	
Importance	11
Preparedness	2
Strategic Gap	20

- The higher the importance ranking, the more important the issue is to respondents.
- The higher the readiness ranking, the better the respondents view the preparedness of their institutions.
- "Strategic gap" refers to the difference between importance and preparedness.
- The rank refers to the rank of the issues out of the 21 included in the survey. Ranks are given for importance, readiness, and strategic gap. The highest rank is 1; the lowest rank is 21.

Regional Results

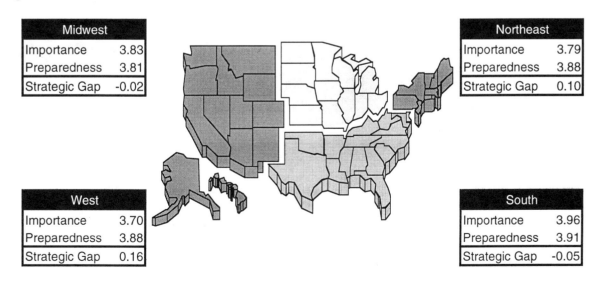

Midwest	
Importance	3.83
Preparedness	3.81
Strategic Gap	-0.02

Northeast	
Importance	3.79
Preparedness	3.88
Strategic Gap	0.10

West	
Importance	3.70
Preparedness	3.88
Strategic Gap	0.16

South	
Importance	3.96
Preparedness	3.91
Strategic Gap	-0.05

Strategic Readiness　　　　　　　　　　　**Credentialing and Liability**

Hospital Executives
Importance vs. Preparedness

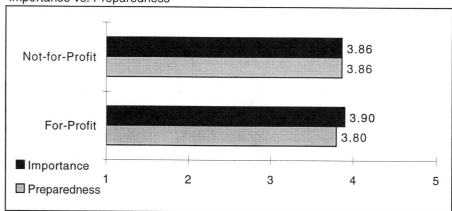

Rank	
Importance	12
Preparedness	3
Strategic Gap	20

Strategic Gap	
Not-for-profit	0.00
For-profit	-0.10

Managed Care Executives
Importance vs. Preparedness

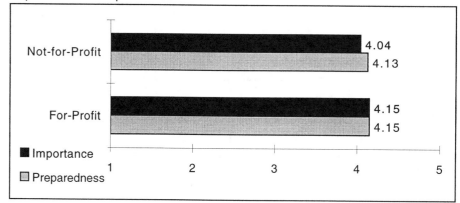

Rank	
Importance	9
Preparedness	1
Strategic Gap	13

Strategic Gap	
Not-for-profit	0.09
For-profit	0.00

Physician Group Practice Executives
Importance vs. Preparedness

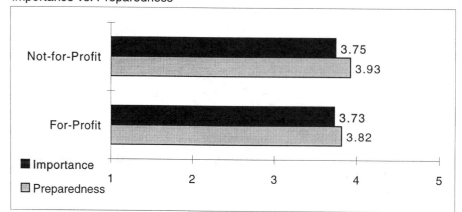

Rank	
Importance	9
Preparedness	2
Strategic Gap	19

Strategic Gap	
Not-for-profit	0.18
For-profit	0.09

Strategic Readiness   Dealing with Physician Management Companies

Overall Results

Importance vs. Preparedness

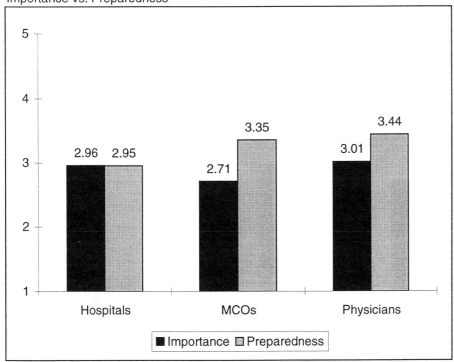

Strategic Gap	
Hospitals	0.00
MCOs	0.65
Physicians	0.42

Rank	
Importance	21
Preparedness	20
Strategic Gap	21

- The higher the importance ranking, the more important the issue is to respondents.
- The higher the readiness ranking, the better the respondents view the preparedness of their institutions.
- "Strategic gap" refers to the difference between importance and preparedness.
- The rank refers to the rank of the issues out of the 21 included in the survey. Ranks are given for importance, readiness, and strategic gap. The highest rank is 1; the lowest rank is 21.

Regional Results

Midwest	
Importance	2.91
Preparedness	2.92
Strategic Gap	0.00

Northeast	
Importance	3.01
Preparedness	3.14
Strategic Gap	0.13

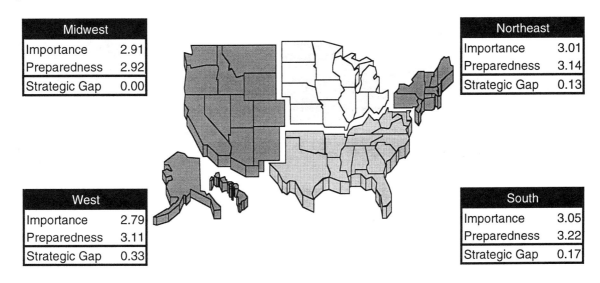

West	
Importance	2.79
Preparedness	3.11
Strategic Gap	0.33

South	
Importance	3.05
Preparedness	3.22
Strategic Gap	0.17

Strategic Readiness   Dealing with Physician Management Companies

Hospital Executives

Importance vs. Preparedness

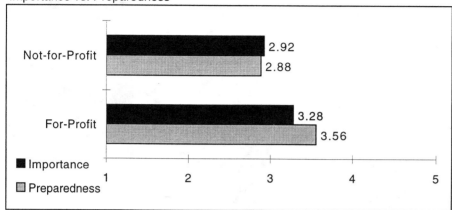

Rank	
Importance	21
Preparedness	21
Strategic Gap	21

Strategic Gap	
Not-for-profit	-0.03
For-profit	0.28

Managed Care Executives

Importance vs. Preparedness

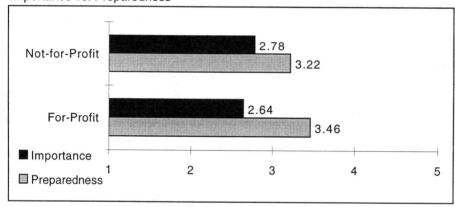

Rank	
Importance	21
Preparedness	20
Strategic Gap	21

Strategic Gap	
Not-for-profit	0.43
For-profit	0.82

Physician Group Practice Executives

Importance vs. Preparedness

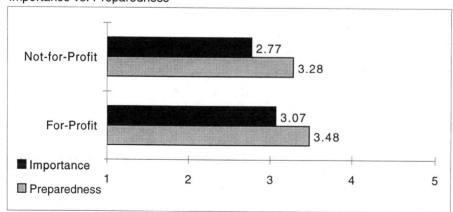

Rank	
Importance	20
Preparedness	14
Strategic Gap	21

Strategic Gap	
Not-for-profit	0.51
For-profit	0.41

Strategic Readiness | Direct Contracting with Employers

Overall Results

Importance vs. Preparedness

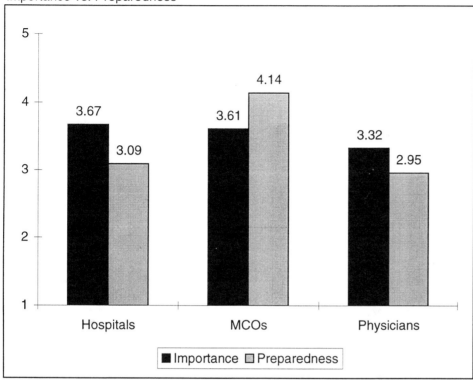

Strategic Gap	
Hospitals	-0.59
MCOs	0.53
Physicians	-0.37

Rank	
Importance	15
Preparedness	19
Strategic Gap	7

- The higher the importance ranking, the more important the issue is to respondents.
- The higher the readiness ranking, the better the respondents view the preparedness of their institutions.
- "Strategic gap" refers to the difference between importance and preparedness.
- The rank refers to the rank of the issues out of the 21 included in the survey. Ranks are given for importance, readiness, and strategic gap. The highest rank is 1; the lowest rank is 21.

Regional Results

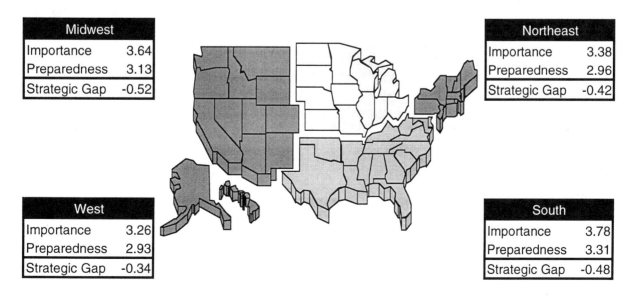

Midwest	
Importance	3.64
Preparedness	3.13
Strategic Gap	-0.52

Northeast	
Importance	3.38
Preparedness	2.96
Strategic Gap	-0.42

West	
Importance	3.26
Preparedness	2.93
Strategic Gap	-0.34

South	
Importance	3.78
Preparedness	3.31
Strategic Gap	-0.48

Strategic Readiness   **Direct Contracting with Employers**

Hospital Executives

Importance vs. Preparedness

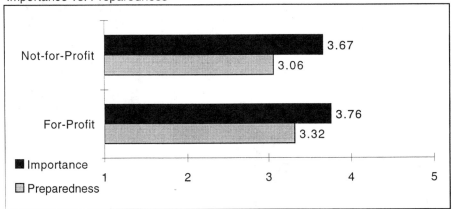

Rank	
Importance	15
Preparedness	19
Strategic Gap	6

Strategic Gap	
Not-for-profit	-0.60
For-profit	-0.44

Managed Care Executives

Importance vs. Preparedness

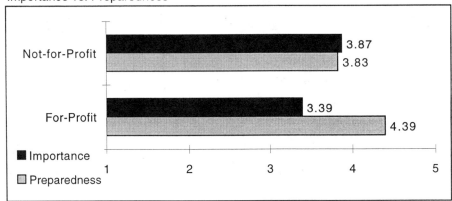

Rank	
Importance	13
Preparedness	2
Strategic Gap	20

Strategic Gap	
Not-for-profit	-0.04
For-profit	1.00

Physician Group Practice Executives

Importance vs. Preparedness

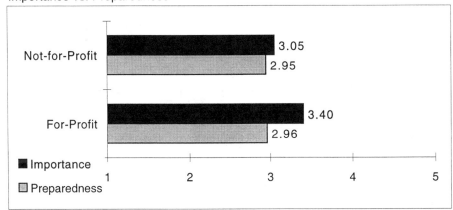

Rank	
Importance	17
Preparedness	21
Strategic Gap	5

Strategic Gap	
Not-for-profit	-0.10
For-profit	-0.44

Strategic Readiness | Educating the Board

Overall Results

Importance vs. Preparedness

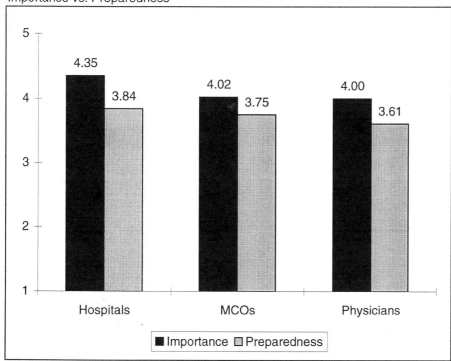

Strategic Gap	
Hospitals	-0.51
MCOs	-0.27
Physicians	-0.39

Rank	
Importance	4
Preparedness	4
Strategic Gap	6

• The higher the importance ranking, the more important the issue is to respondents.
• The higher the readiness ranking, the better the respondents view the preparedness of their institutions.
• "Strategic gap" refers to the difference between importance and preparedness.
• The rank refers to the rank of the issues out of the 21 included in the survey. Ranks are given for importance, readiness, and strategic gap. The highest rank is 1; the lowest rank is 21.

Regional Results

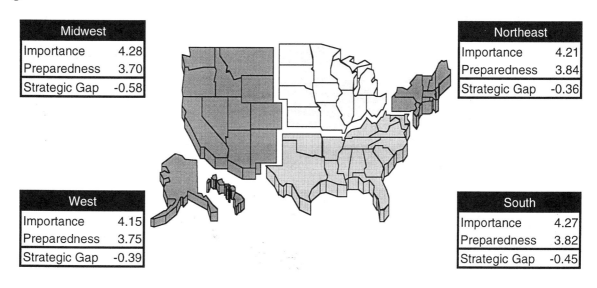

Midwest	
Importance	4.28
Preparedness	3.70
Strategic Gap	-0.58

Northeast	
Importance	4.21
Preparedness	3.84
Strategic Gap	-0.36

West	
Importance	4.15
Preparedness	3.75
Strategic Gap	-0.39

South	
Importance	4.27
Preparedness	3.82
Strategic Gap	-0.45

Strategic Readiness   **Educating the Board**

Hospital Executives

Importance vs. Preparedness

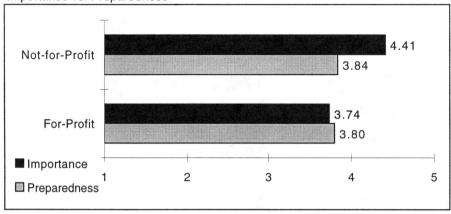

Rank	
Importance	4
Preparedness	4
Strategic Gap	8

Strategic Gap	
Not-for-profit	-0.57
For-profit	0.06

Managed Care Executives

Importance vs. Preparedness

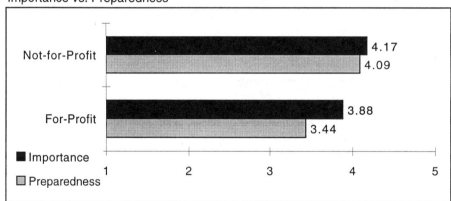

Rank	
Importance	10
Preparedness	9
Strategic Gap	9

Strategic Gap	
Not-for-profit	-0.09
For-profit	-0.44

Physician Group Practice Executives

Importance vs. Preparedness

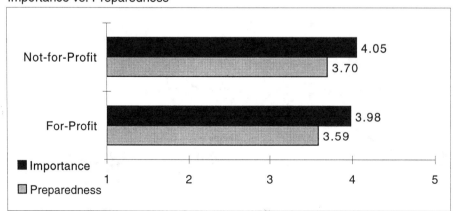

Rank	
Importance	6
Preparedness	9
Strategic Gap	4

Strategic Gap	
Not-for-profit	-0.35
For-profit	-0.38

Strategic Readiness   ERISA Revisions

Overall Results

Importance vs. Preparedness

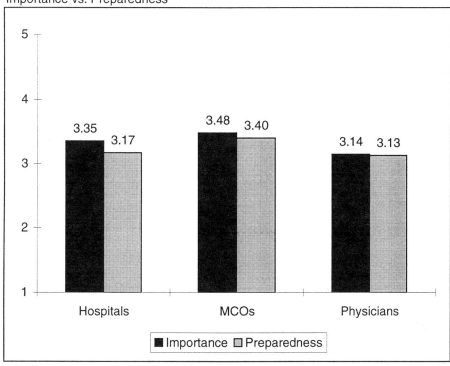

Strategic Gap	
Hospitals	-0.18
MCOs	-0.08
Physicians	-0.02

Rank	
Importance	19
Preparedness	18
Strategic Gap	15

- The higher the importance ranking, the more important the issue is to respondents.
- The higher the readiness ranking, the better the respondents view the preparedness of their institutions.
- "Strategic gap" refers to the difference between importance and preparedness.
- The rank refers to the rank of the issues out of the 21 included in the survey. Ranks are given for importance, readiness, and strategic gap. The highest rank is 1; the lowest rank is 21.

Regional Results

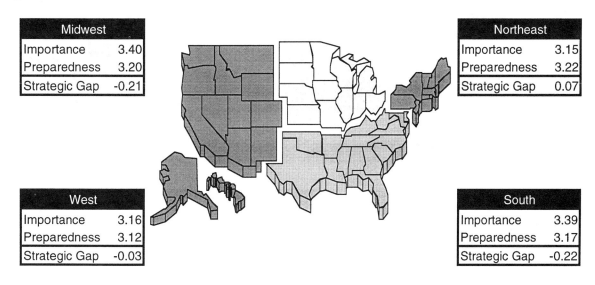

Midwest	
Importance	3.40
Preparedness	3.20
Strategic Gap	-0.21

Northeast	
Importance	3.15
Preparedness	3.22
Strategic Gap	0.07

West	
Importance	3.16
Preparedness	3.12
Strategic Gap	-0.03

South	
Importance	3.39
Preparedness	3.17
Strategic Gap	-0.22

Strategic Readiness   ERISA Revisions

Hospital Executives
Importance vs. Preparedness

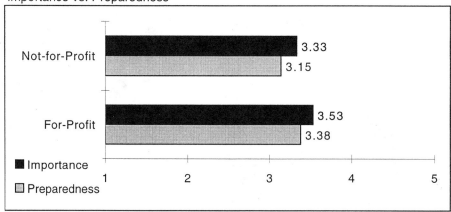

Rank	
Importance	18
Preparedness	18
Strategic Gap	14

Strategic Gap	
Not-for-profit	-0.19
For-profit	-0.16

Managed Care Executives
Importance vs. Preparedness

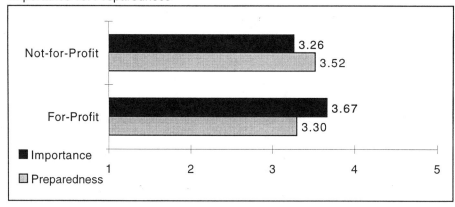

Rank	
Importance	16
Preparedness	19
Strategic Gap	11

Strategic Gap	
Not-for-profit	0.26
For-profit	-0.37

Physician Group Practice Executives
Importance vs. Preparedness

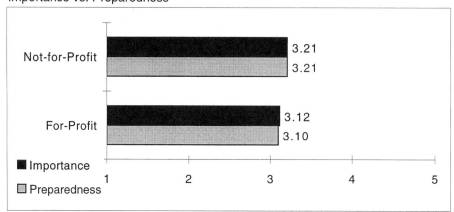

Rank	
Importance	19
Preparedness	19
Strategic Gap	16

Strategic Gap	
Not-for-profit	0.00
For-profit	-0.02

Strategic Readiness · Expanding Physician Networks

Overall Results

Importance vs. Preparedness

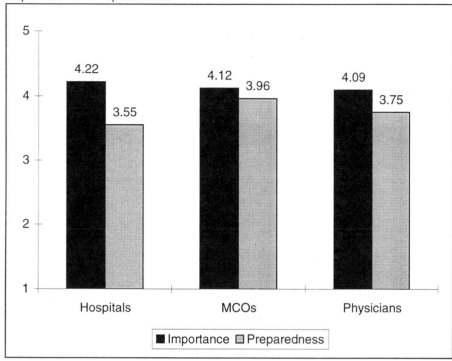

Strategic Gap	
Hospitals	-0.67
MCOs	-0.16
Physicians	-0.34

Rank	
Importance	7
Preparedness	8
Strategic Gap	4

- The higher the importance ranking, the more important the issue is to respondents.
- The higher the readiness ranking, the better the respondents view the preparedness of their institutions.
- "Strategic gap" refers to the difference between importance and preparedness.
- The rank refers to the rank of the issues out of the 21 included in the survey. Ranks are given for importance, readiness, and strategic gap. The highest rank is 1; the lowest rank is 21.

Regional Results

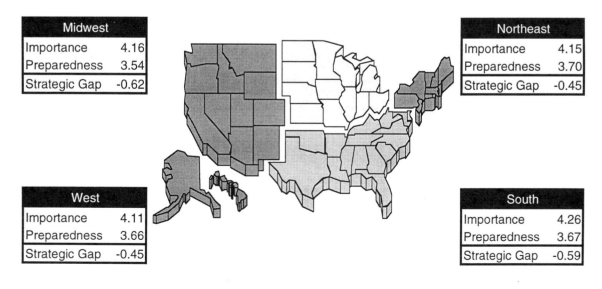

Midwest	
Importance	4.16
Preparedness	3.54
Strategic Gap	-0.62

Northeast	
Importance	4.15
Preparedness	3.70
Strategic Gap	-0.45

West	
Importance	4.11
Preparedness	3.66
Strategic Gap	-0.45

South	
Importance	4.26
Preparedness	3.67
Strategic Gap	-0.59

Hospital Executives
Importance vs. Preparedness

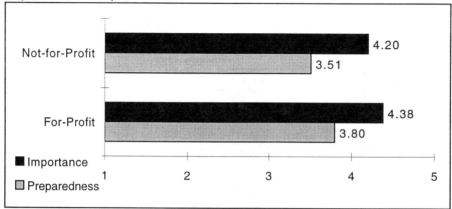

Rank	
Importance	7
Preparedness	9
Strategic Gap	4

Strategic Gap	
Not-for-profit	-0.69
For-profit	-0.58

Managed Care Executives
Importance vs. Preparedness

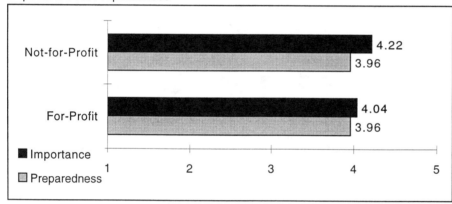

Rank	
Importance	7
Preparedness	5
Strategic Gap	10

Strategic Gap	
Not-for-profit	-0.26
For-profit	-0.08

Physician Group Practice Executives
Importance vs. Preparedness

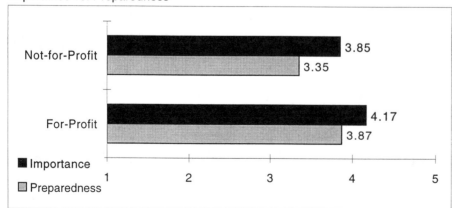

Rank	
Importance	4
Preparedness	3
Strategic Gap	7

Strategic Gap	
Not-for-profit	-0.50
For-profit	-0.29

| Strategic Readiness • | Information Technology |

Overall Results

Importance vs. Preparedness

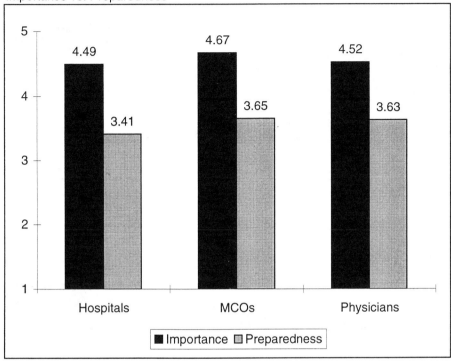

Strategic Gap	
Hospitals	-1.08
MCOs	-1.02
Physicians	-0.89

Rank	
Importance	2
Preparedness	11
Strategic Gap	1

• The higher the importance ranking, the more important the issue is to respondents.
• The higher the readiness ranking, the better the respondents view the preparedness of their institutions.
• "Strategic gap" refers to the difference between importance and preparedness.
• The rank refers to the rank of the issues out of the 21 included in the survey. Ranks are given for importance, readiness, and strategic gap. The highest rank is 1; the lowest rank is 21.

Regional Results

Midwest	
Importance	4.47
Preparedness	3.38
Strategic Gap	-1.09

Northeast	
Importance	4.67
Preparedness	3.64
Strategic Gap	-1.03

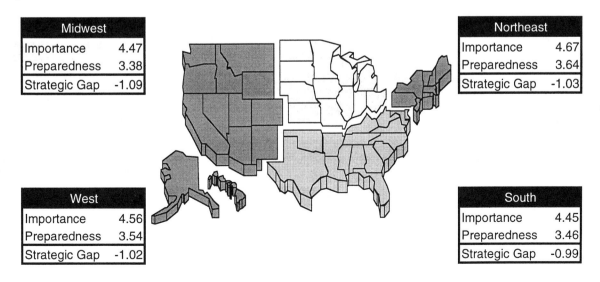

West	
Importance	4.56
Preparedness	3.54
Strategic Gap	-1.02

South	
Importance	4.45
Preparedness	3.46
Strategic Gap	-0.99

Hospital Executives
Importance vs. Preparedness

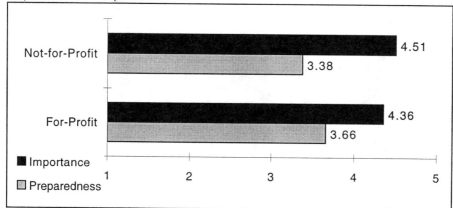

Rank	
Importance	2
Preparedness	12
Strategic Gap	1

Strategic Gap	
Not-for-profit	-1.13
For-profit	-0.70

Managed Care Executives
Importance vs. Preparedness

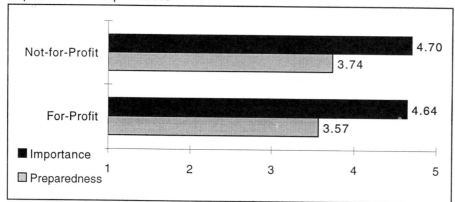

Rank	
Importance	1
Preparedness	12
Strategic Gap	1

Strategic Gap	
Not-for-profit	-0.96
For-profit	-1.07

Physician Group Practice Executives
Importance vs. Preparedness

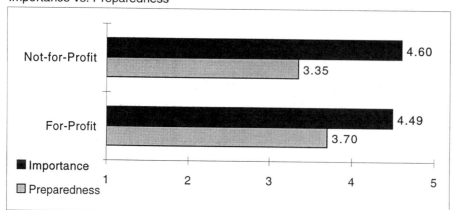

Rank	
Importance	1
Preparedness	8
Strategic Gap	1

Strategic Gap	
Not-for-profit	-1.25
For-profit	-0.79

Strategic Readiness — Measuring Quality of Care/Outcomes

Overall Results

Importance vs. Preparedness

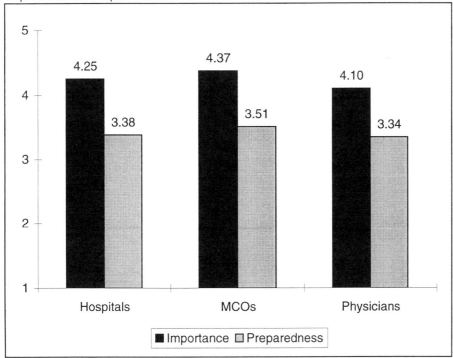

Strategic Gap	
Hospitals	-0.87
MCOs	-0.86
Physicians	-0.76

Rank	
Importance	6
Preparedness	14
Strategic Gap	2

- The higher the importance ranking, the more important the issue is to respondents.
- The higher the readiness ranking, the better the respondents view the preparedness of their institutions.
- "Strategic gap" refers to the difference between importance and preparedness.
- The rank refers to the rank of the issues out of the 21 included in the survey. Ranks are given for importance, readiness, and strategic gap. The highest rank is 1; the lowest rank is 21.

Regional Results

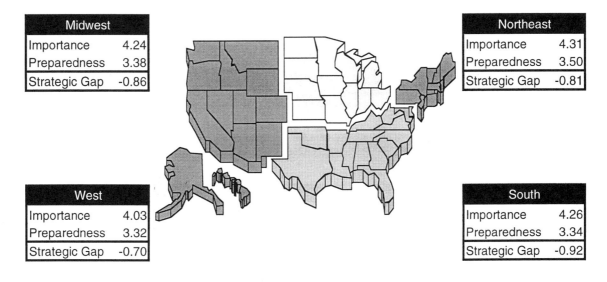

Midwest	
Importance	4.24
Preparedness	3.38
Strategic Gap	-0.86

Northeast	
Importance	4.31
Preparedness	3.50
Strategic Gap	-0.81

West	
Importance	4.03
Preparedness	3.32
Strategic Gap	-0.70

South	
Importance	4.26
Preparedness	3.34
Strategic Gap	-0.92

Strategic Readiness	Measuring Quality of Care/Outcomes

Hospital Executives

Importance vs. Preparedness

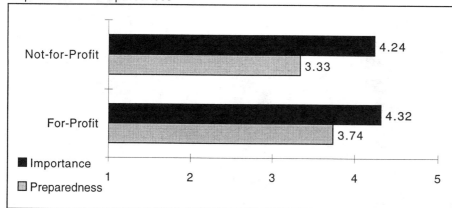

Rank	
Importance	6
Preparedness	13
Strategic Gap	3

Strategic Gap	
Not-for-profit	-0.90
For-profit	-0.58

Managed Care Executives

Importance vs. Preparedness

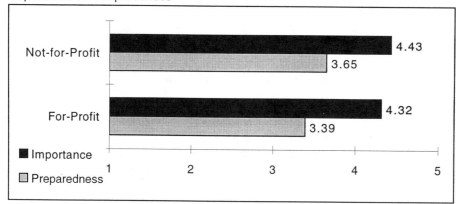

Rank	
Importance	5
Preparedness	15
Strategic Gap	2

Strategic Gap	
Not-for-profit	-0.78
For-profit	-0.93

Physician Group Practice Executives

Importance vs. Preparedness

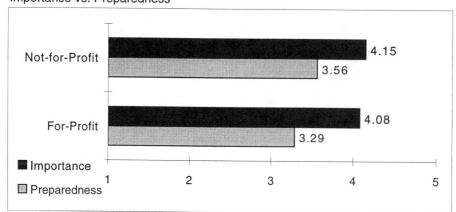

Rank	
Importance	3
Preparedness	16
Strategic Gap	2

Strategic Gap	
Not-for-profit	-0.59
For-profit	-0.79

Strategic Readiness | Medical Savings Accounts

Overall Results

Importance vs. Preparedness

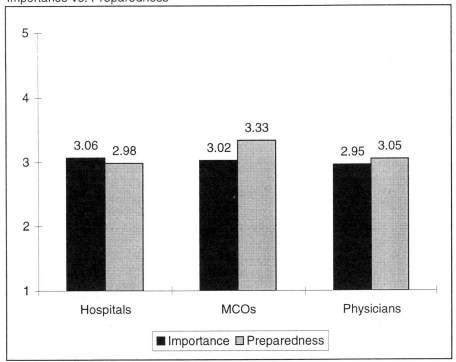

Strategic Gap	
Hospitals	-0.08
MCOs	0.31
Physicians	0.09

Rank	
Importance	20
Preparedness	21
Strategic Gap	19

- The higher the importance ranking, the more important the issue is to respondents.
- The higher the readiness ranking, the better the respondents view the preparedness of their institutions.
- "Strategic gap" refers to the difference between importance and preparedness.
- The rank refers to the rank of the issues out of the 21 included in the survey. Ranks are given for importance, readiness, and strategic gap. The highest rank is 1; the lowest rank is 21.

Regional Results

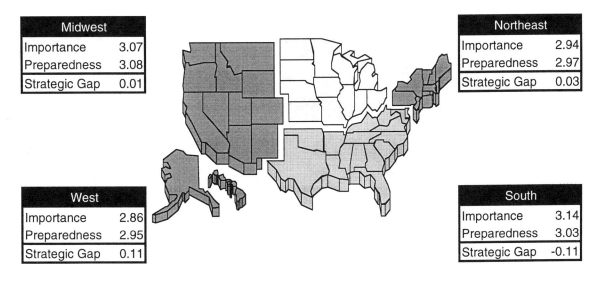

Midwest	
Importance	3.07
Preparedness	3.08
Strategic Gap	0.01

Northeast	
Importance	2.94
Preparedness	2.97
Strategic Gap	0.03

West	
Importance	2.86
Preparedness	2.95
Strategic Gap	0.11

South	
Importance	3.14
Preparedness	3.03
Strategic Gap	-0.11

Hospital Executives

Importance vs. Preparedness

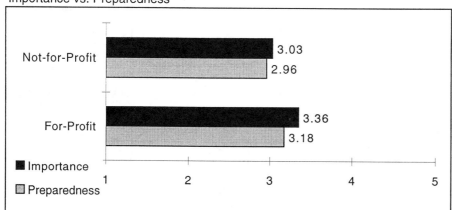

Rank	
Importance	20
Preparedness	20
Strategic Gap	19

Strategic Gap	
Not-for-profit	-0.07
For-profit	-0.18

Managed Care Executives

Importance vs. Preparedness

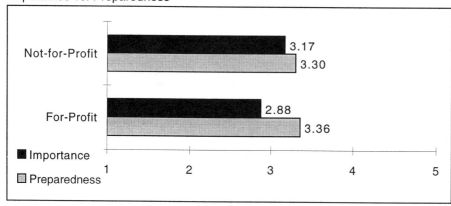

Rank	
Importance	19
Preparedness	21
Strategic Gap	18

Strategic Gap	
Not-for-profit	0.13
For-profit	0.48

Physician Group Practice Executives

Importance vs. Preparedness

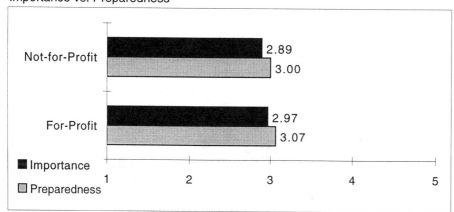

Rank	
Importance	21
Preparedness	20
Strategic Gap	18

Strategic Gap	
Not-for-profit	0.11
For-profit	0.09

Strategic Readiness   Medicare/Medicaid Managed Care Contracting

Overall Results

Importance vs. Preparedness

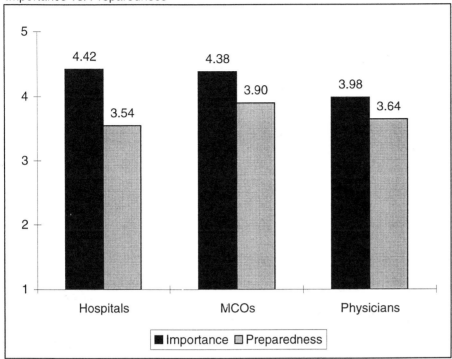

Strategic Gap	
Hospitals	-0.87
MCOs	-0.48
Physicians	-0.34

Rank	
Importance	3
Preparedness	10
Strategic Gap	3

- The higher the importance ranking, the more important the issue is to respondents.
- The higher the readiness ranking, the better the respondents view the preparedness of their institutions.
- "Strategic gap" refers to the difference between importance and preparedness.
- The rank refers to the rank of the issues out of the 21 included in the survey. Ranks are given for importance, readiness, and strategic gap. The highest rank is 1; the lowest rank is 21.

Regional Results

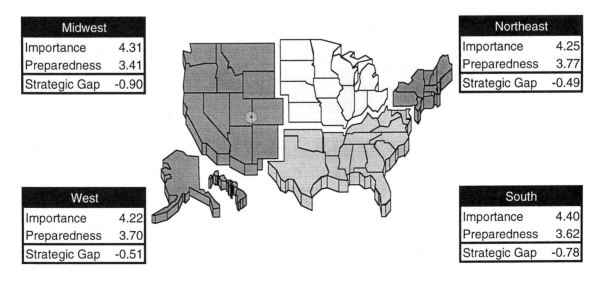

Midwest	
Importance	4.31
Preparedness	3.41
Strategic Gap	-0.90

Northeast	
Importance	4.25
Preparedness	3.77
Strategic Gap	-0.49

West	
Importance	4.22
Preparedness	3.70
Strategic Gap	-0.51

South	
Importance	4.40
Preparedness	3.62
Strategic Gap	-0.78

Strategic Readiness   Medicare/Medicaid Managed Care Contracting

Hospital Executives
Importance vs. Preparedness

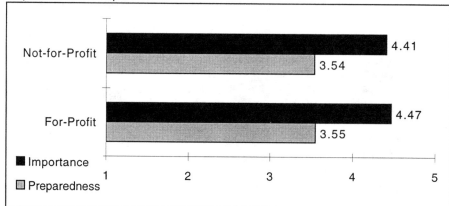

Rank	
Importance	3
Preparedness	10
Strategic Gap	2

Strategic Gap	
Not-for-profit	-0.87
For-profit	-0.92

Managed Care Executives
Importance vs. Preparedness

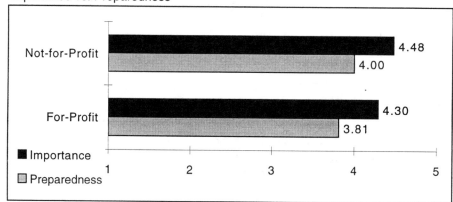

Rank	
Importance	4
Preparedness	7
Strategic Gap	4

Strategic Gap	
Not-for-profit	-0.48
For-profit	-0.48

Physician Group Practice Executives
Importance vs. Preparedness

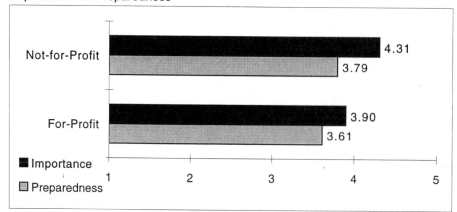

Rank	
Importance	8
Preparedness	6
Strategic Gap	6

Strategic Gap	
Not-for-profit	-0.51
For-profit	-0.29

Strategic Readiness | New Utilization Review Laws

Overall Results

Importance vs. Preparedness

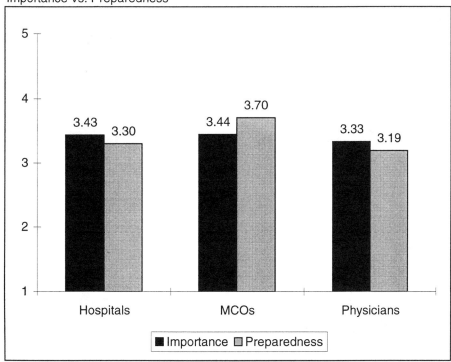

Strategic Gap	
Hospitals	-0.14
MCOs	0.26
Physicians	-0.14

Rank	
Importance	17
Preparedness	16
Strategic Gap	16

• The higher the importance ranking, the more important the issue is to respondents.
• The higher the readiness ranking, the better the respondents view the preparedness of their institutions.
• "Strategic gap" refers to the difference between importance and preparedness.
• The rank refers to the rank of the issues out of the 21 included in the survey. Ranks are given for importance, readiness, and strategic gap. The highest rank is 1; the lowest rank is 21.

Regional Results

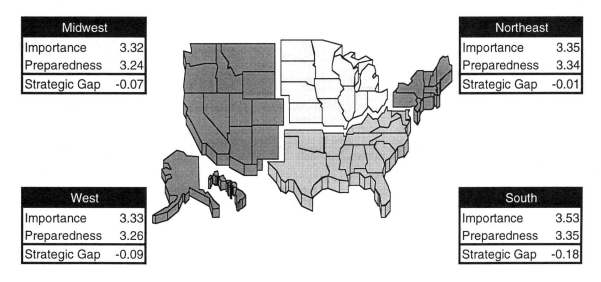

Midwest	
Importance	3.32
Preparedness	3.24
Strategic Gap	-0.07

Northeast	
Importance	3.35
Preparedness	3.34
Strategic Gap	-0.01

West	
Importance	3.33
Preparedness	3.26
Strategic Gap	-0.09

South	
Importance	3.53
Preparedness	3.35
Strategic Gap	-0.18

Strategic Readiness	New Utilization Review Laws

Hospital Executives

Importance vs. Preparedness

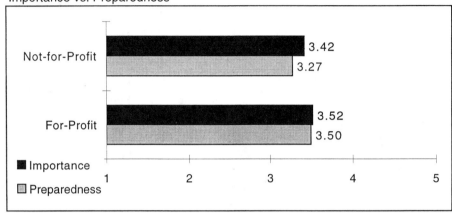

Rank	
Importance	17
Preparedness	16
Strategic Gap	17

Strategic Gap	
Not-for-profit	-0.15
For-profit	-0.02

Managed Care Executives

Importance vs. Preparedness

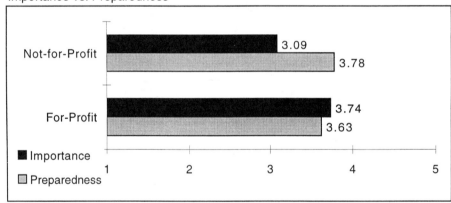

Rank	
Importance	17
Preparedness	10
Strategic Gap	17

Strategic Gap	
Not-for-profit	0.70
For-profit	-0.11

Physician Group Practice Executives

Importance vs. Preparedness

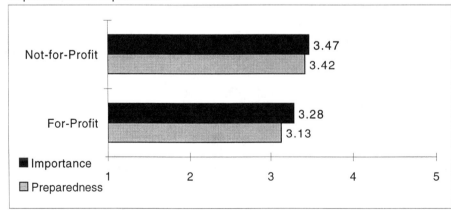

Rank	
Importance	16
Preparedness	18
Strategic Gap	12

Strategic Gap	
Not-for-profit	-0.05
For-profit	-0.15

Strategic Readiness   Partnering and Integration

Overall Results

Importance vs. Preparedness

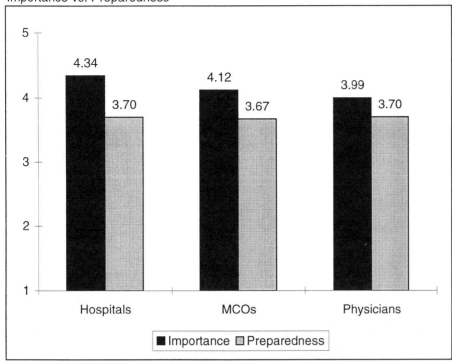

Strategic Gap	
Hospitals	-0.64
MCOs	-0.45
Physicians	-0.30

Rank	
Importance	5
Preparedness	6
Strategic Gap	5

• The higher the importance ranking, the more important the issue is to respondents.
• The higher the readiness ranking, the better the respondents view the preparedness of their institutions.
• "Strategic gap" refers to the difference between importance and preparedness.
• The rank refers to the rank of the issues out of the 21 included in the survey. Ranks are given for importance, readiness, and strategic gap. The highest rank is 1; the lowest rank is 21.

Regional Results

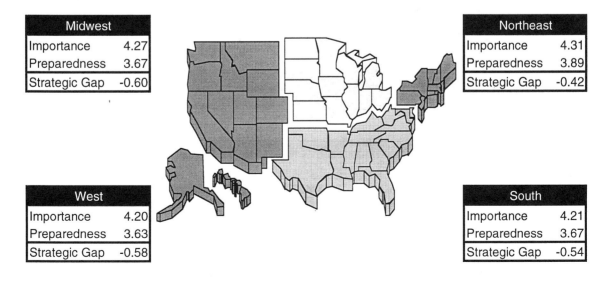

Midwest	
Importance	4.27
Preparedness	3.67
Strategic Gap	-0.60

Northeast	
Importance	4.31
Preparedness	3.89
Strategic Gap	-0.42

West	
Importance	4.20
Preparedness	3.63
Strategic Gap	-0.58

South	
Importance	4.21
Preparedness	3.67
Strategic Gap	-0.54

Strategic Readiness	Partnering and Integration

Hospital Executives

Importance vs. Preparedness

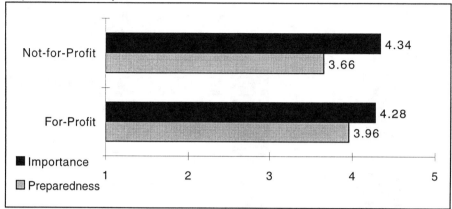

Rank	
Importance	5
Preparedness	7
Strategic Gap	5

Strategic Gap	
Not-for-profit	-0.68
For-profit	-0.32

Managed Care Executives

Importance vs. Preparedness

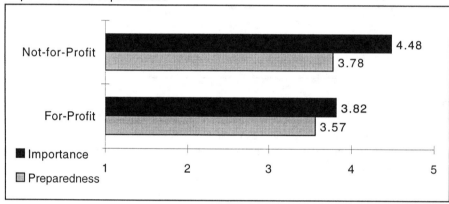

Rank	
Importance	8
Preparedness	11
Strategic Gap	5

Strategic Gap	
Not-for-profit	-0.70
For-profit	-0.25

Physician Group Practice Executives

Importance vs. Preparedness

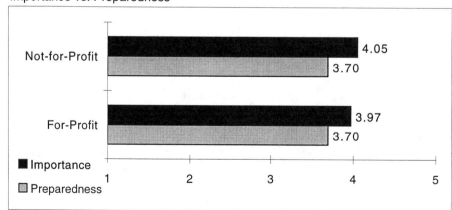

Rank	
Importance	7
Preparedness	5
Strategic Gap	10

Strategic Gap	
Not-for-profit	-0.35
For-profit	-0.27

| Strategic Readiness | Provider-Sponsored Networks |

Overall Results

Importance vs. Preparedness

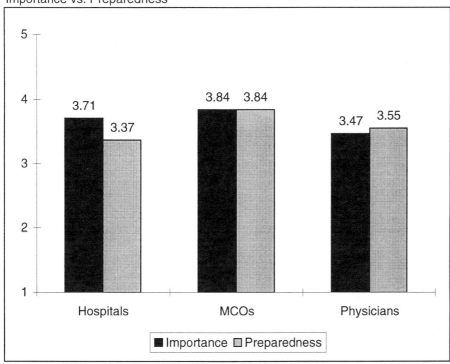

Strategic Gap	
Hospitals	-0.33
MCOs	0.00
Physicians	0.09

Rank	
Importance	14
Preparedness	12
Strategic Gap	13

• The higher the importance ranking, the more important the issue is to respondents.
• The higher the readiness ranking, the better the respondents view the preparedness of their institutions.
• "Strategic gap" refers to the difference between importance and preparedness.
• The rank refers to the rank of the issues out of the 21 included in the survey. Ranks are given for importance, readiness, and strategic gap. The highest rank is 1; the lowest rank is 21.

Regional Results

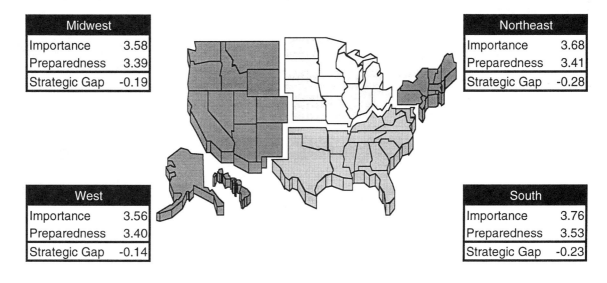

Midwest	
Importance	3.58
Preparedness	3.39
Strategic Gap	-0.19

Northeast	
Importance	3.68
Preparedness	3.41
Strategic Gap	-0.28

West	
Importance	3.56
Preparedness	3.40
Strategic Gap	-0.14

South	
Importance	3.76
Preparedness	3.53
Strategic Gap	-0.23

Strategic Readiness   **Provider-Sponsored Networks**

Hospital Executives
Importance vs. Preparedness

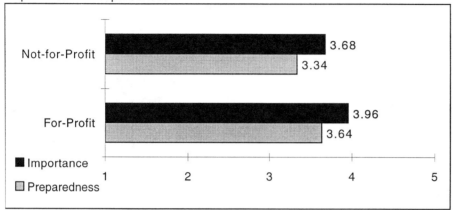

Rank	
Importance	14
Preparedness	14
Strategic Gap	11

Strategic Gap	
Not-for-profit	-0.34
For-profit	-0.32

Managed Care Executives
Importance vs. Preparedness

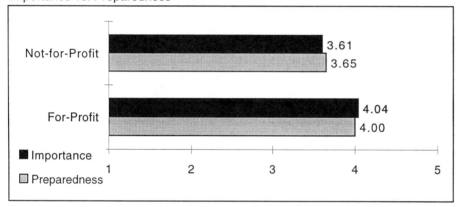

Rank	
Importance	12
Preparedness	8
Strategic Gap	12

Strategic Gap	
Not-for-profit	0.04
For-profit	-0.04

Physician Group Practice Executives
Importance vs. Preparedness

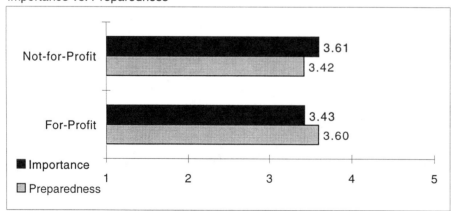

Rank	
Importance	15
Preparedness	10
Strategic Gap	17

Strategic Gap	
Not-for-profit	-0.18
For-profit	0.17

Strategic Readiness   Recruiting Qualified Senior Managers

Overall Results

Importance vs. Preparedness

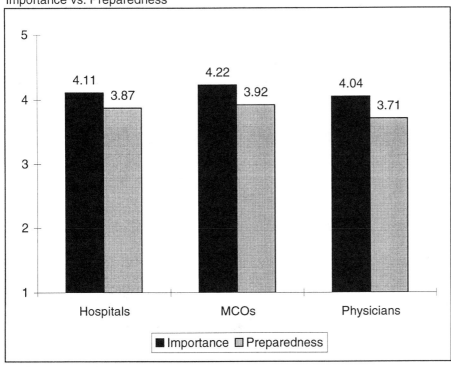

Strategic Gap	
Hospitals	-0.23
MCOs	-0.31
Physicians	-0.34

Rank	
Importance	8
Preparedness	3
Strategic Gap	12

- The higher the importance ranking, the more important the issue is to respondents.
- The higher the readiness ranking, the better the respondents view the preparedness of their institutions.
- "Strategic gap" refers to the difference between importance and preparedness.
- The rank refers to the rank of the issues out of the 21 included in the survey. Ranks are given for importance, readiness, and strategic gap. The highest rank is 1; the lowest rank is 21.

Regional Results

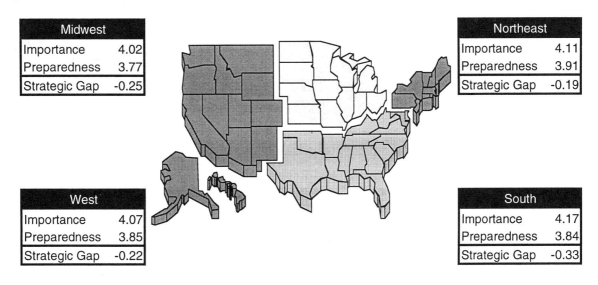

Midwest	
Importance	4.02
Preparedness	3.77
Strategic Gap	-0.25

Northeast	
Importance	4.11
Preparedness	3.91
Strategic Gap	-0.19

West	
Importance	4.07
Preparedness	3.85
Strategic Gap	-0.22

South	
Importance	4.17
Preparedness	3.84
Strategic Gap	-0.33

Strategic Readiness | **Recruiting Qualified Senior Managers**

Hospital Executives
Importance vs. Preparedness

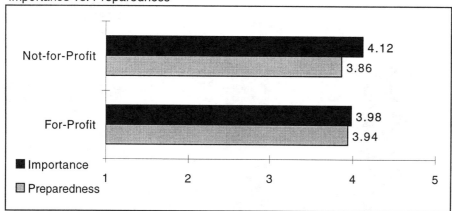

Rank	
Importance	8
Preparedness	2
Strategic Gap	13

Strategic Gap	
Not-for-profit	-0.26
For-profit	-0.04

Managed Care Executives
Importance vs. Preparedness

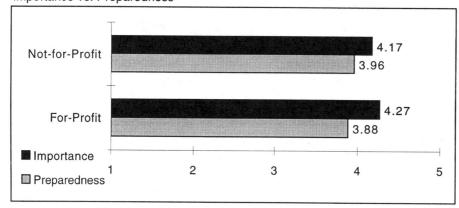

Rank	
Importance	6
Preparedness	6
Strategic Gap	8

Strategic Gap	
Not-for-profit	-0.22
For-profit	-0.38

Physician Group Practice Executives
Importance vs. Preparedness

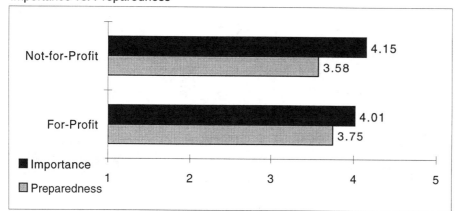

Rank	
Importance	5
Preparedness	4
Strategic Gap	8

Strategic Gap	
Not-for-profit	-0.58
For-profit	-0.27

Strategic Readiness   Responding to Community Health Needs

Overall Results

Importance vs. Preparedness

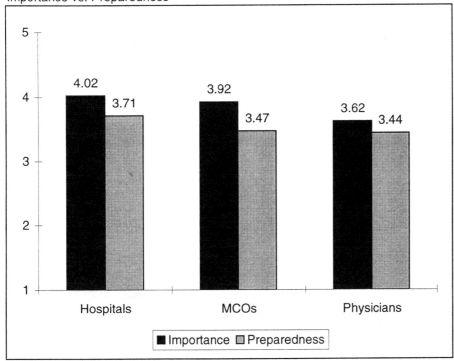

Strategic Gap	
Hospitals	-0.31
MCOs	-0.45
Physicians	-0.18

Rank	
Importance	10
Preparedness	9
Strategic Gap	11

- The higher the importance ranking, the more important the issue is to respondents.
- The higher the readiness ranking, the better the respondents view the preparedness of their institutions.
- "Strategic gap" refers to the difference between importance and preparedness.
- The rank refers to the rank of the issues out of the 21 included in the survey. Ranks are given for importance, readiness, and strategic gap. The highest rank is 1; the lowest rank is 21.

Regional Results

Midwest	
Importance	4.00
Preparedness	3.63
Strategic Gap	-0.37

Northeast	
Importance	4.00
Preparedness	3.71
Strategic Gap	-0.29

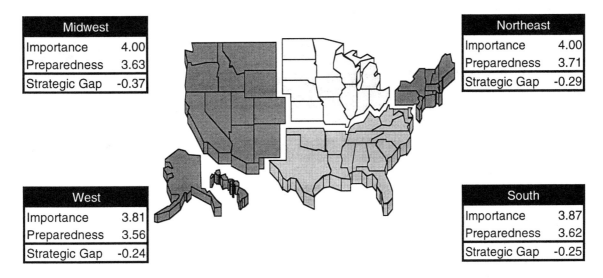

West	
Importance	3.81
Preparedness	3.56
Strategic Gap	-0.24

South	
Importance	3.87
Preparedness	3.62
Strategic Gap	-0.25

Strategic Readiness   **Responding to Community Health Needs**

Hospital Executives
Importance vs. Preparedness

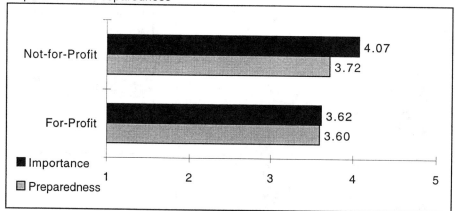

Rank	
Importance	9
Preparedness	6
Strategic Gap	12

Strategic Gap	
Not-for-profit	-0.35
For-profit	-0.02

Managed Care Executives
Importance vs. Preparedness

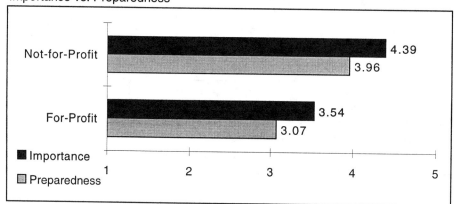

Rank	
Importance	11
Preparedness	17
Strategic Gap	6

Strategic Gap	
Not-for-profit	-0.43
For-profit	-0.46

Physician Group Practice Executives
Importance vs. Preparedness

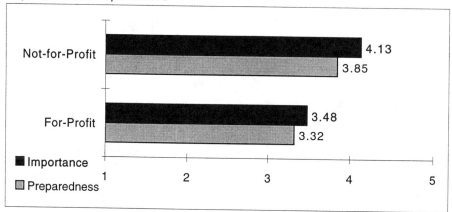

Rank	
Importance	11
Preparedness	13
Strategic Gap	11

Strategic Gap	
Not-for-profit	-0.28
For-profit	-0.16

Strategic Readiness | State-Mandated Reforms

Overall Results

Importance vs. Preparedness

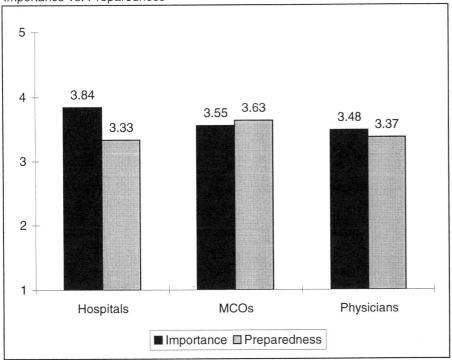

Strategic Gap	
Hospitals	-0.51
MCOs	0.08
Physicians	-0.11

Rank	
Importance	13
Preparedness	15
Strategic Gap	9

- The higher the importance ranking, the more important the issue is to respondents.
- The higher the readiness ranking, the better the respondents view the preparedness of their institutions.
- "Strategic gap" refers to the difference between importance and preparedness.
- The rank refers to the rank of the issues out of the 21 included in the survey. Ranks are given for importance, readiness, and strategic gap. The highest rank is 1; the lowest rank is 21.

Regional Results

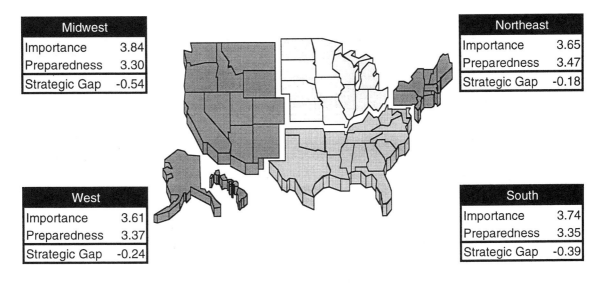

Midwest	
Importance	3.84
Preparedness	3.30
Strategic Gap	-0.54

Northeast	
Importance	3.65
Preparedness	3.47
Strategic Gap	-0.18

West	
Importance	3.61
Preparedness	3.37
Strategic Gap	-0.24

South	
Importance	3.74
Preparedness	3.35
Strategic Gap	-0.39

Strategic Readiness   **State-Mandated Reforms**

Hospital Executives
Importance vs. Preparedness

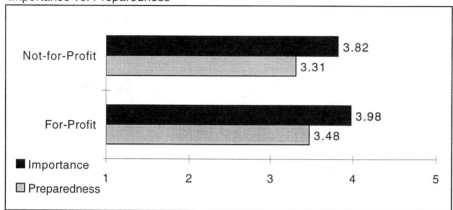

Rank	
Importance	13
Preparedness	15
Strategic Gap	7

Strategic Gap	
Not-for-profit	-0.52
For-profit	-0.50

Managed Care Executives
Importance vs. Preparedness

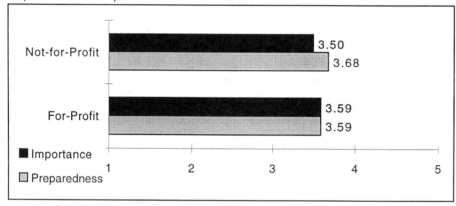

Rank	
Importance	14
Preparedness	13
Strategic Gap	15

Strategic Gap	
Not-for-profit	0.18
For-profit	0.00

Physician Group Practice Executives
Importance vs. Preparedness

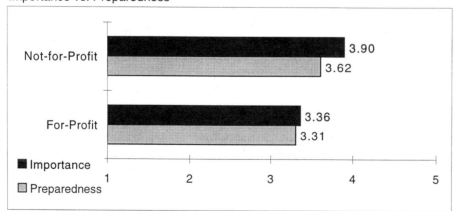

Rank	
Importance	14
Preparedness	15
Strategic Gap	13

Strategic Gap	
Not-for-profit	-0.28
For-profit	-0.06

Strategic Readiness | Working with Business Coalitions

Overall Results

Importance vs. Preparedness

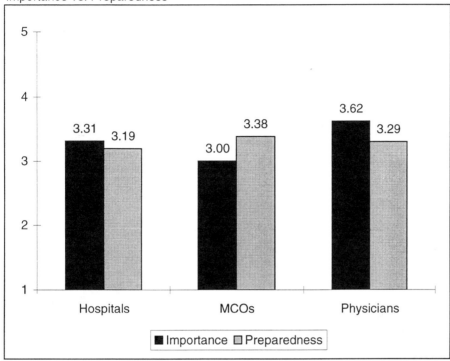

Strategic Gap	
Hospitals	-0.12
MCOs	0.38
Physicians	-0.32

Rank	
Importance	18
Preparedness	17
Strategic Gap	14

- The higher the importance ranking, the more important the issue is to respondents.
- The higher the readiness ranking, the better the respondents view the preparedness of their institutions.
- "Strategic gap" refers to the difference between importance and preparedness.
- The rank refers to the rank of the issues out of the 21 included in the survey. Ranks are given for importance, readiness, and strategic gap. The highest rank is 1; the lowest rank is 21.

Regional Results

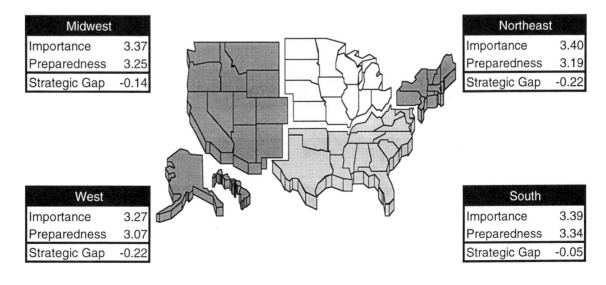

Midwest	
Importance	3.37
Preparedness	3.25
Strategic Gap	-0.14

Northeast	
Importance	3.40
Preparedness	3.19
Strategic Gap	-0.22

West	
Importance	3.27
Preparedness	3.07
Strategic Gap	-0.22

South	
Importance	3.39
Preparedness	3.34
Strategic Gap	-0.05

Hospital Executives
Importance vs. Preparedness

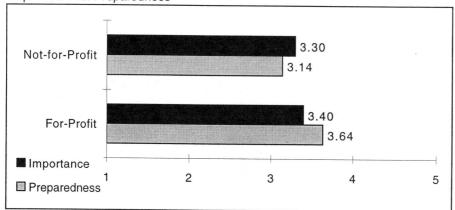

Rank	
Importance	19
Preparedness	17
Strategic Gap	18

Strategic Gap	
Not-for-profit	-0.16
For-profit	0.24

Managed Care Executives
Importance vs. Preparedness

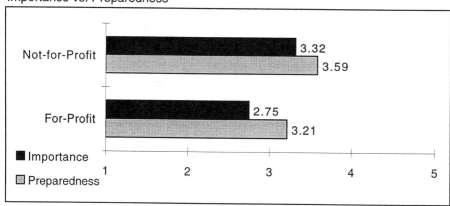

Rank	
Importance	20
Preparedness	18
Strategic Gap	19

Strategic Gap	
Not-for-profit	0.27
For-profit	0.46

Physician Group Practice Executives
Importance vs. Preparedness

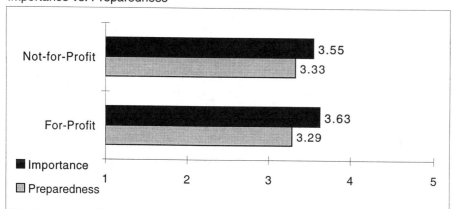

Rank	
Importance	12
Preparedness	17
Strategic Gap	9

Strategic Gap	
Not-for-profit	-0.23
For-profit	-0.35

Which of These Are Issues in Your Local Communities?

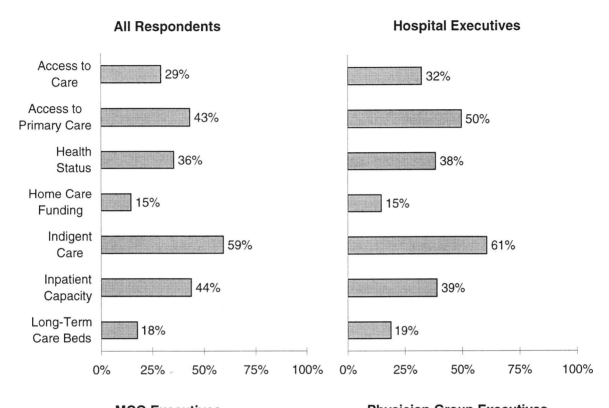

All Respondents

Access to Care	29%
Access to Primary Care	43%
Health Status	36%
Home Care Funding	15%
Indigent Care	59%
Inpatient Capacity	44%
Long-Term Care Beds	18%

Hospital Executives

Access to Care	32%
Access to Primary Care	50%
Health Status	38%
Home Care Funding	15%
Indigent Care	61%
Inpatient Capacity	39%
Long-Term Care Beds	19%

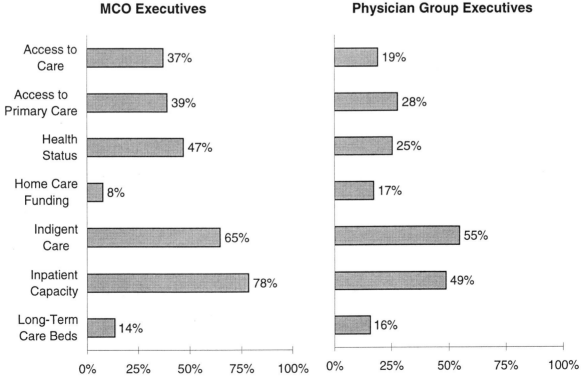

MCO Executives

Access to Care	37%
Access to Primary Care	39%
Health Status	47%
Home Care Funding	8%
Indigent Care	65%
Inpatient Capacity	78%
Long-Term Care Beds	14%

Physician Group Executives

Access to Care	19%
Access to Primary Care	28%
Health Status	25%
Home Care Funding	17%
Indigent Care	55%
Inpatient Capacity	49%
Long-Term Care Beds	16%

• Percent of respondents identifying each area; multiple responses allowed.

3

Partnerships

Kevin Lumsdon

Analysts and journalists often use the words "frenzy" and "mania" to describe the pace of consolidation and deal making in health care today. But there's much more than hype behind those words: The speed and the results are dramatic, signaling vast changes as players in the marketplace struggle both to expand geographically and to shrink the costs of doing business. These partnerships and alliances take various forms, including long-term contracts, loose affiliations, and full-asset mergers.

Fundamentally, health care's deal frenzy is about clout. Jockeying for managed care contracts, achieving economies of scale, and expanding market share top the list of motivations among all three sectors, hospitals, health plans, and physician groups. Partnerships are not only driven by shifting market conditions—such as tighter, fixed payments and growth in managed care—but they also drive new alliances to form. "Mergers aren't the ends but the means" to leaner cost structures and fewer duplicated services, consultant Gerald McManis recently argued.[1] But once a deal closes, he pointed out, the hard work of consolidating services can take five years or more to pull off. Politics, turf issues, tradition, and egos all factor into the equation. "Still, I don't say we're trying to do too much too soon," McManis continued. "If anything, we started too late."

Respondents affirm partnering activity as a core strategy. In the last five years, hospitals, medical groups, and managed care plans have frequently crossed into new structural terrain. More than a quarter of respondents have joined a hospital or health system; more than 18 percent have acquired another organization; and nearly 20 percent have formed an equal partnership. But many made their moves even earlier; 71.4 percent say they already belong to an integrated delivery network or some type of alliance.

Health care executives overwhelmingly place importance on the scramble for partners and see these moves as key to their future success. Some are readier than others to handle the realities of the morning after and to strike out with new partnerships in the future. Change produces anxiety and uncertainty, a sentiment echoed again and again in the survey. So far, however, the evidence suggests that the pace of new partnerships will remain brisk, despite uncertain outcomes and recent criticism about the value being gained. For example, the accounting firm Deloitte & Touche has warned that recently merged hospitals were not combining clinical services fast enough.[2]

Whatever the postmerger hurdles, hospital consolidation has accelerated dramatically in the past few years. Between 1994 and 1996, nearly 400 such transactions were announced, a figure that far outdistances the 195 mergers reported between 1980 and 1991. Moreover, 1997 was off to a record-shattering start, with hospitals unveiling plans for nearly 100 mergers in the first half of the year alone.[3] Looser business arrangements are not as closely tracked or announced with as much fanfare, but they are equally important agents of change. The management consulting firm Bedford Health Associates has gone as far as projecting that 90 percent of the nation's hospitals will belong to regional health networks by 2000.[4]

The consolidation trend goes beyond hospitals. Deal making is intense across all sectors. The first quarter of 1997 saw a record 315 transactions. Merger and acquisition volume slowed about 14 percent in the second quarter, but it still represented the third highest three-month period on record.[5] Doctors and hospitals account for most of today's matchups—more than 40 percent in recent periods—perhaps simply because they outnumber managed care plans. Hospital transactions and physician group mergers have numbered in the hundreds in recent years, while deals involving HMOs have hovered in the double digits. In the 10 years from 1985 to 1995, the number of medical group practices climbed from 15,485 to 19,787, as more and more doctors left solo practice. Yet most of today's physician groups remain small; 69 percent have no more than six doctors.[6]

Because insurers need especially large enrollments to compete in the marketplace, a few plans tend to dominate over time in most regions. HMO deals tend to be much larger and more dramatic, such as the national powerhouses created by last year's PacifiCare/FHP merger and by the merger of Aetna Health Plans and U.S. Healthcare. At the same time, the number of new HMOs has climbed significantly, particularly those started by hospitals and health systems. From December 1994 to July 1996, the number of HMOs belonging to integrated networks soared by 207 percent.[7] Interest in buying and selling managed care plans, however, may be waning, with greater interest in alliances among hospitals, medical groups, and health plans.

Supply and demand also play prominent roles in deals of all types. Although hospitals in many urban markets have already mothballed large numbers of beds and even entire facilities, insurers continue to squeeze hospital admissions and lengths of stay. Forecasts of markets dominated by managed care show that facilities in many regions have their work cut out for them, as hospital days per thousand patients decline by half or more. This factor will spur more mergers and alliances. (See table 3-1.)

Doctors also must contend with oversupply in their ranks, particularly specialists. When the numbers of specialists in physician networks of large HMOs are used as the standard, the nation's oversupply stands at 76 percent among all specialists. General surgeons (115 percent) and cardiologists (147 percent) lead the pack.[8] Participation in networks, independent practice associations, and group practices are among the remedies physicians use to ensure sufficient flow of patients and specialty referrals, and to escape from administrative burdens.

ISSUES FOR HOSPITAL EXECUTIVES

Hospitals are partnership mavens. More than three-quarters of responding hospitals already belong to an alliance or integrated delivery network, though less than a third have done so in the past five years. Of that group, most of them apparently prefer to keep their deals even by sharing control: About one-fifth say that they formed an equal partnership during the period.

Outright acquisitions of hospitals occurred less frequently than did other partnership moves: 10.1 percent of respondents have been acquired by another organization, while nearly 16 percent say they did the acquiring. But among for-profit hospitals, the growth of large national chains such as Columbia/HCA and Tenet Healthcare is especially pronounced. Nearly two-thirds of for-profits have been purchased in the last five years, and 16 percent have bought another organization. Not-for-profits, meanwhile, are much more likely to have joined a hospital or health system—nearly a third of them.

The percentage of hospitals reporting membership in existing networks and alliances is somewhat higher here than in other recent national surveys. But definitions and timing may explain the differences. As of February 1996, SMG Marketing Group reported that a third of all U.S. hospitals belonged to integrated networks.[9] The *Hospitals & Health Networks* Leadership Survey, however, was carried out more than a year later. More important, it allowed

Table 3-1. Hospital Bed Supply and Demand—Current and Future

Market	Staffed beds per 1,000 pop., 1994	Need for beds per 1,000, current market	Estimated demand for beds per 1,000, 100% managed care
Boston	6.1	3.2	1.6
Pittsburgh	6.0	3.8	1.9
New York	5.5	3.3	1.6
Cleveland	5.4	2.5	1.7
Tampa	5.1	2.7	2.2
Philadelphia	5.0	3.2	1.6
St. Louis	5.0	2.4	1.6
Miami	5.0	2.3	1.8
Chicago	4.3	2.2	1.5
Houston	4.3	2.0	1.3
Detroit	4.0	2.3	1.5
San Francisco	4.0	1.6	1.4
Los Angeles	3.7	1.5	1.3
Dallas	3.6	2.0	1.4
Atlanta	3.5	2.1	1.4
Phoenix	3.2	1.6	1.5
Minneapolis	2.8	1.8	1.5
San Diego	2.8	1.5	1.3
Seattle	2.5	1.5	1.4

Source: The Sachs Group, 1995.

respondents to include other types of partnerships in their answers and counted looser affiliations and joint ventures. The figure also includes members of large national and regional hospital systems.

Three-quarters of hospital respondents are already in networks or systems; more than a third of these were acquired by larger organizations (including integrated networks) in the past two years, while nearly as many have joined provider networks without combining assets.[10]

Hospitals are most often aligning horizontally; nearly all say the deal included another hospital. Horizontal integration is more prevalent among not-for-profits than for-profits—89.2 percent versus 56.3 percent. Vertical alignments are fairly common, too, with no significant differences by tax status. More than half of these partnerships operate home health agencies, and nearly as many include a physician group practice. Physician-hospital organizations and managed care organizations (MCOs) are also popular components.

Managed care contracting is the number one driver of all this activity; 82.5 percent of hospitals list this reason. Other big motivators include economies of scale, increased market share, and better geographic reach. Only 11.6 percent say they aim to cut excess capacity by partnering. This finding jibes with the 1996 Deloitte & Touche study, which took hospitals to task for failing to combine clinical services postmerger. Tax status makes little difference here, although not-for-profits are more interested in economies of scale than are their for-profit counterparts.

Future partnerships seem likely for most hospitals, but apparently through contracts rather than purchases. Nearly two-thirds of hospitals say their current strategies include alliances with other hospitals, while just 12.7 percent are interested in acquiring an acute care facility. Few say they will be acquired by another entity. For-profits, however, remain much more interested than not-for-profits in hospital consolidation—36 percent versus 10.2 percent. On the whole, purchases of practices may be waning. Only a quarter of hospitals say their strategies include such a move, though not-for-profits are slightly more interested. The mounting evidence that hospitals lose money on these deals may be having an impact. Instead, more than half plan to form alliances with physician groups and health plans.

Interest and readiness are different animals for hospital leaders. They reported sizable differences between the importance rating and their self-described preparedness for all forms of alliances. Nearly all consider partnerships with doctors somewhat or extremely important, for example, but about one-third fewer consider themselves ready to act. Hospitals feel least prepared to move forward with alliances involving all three parties—themselves, doctors, and MCOs. Meanwhile, experience with managed care contracting may be boosting their confidence in health plan partnerships, which represented the smallest strategic gap.

ISSUES FOR MANAGED CARE EXECUTIVES

Although partnerships are prevalent in other sectors, most health plans have gone about their business quietly and without accompaniment the past five years. While 60 percent already belong to an alliance or an integrated delivery network, less than 20 percent have joined one in the past five years. Overall, the average time in an alliance is 7.5 years. But not-for-profits are more than twice as likely to belong to an integrated network than are investor-owned health plans.

Rather than joining alliances and networks, health plans are slightly more likely to have acquired another organization (31.4 percent) or formed an equal partnership (25.5 percent) in the past five years. As for those getting acquired, tax status makes a difference; a quarter of for-profits report being purchased, while this activity was entirely absent among not-for-profits.

Hospitals and physician groups are the most common elements of alliances reported by MCOs. More than a third of for-profit plans include physician groups in their partnerships, and three-quarters of not-for-profits do so. This difference could reflect recent moves by health plans to divest medical groups, though it is not clear how many of these alliances involve ownership arrangements.

Market share is the big motivator for deals involving health plans. More than three-quarters give that as the top reason for their partnering and integration moves. Better positioning for managed care contracts, economies of scale, and geographic reach are also big draws. Slightly more than a third pursue partnerships to improve access to capital.

Though the past five years have been relatively quiet on the partnership front for MCOs, that may change in the coming years. More than half say their current strategies include entering alliances. Most of them are eyeing other health plans, but more often as partners than as acquisition targets. Close to half foresee such alliances with other managed care plans. Health plans express similar levels of interest in developing new partnerships with hospitals and physician groups but seldom in buying them. Interest in these ventures is stronger among not-for-profits; only about 40 percent of for-profits want to pursue alliances with either physician groups or hospitals.

Managed care respondents are confident about their readiness for partnerships with hospitals, but for-profits give only middling importance to such deals. For-profits place more weight on alliances with doctors. The confidence ends with hospital deals, however. Health plans feel unprepared for new alliances with doctors and least of all for deals bringing all three parties to the table.

ISSUES FOR GROUP PRACTICE EXECUTIVES

Networking with their own kind has been the most common form of partnering among doctors during the past five years. Nearly half of the medical group respondents say they joined a physician network in that time, and the average alliance got off the ground 4.5 years ago. Less than two-thirds currently belong to an integrated delivery network or alliance, and about one-fifth have joined a hospital or health system in the past five years. Consolidation is also evident; 21.5 percent say they acquired another organization during the period. Less than one-tenth were acquired by someone else.

Differences surface when comparing for-profit with not-for-profit groups. More than half of for-profits have joined a physician network in the past five years, compared with 27.5 percent of not-for-profits. For-profits are also more likely to have acquired another organization. Meanwhile, not-for-profits are nearly twice as likely to have joined a hospital or health system in the past five years. One reason for these differences may be that respondents include leaders from physician-hospital organizations as well as those heading multispecialty groups of merged practices.

Medical groups in alliances are most likely to have teamed only with other medical groups in the last five years. Their alliance partners include hospitals less than half the time, and even fewer partnerships include MCOs (37.3 percent), freestanding clinics (24.5 percent), and other components. Again, the partnership picture among not-for-profits is drawn differently; nearly three-quarters of not-for-profit medical groups include hospitals, and more than half include MCOs.

Contracting clout with managed care firms led more than three-quarters of medical groups to pursue partnership deals. Market share, referrals, and economies of scale were other prominent reasons. Motivation varies little by tax status, except that for-profits (44.6 percent) are twice as likely to identify geographic reach as a benefit.

Medical groups see more alliances coming, but interest in partners diverges widely by tax status. More than 67 percent of for-profits intend to link with other medical groups, as opposed to 37.5 percent of not-for-profits. And more than 62 percent of for-profits include hospitals in their alliance strategies, versus 40 percent of not-for-profits. Virtually nobody expresses interest in being taken over by a larger network or organization. Only a handful plan to sell their practices to hospitals or other physician groups, but nearly one-fourth of for-profit medical groups aim to buy other practices, a strategy favored by fewer not-for-profits.

Not-for-profits clearly see their continued success more closely linked to hospitals than do for-profit groups. About 84 percent say those alliances are either somewhat or extremely important, while slightly more than half of for-profits shared that sentiment. The two came closer in rating the value of their future alliances with health plans. More than three-quarters of for-profits agree that such deals with health plans are somewhat or extremely important, and nearly two-thirds of not-for-profits take that position. Not-for-profits are far more bullish in their rating of alliances among hospitals, health plans, and doctors. Nevertheless, they do not all feel ready to handle the challenges implicit in such deals. A comparison between importance and preparedness shows negative strategic gaps for all forms of partnerships, with the most pronounced strategic gaps for deals that bring all three parties to the table.

KEY COMPARISONS

Joining a hospital or health system during the past five years was largely a not-for-profit strategy. Both tax-exempt hospitals and physician groups took that route in greater numbers than did their for-profit counterparts—about one-third of both groups. Health plans, meanwhile, were much more likely to be out prospecting for acquisition targets; similar percentages of for-profits and not-for-profits report buying other organizations. And for-profit group practices were busy building leverage another way, joining physician networks at twice the rate not-for-profit groups did.

The survey also asked respondents to project the growth of for-profit hospitals by 2000 and by 2007. The percentage of investor-owned facilities is currently 13.7 percent. All respondents foresee significant growth, though not-for-profit hospitals peg the coming percentages lower than did other respondents: 18.6 percent by 2000 and 29.4 percent by 2007. But all hospitals foresee slower growth than the other groups. Executives in for-profit health plans expect the biggest growth. They see for-profit hospitals grabbing nearly 35 percent of the market by 2007, while not-for-profit medical group leaders set the figure at 33 percent.

As for the effects of this consolidation, respondents agree that access to capital will improve and that prices to payers will rise. Both hospitals and health plans say hospitals will benefit as the cost of care decreases. But they part company over the perceived effects on quality. Not-for-profits see both quality and access suffering. For-profits agree about access but not quality, predicting that their growth will improve it. Meanwhile, only a slight percentage of doctors expect that access to care will suffer.

Alliances and networks are deeply entrenched. Except for for-profit health plans (which have not joined alliances at the same rate), more than 60 percent of respondents say they already belong to one. It is notable that MCOs that have joined alliances have longer track records—an average of 7.5 years, 3 years longer than the overall average.

Partners see different advantages to making these deals. These discrepancies are not terribly surprising; a mix of incentives are present in almost every business dealing. Health plans are more often motivated by the lure of bigger market share than are others, while hospitals overwhelmingly aim to better position themselves to negotiate managed care contracts. Hospitals, particularly the tax-exempt, are moved by economies of scale more than any other group. For-profit facilities, meanwhile, eye market share as much as health plans do. This could result from a more intense business orientation than the one shaping not-for-profit decisions or the need to catch up with competitors in new markets.

Doctors win the partnership popularity contest. They are sought after by the majority of all respondents. However, only 34 percent of for-profit and less than 25 percent of not-for-profit hospitals say they intend to buy practices. In fact, hospitals remain even more interested in acquiring practices than do other medical groups. But those figures hardly point to a mass movement. With few exceptions, acquisitions are out and partnerships are in, signaling a sharp turn toward virtual integration. On other fronts, for example, only for-profit hospitals (at 36 percent) expressed notable interest in acquiring other hospitals.

Though interest is high, few are prepared for a virtual future. When asked about the likelihood of alliances between providers and health plans becoming widespread, 55 percent say that it is somewhat likely—not yet a ringing endorsement. Furthermore, across the three groups of respondents, there were significant strategic gaps for all four types of partnerships—whether between hospitals and MCOs, medical groups and health plans, hospitals and medical groups, or a combination of all three. Complexity breeds uncertainty in this case. All groups gave the latter combination the biggest strategic gap.

Executives see differences in importance and readiness as they take stock of partnerships other than their own. Hospitals suffer the largest strategic gaps, even in deals where others see a good match. For example, they consider themselves much less prepared for partnerships with doctors than do not-for-profit health plans. And though respondents report the greatest readiness for partnerships involving hospitals and health plans, hospitals do not see things that way. Their strategic gap falls below that of respondents overall. For their part, MCOs give their ventures with hospitals their only positive score. Perhaps, as seen elsewhere in the survey, health plans still seem to have the upper hand in contract negotiations. Power leads to positive thinking.

IMPLICATIONS

Health care futurist Jeff Goldsmith and other observers have urged system leaders for several years to reverse the acquisition frenzy—to stop buying up more hospitals, more medical practices, more everything, and concentrate instead on trimming their costs and improving what they started with. "The idea that you can wheel and deal yourself into a competitive position is something that will disappear," Goldsmith told *Hospitals & Health Networks* last year. "Health care executives right now are consumed in the deal and are not looking at how to create value."[11]

His exhortations may be sinking in; this survey indicates a widespread increase in interest in partnerships and alliances that go beyond traditional acquisitions. But there are consequences and insecurities behind this trend, evident in the strategic gaps shown toward all forms of partnerships. Competing motivations and expectations are not easily resolved, and experience is scant in dealing with conflicts. Long-term contracts do not necessarily secure anyone's future. In light of the apparent momentum toward alliances, health care leaders might simply have to get over that insecurity. And if they intend to act on their interest in partnerships, they will need help learning the fine art of negotiating.

Plenty of blowups are likely to result, however skilled the negotiators become. As partners come and go, improvements in care and products developed in one virtual system can be easily exported to a competing one. Contractual relationships also take time and finesse. Control must be shared. "It's very different from a direct reporting relationship. And yet, the not-for-profit sector of health care is out there setting up a plethora of alliances and strategic relationships. They are different animals in terms of time, talent, and management techniques," said Judith Pelham, CEO of Mercy Health Services in Farmington Hills, Michigan.[12]

As these relationships play out, it's clear that some consolidation through horizontal integration will continue. Survey respondents see the ranks of for-profits doubling over the next 10 years. Certain events that occurred after the present survey was conducted may change that. The federal investigation of, and executive departures at, Columbia/HCA Healthcare have changed the for-profit giant's position in the market. Columbia's new chief, Thomas Frist, not only has a less aggressive style than his predecessor but also a less voracious appetite for acquisitions. Tenet Healthcare, the number two chain, bills itself as kinder and gentler. Wall Street has an unforgiving way of dealing with both financial setbacks and strategic shifts. Falling stock prices and lower credit ratings may slow the growth of these companies, at least in the short term.[13]

Despite these developments, changes in the for-profit mix are not likely to slow partnerships overall—not with the level of interest that respondents expressed. Nor is the pressure for cost-efficiency abating. As employers and the government push for proof that they are getting their money's worth, cost and quality concerns will intersect. The drive for greater efficiency and standards of care will likely bring more partners to the table. Though loose affiliations may come first, it is possible that long-term contracts may prompt some partners to form even closer ties, leading to new mergers down the road. But these deals will likely face new standards. Value will be the pivotal issue. Can these new entitites give the market something it wants? That's the ultimate test.

References

1. Kevin Lumsdon, "Deals That Went Down the Drain," *Hospitals & Health Networks* 70, no. 22 (November 20, 1996): 24.

2. *U.S. Hospitals and the Future of Health Care: A Continuing Opinion Survey* (Philadelphia: Deloitte & Touche, 1996), p. 4.

3. *The Health Care Merger & Acquisition Report* (New Canaan, Conn.: Irving Levin Associates, 1997).

4. *Redesigning Health Care for the New Millennium: An Assessment of the Health Care Environment in the United States* (Irving, Tex.: VHA Inc., 1997), p. 27.

5. *The Health Care Merger & Acquisition Report.*

6. *Redesigning Health Care for the New Millennium,* pp. 32–33.

7. *Market Letter* (Chicago: SMG Marketing Group, 1996).

8. *The Dartmouth Atlas of Health Care* (Chicago: American Hospital Publishing, 1996), p. 149.

9. *Market Letter.*

10. *U.S. Hospitals and the Future of Health Care.*

11. "Look at It This Way," *Hospitals & Health Networks* 70, no. 14 (July 20, 1996): 68.

12. Kevin Lumsdon, "Talk Shows," *Hospitals & Health Networks* 70, no. 14 (July 20, 1996): 52.

13. Eva M. Rodriguez and Laurie McGinley, "Move to Widen Columbia/HCA Inquiry Undertaken by Justice Department," *Wall Street Journal* (September 9, 1997): A2; 14. Lucette Lagnado, "Columbia/HCA Warns of Profit Decline," *Wall Street Journal* (September 10, 1997): A3.

Tactics Used by All Respondents in the Last Five Years

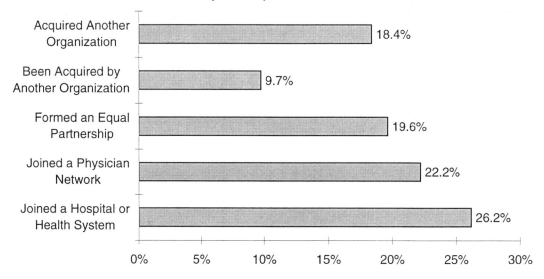

Part of an Integrated Delivery Network--All Respondents

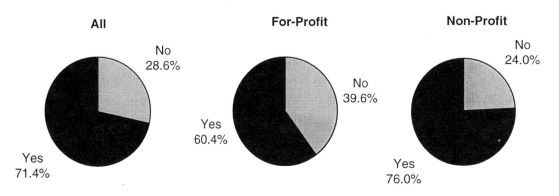

Average Years in an Alliance or Partnership--All Respondents

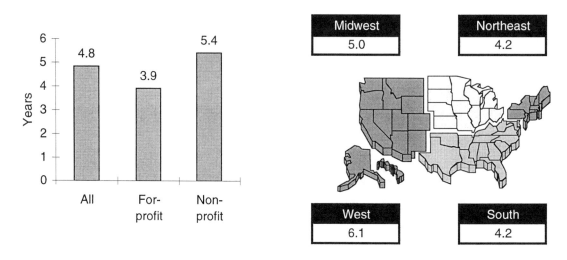

Reasons for Partnering and Integration--All Respondents

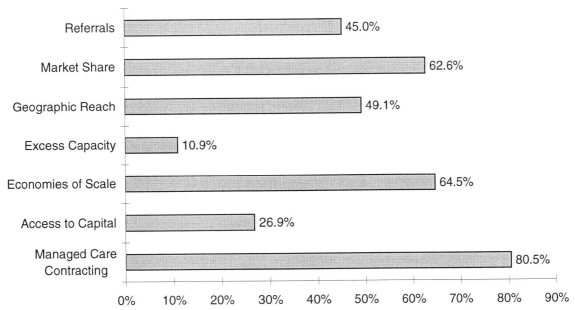

Components of the Organization's Network--All Respondents

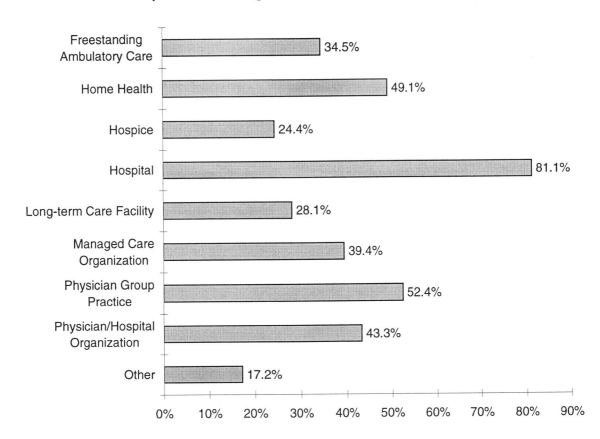

Partnerships   **Tactics**

Partnering Strategies

What all respondents say they'll do with . . .

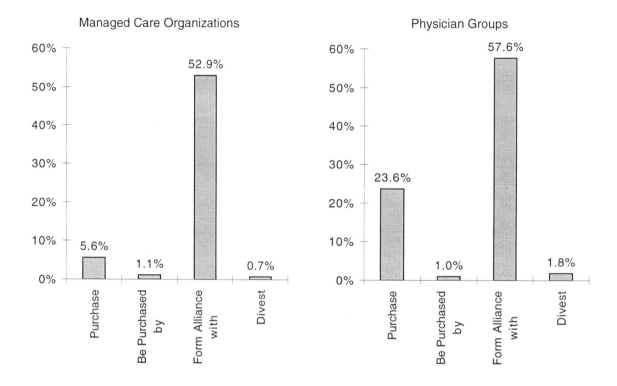

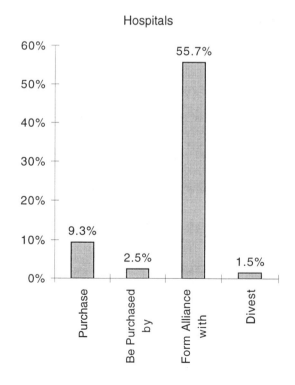

Tactics Used by Hospital Executives in the Last Five Years

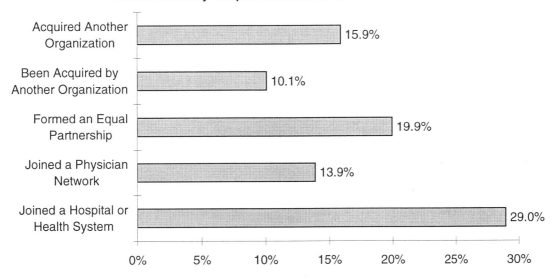

Part of an Integrated Delivery Network--Hospital Executives

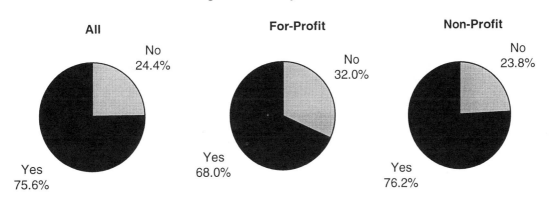

Average Years in an Alliance or Partnership--Hospital Executives

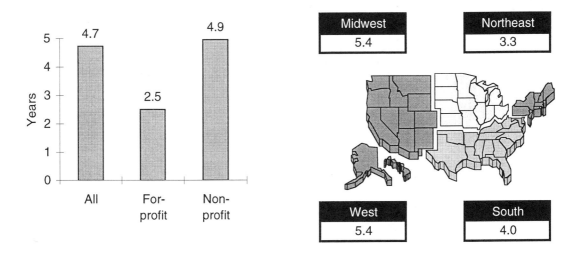

Partnerships   **Tactics**

Reasons for Partnering and Integration--Hospital Executives

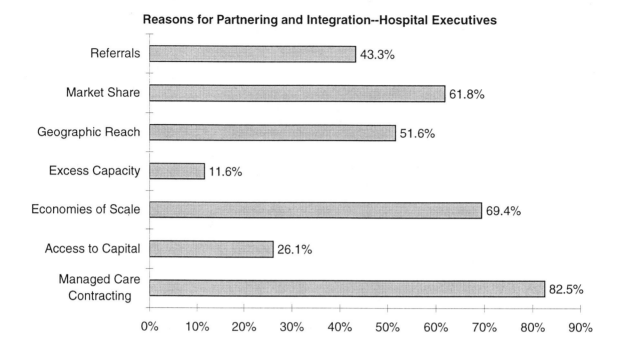

Referrals	43.3%
Market Share	61.8%
Geographic Reach	51.6%
Excess Capacity	11.6%
Economies of Scale	69.4%
Access to Capital	26.1%
Managed Care Contracting	82.5%

Components of the Organization's Network--Hospital Executives

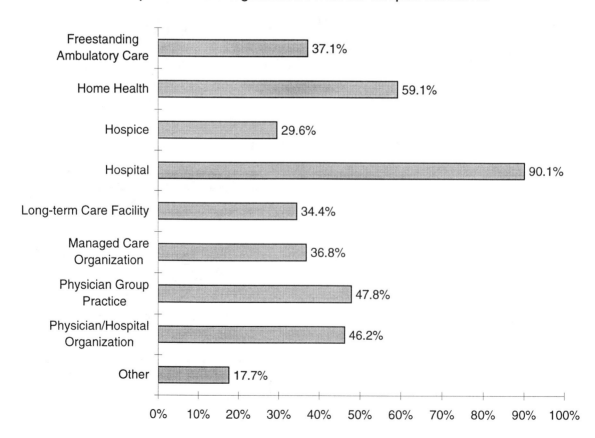

Freestanding Ambulatory Care	37.1%
Home Health	59.1%
Hospice	29.6%
Hospital	90.1%
Long-term Care Facility	34.4%
Managed Care Organization	36.8%
Physician Group Practice	47.8%
Physician/Hospital Organization	46.2%
Other	17.7%

Partnering Strategies

What hospital executives say they'll do with . . .

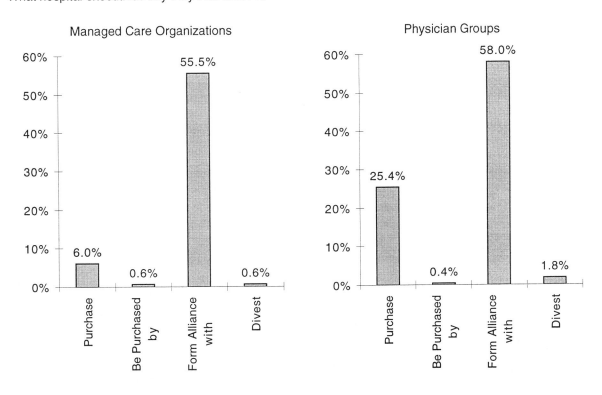

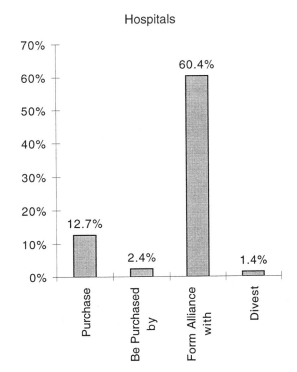

Tactics Used by Managed Care Executives in the Last Five Years

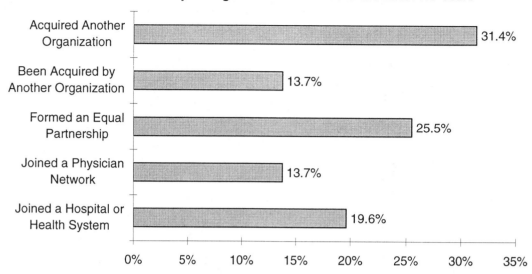

Part of an Integrated Delivery Network--Managed Care Executives

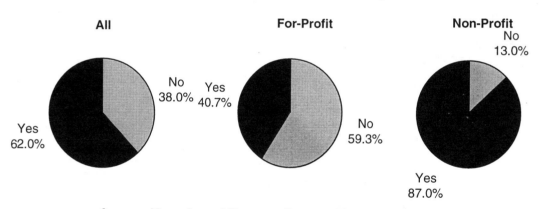

Average Years in an Alliance or Partnership--Managed Care Executives

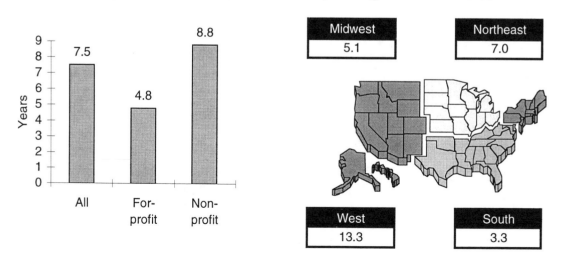

Reasons for Partnering and Integration--Managed Care Executives

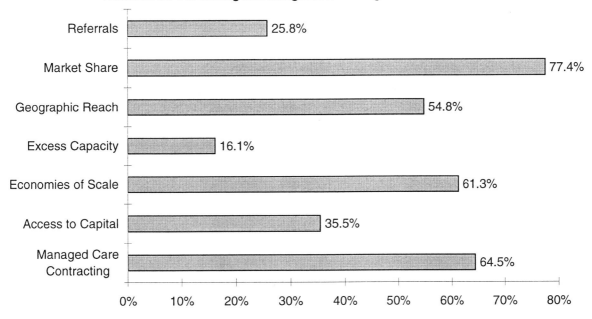

Referrals	25.8%
Market Share	77.4%
Geographic Reach	54.8%
Excess Capacity	16.1%
Economies of Scale	61.3%
Access to Capital	35.5%
Managed Care Contracting	64.5%

Components of the Organization's Network--Managed Care Executives

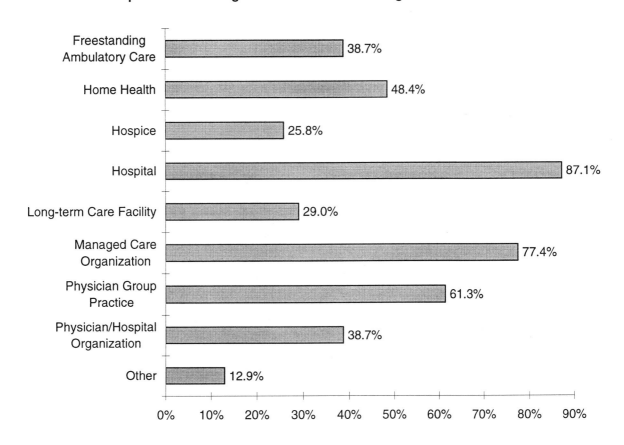

Freestanding Ambulatory Care	38.7%
Home Health	48.4%
Hospice	25.8%
Hospital	87.1%
Long-term Care Facility	29.0%
Managed Care Organization	77.4%
Physician Group Practice	61.3%
Physician/Hospital Organization	38.7%
Other	12.9%

Partnerships   **Tactics**

Partnering Strategies

What managed care executives say they'll do with . . .

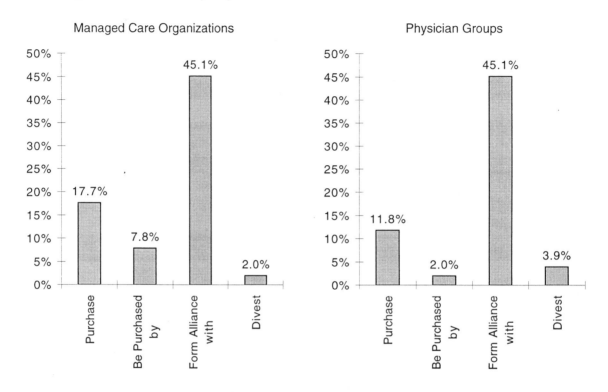

Managed Care Organizations

Physician Groups

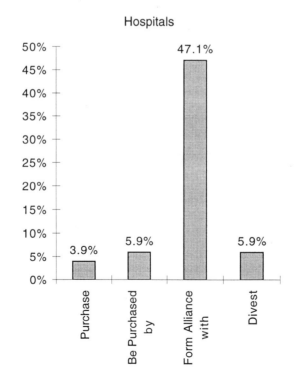

Hospitals

Partnerships   **Tactics**

Tactics Used by Physician Group Executives in the Last Five Years

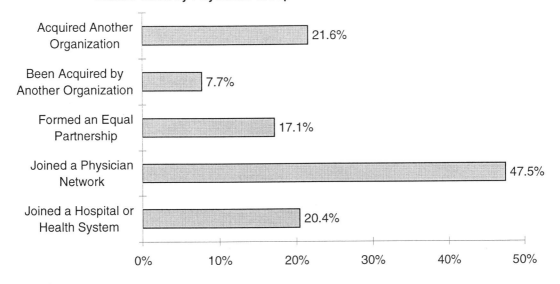

Acquired Another Organization	21.6%
Been Acquired by Another Organization	7.7%
Formed an Equal Partnership	17.1%
Joined a Physician Network	47.5%
Joined a Hospital or Health System	20.4%

Part of an Integrated Delivery Network--Physician Group Executives

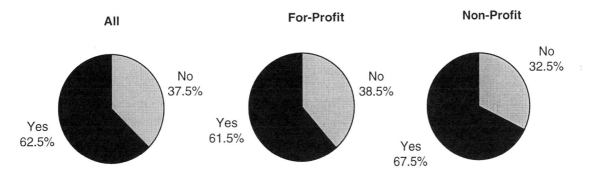

All
No 37.5%
Yes 62.5%

For-Profit
No 38.5%
Yes 61.5%

Non-Profit
No 32.5%
Yes 67.5%

Average Years in an Alliance or Partnership--Physician Group Executives

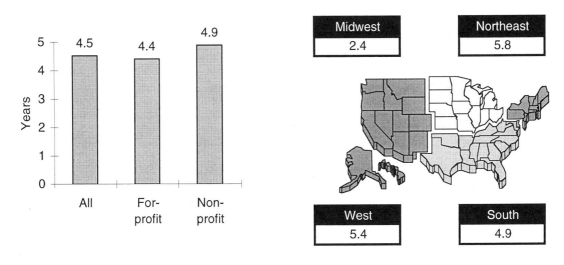

	Years
All	4.5
For-profit	4.4
Non-profit	4.9

Midwest 2.4

Northeast 5.8

West 5.4

South 4.9

Reasons for Partnering and Integration--Physician Group Executives

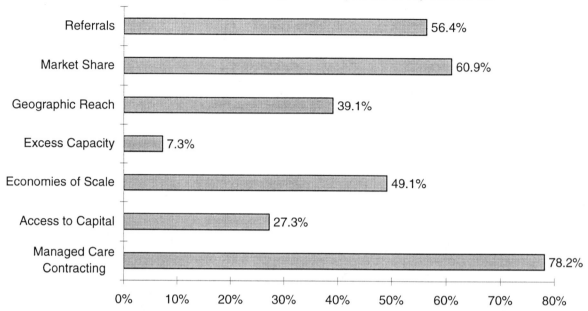

Components of the Organization's Network--Physician Group Executives

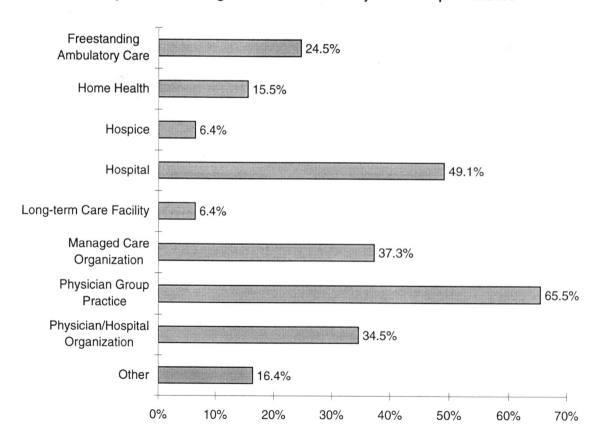

Partnerships **Tactics**

Partnering Strategies

What physician group executives say they'll do with . . .

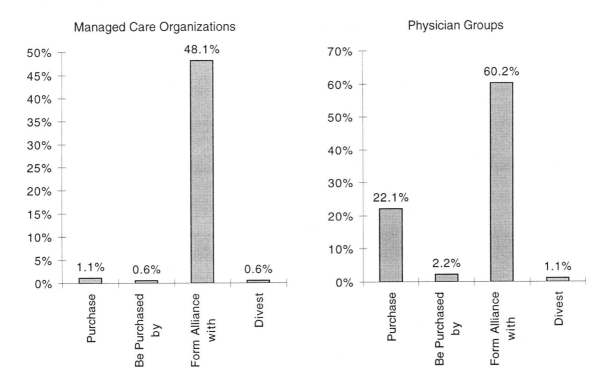

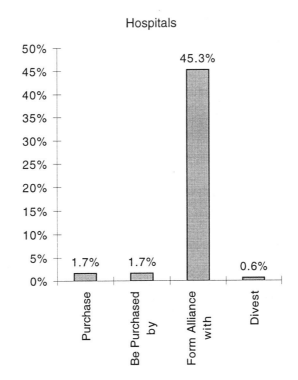

Partnerships   **Ranking of Combinations**

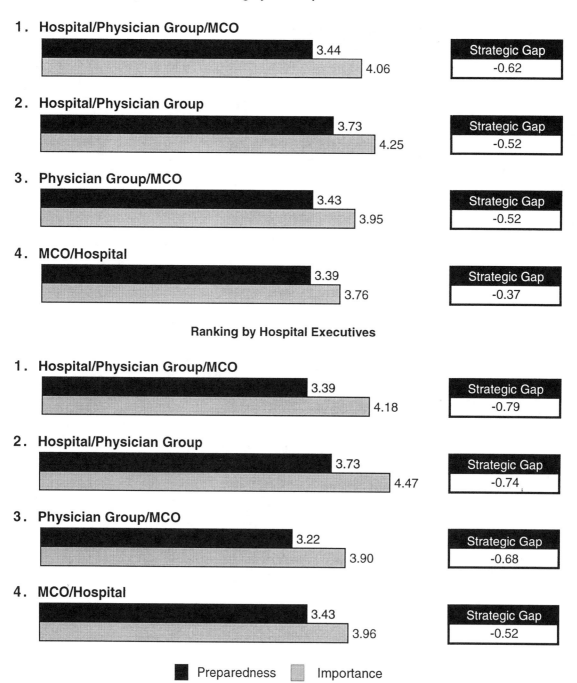

Ranking by All Respondents

1. Hospital/Physician Group/MCO

3.44
4.06

| Strategic Gap |
| -0.62 |

2. Hospital/Physician Group

3.73
4.25

| Strategic Gap |
| -0.52 |

3. Physician Group/MCO

3.43
3.95

| Strategic Gap |
| -0.52 |

4. MCO/Hospital

3.39
3.76

| Strategic Gap |
| -0.37 |

Ranking by Hospital Executives

1. Hospital/Physician Group/MCO

3.39
4.18

| Strategic Gap |
| -0.79 |

2. Hospital/Physician Group

3.73
4.47

| Strategic Gap |
| -0.74 |

3. Physician Group/MCO

3.22
3.90

| Strategic Gap |
| -0.68 |

4. MCO/Hospital

3.43
3.96

| Strategic Gap |
| -0.52 |

■ Preparedness   ▨ Importance

- Respondents ranked the importance of four partnership combinations for developing their strategies.
- Respondents also ranked their preparedness for dealing with these partnership combinations.
- Combinations are ranked from largest to smallest strategic gap.
- Small discrepancies between the strategic gap and the rankings may occur due to rounding.

Partnerships   **Ranking of Combinations**

Ranking by Managed Care Executives

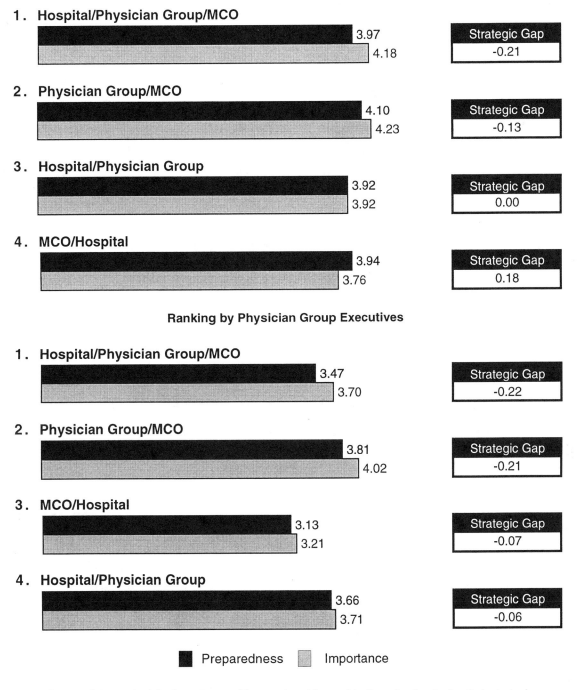

1. **Hospital/Physician Group/MCO**

   3.97
   4.18

   Strategic Gap
   -0.21

2. **Physician Group/MCO**

   4.10
   4.23

   Strategic Gap
   -0.13

3. **Hospital/Physician Group**

   3.92
   3.92

   Strategic Gap
   0.00

4. **MCO/Hospital**

   3.94
   3.76

   Strategic Gap
   0.18

Ranking by Physician Group Executives

1. **Hospital/Physician Group/MCO**

   3.47
   3.70

   Strategic Gap
   -0.22

2. **Physician Group/MCO**

   3.81
   4.02

   Strategic Gap
   -0.21

3. **MCO/Hospital**

   3.13
   3.21

   Strategic Gap
   -0.07

4. **Hospital/Physician Group**

   3.66
   3.71

   Strategic Gap
   -0.06

■ Preparedness   ▨ Importance

- Respondents ranked the importance of four partnership combinations for developing their strategies.
- Respondents also ranked their preparedness for dealing with these partnership combinations.
- Combinations are ranked from largest to smallest strategic gap.
- Small discrepancies between the strategic gap and the rankings may occur due to rounding.

Partnerships   Hospital/Physician Group Alliances

Overall Results

Importance vs. Preparedness

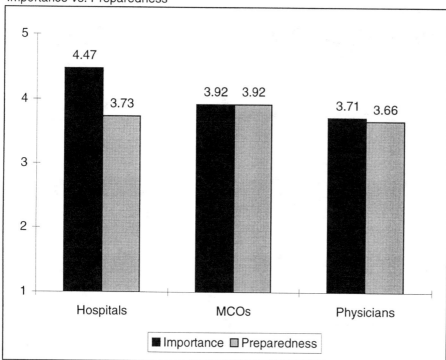

Strategic Gap	
Hospitals	-0.74
MCOs	0.00
Physicians	-0.06

Rank	
Importance	1
Preparedness	1
Strategic Gap	2

- The higher the importance ranking, the more important the combination is to respondents.
- The higher the readiness ranking, the better the respondents view the preparedness of their institutions.
- "Strategic gap" refers to the difference between importance and preparedness.
- The rank refers to the rank of the alliances out of the 4 combinations in the survey. Ranks are given for importance, readiness, and strategic gap. The highest rank is 1; the lowest rank is 4.

Regional Results

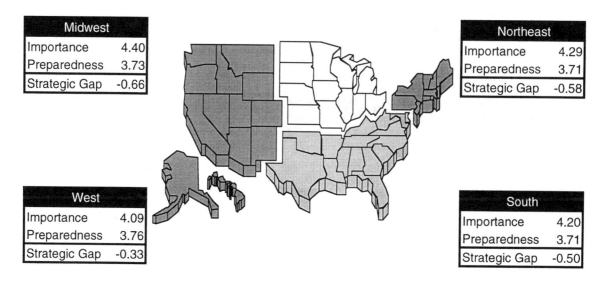

Midwest	
Importance	4.40
Preparedness	3.73
Strategic Gap	-0.66

Northeast	
Importance	4.29
Preparedness	3.71
Strategic Gap	-0.58

West	
Importance	4.09
Preparedness	3.76
Strategic Gap	-0.33

South	
Importance	4.20
Preparedness	3.71
Strategic Gap	-0.50

Partnerships · Hospital/Physician Group Alliances

Hospital Executives

Importance vs. Preparedness

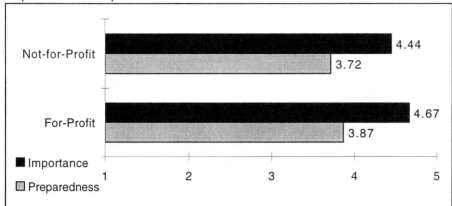

Rank	
Importance	1
Preparedness	1
Strategic Gap	2

Strategic Gap	
Not-for-profit	-0.73
For-profit	-0.80

Managed Care Executives

Importance vs. Preparedness

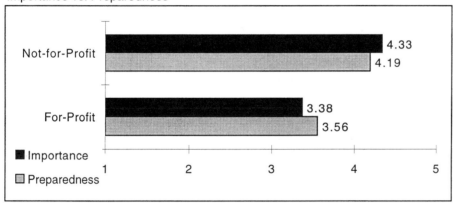

Rank	
Importance	3
Preparedness	4
Strategic Gap	3

Strategic Gap	
Not-for-profit	-0.14
For-profit	0.19

Physician Group Practice Executives

Importance vs. Preparedness

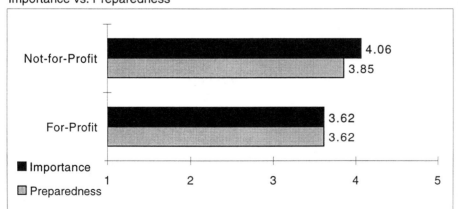

Rank	
Importance	2
Preparedness	2
Strategic Gap	4

Strategic Gap	
Not-for-profit	-0.21
For-profit	0.00

Partnerships   Physician Group/MCO Alliances

Overall Results

Importance vs. Preparedness

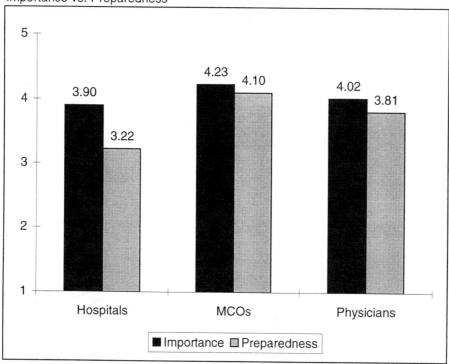

Strategic Gap	
Hospitals	-0.68
MCOs	-0.13
Physicians	-0.21

Rank	
Importance	3
Preparedness	3
Strategic Gap	3

- The higher the importance ranking, the more important the combination is to respondents.
- The higher the readiness ranking, the better the respondents view the preparedness of their institutions.
- "Strategic gap" refers to the difference between importance and preparedness.
- The rank refers to the rank of the alliances out of the 4 combinations in the survey. Ranks are given for importance, readiness, and strategic gap. The highest rank is 1; the lowest rank is 4.

Regional Results

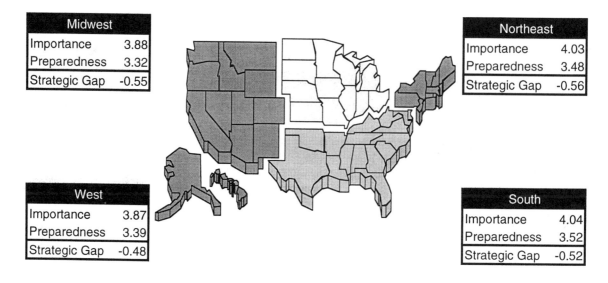

Midwest	
Importance	3.88
Preparedness	3.32
Strategic Gap	-0.55

Northeast	
Importance	4.03
Preparedness	3.48
Strategic Gap	-0.56

West	
Importance	3.87
Preparedness	3.39
Strategic Gap	-0.48

South	
Importance	4.04
Preparedness	3.52
Strategic Gap	-0.52

Partnerships   **Physician Group/MCO Alliances**

Hospital Executives
Importance vs. Preparedness

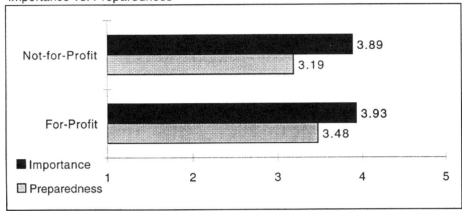

Rank	
Importance	4
Preparedness	4
Strategic Gap	3

Strategic Gap	
Not-for-profit	-0.70
For-profit	-0.45

Managed Care Executives
Importance vs. Preparedness

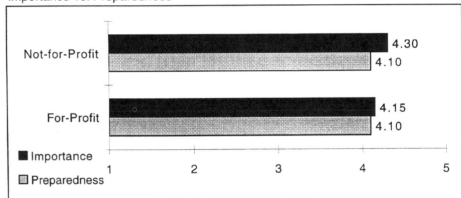

Rank	
Importance	1
Preparedness	1
Strategic Gap	2

Strategic Gap	
Not-for-profit	-0.20
For-profit	-0.05

Physician Group Practice Executives
Importance vs. Preparedness

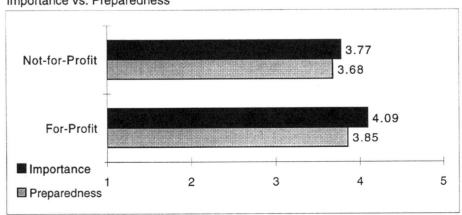

Rank	
Importance	1
Preparedness	1
Strategic Gap	2

Strategic Gap	
Not-for-profit	-0.10
For-profit	-0.24

Partnerships   MCO/Hospital Alliances

Overall Results

Importance vs. Preparedness

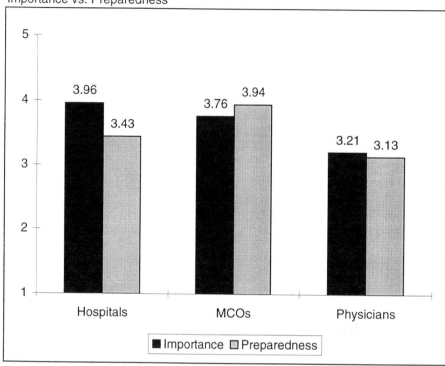

Strategic Gap	
Hospitals	-0.52
MCOs	0.18
Physicians	-0.07

Rank	
Importance	4
Preparedness	4
Strategic Gap	4

- The higher the importance ranking, the more important the combination is to respondents.
- The higher the readiness ranking, the better the respondents view the preparedness of their institutions.
- "Strategic gap" refers to the difference between importance and preparedness.
- The rank refers to the rank of the alliances out of the 4 combinations in the survey. Ranks are given for importance, readiness, and strategic gap. The highest rank is 1; the lowest rank is 4.

Regional Results

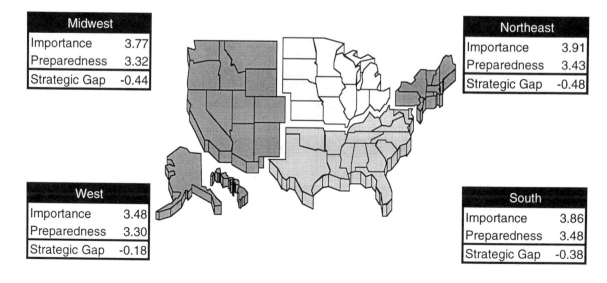

Midwest	
Importance	3.77
Preparedness	3.32
Strategic Gap	-0.44

Northeast	
Importance	3.91
Preparedness	3.43
Strategic Gap	-0.48

West	
Importance	3.48
Preparedness	3.30
Strategic Gap	-0.18

South	
Importance	3.86
Preparedness	3.48
Strategic Gap	-0.38

Hospital Executives
Importance vs. Preparedness

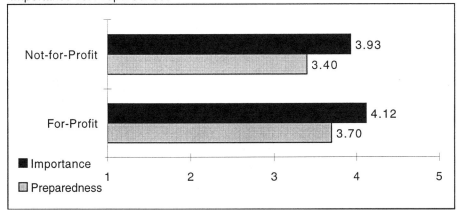

Rank	
Importance	3
Preparedness	2
Strategic Gap	4

Strategic Gap	
Not-for-profit	-0.52
For-profit	-0.42

Managed Care Executives
Importance vs. Preparedness

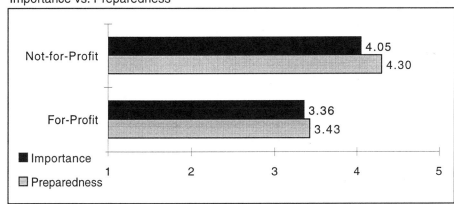

Rank	
Importance	4
Preparedness	3
Strategic Gap	4

Strategic Gap	
Not-for-profit	0.25
For-profit	0.07

Physician Group Practice Executives
Importance vs. Preparedness

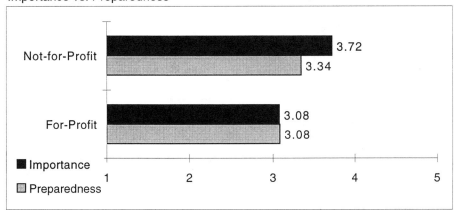

Rank	
Importance	4
Preparedness	4
Strategic Gap	3

Strategic Gap	
Not-for-profit	-0.38
For-profit	0.01

Partnerships   **Hospital/Physician Group/MCO Alliances**

Overall Results

Importance vs. Preparedness

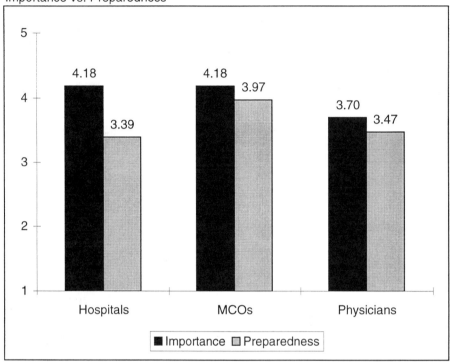

Strategic Gap	
Hospitals	-0.79
MCOs	-0.21
Physicians	-0.22

Rank	
Importance	2
Preparedness	2
Strategic Gap	1

• The higher the importance ranking, the more important the combination is to respondents.
• The higher the readiness ranking, the better the respondents view the preparedness of their institutions.
• "Strategic gap" refers to the difference between importance and preparedness.
• The rank refers to the rank of the alliances out of the 4 combinations in the survey. Ranks are given for importance, readiness, and strategic gap. The highest rank is 1; the lowest rank is 4.

Regional Results

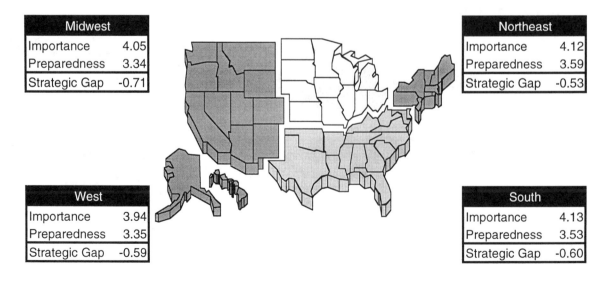

Midwest	
Importance	4.05
Preparedness	3.34
Strategic Gap	-0.71

Northeast	
Importance	4.12
Preparedness	3.59
Strategic Gap	-0.53

West	
Importance	3.94
Preparedness	3.35
Strategic Gap	-0.59

South	
Importance	4.13
Preparedness	3.53
Strategic Gap	-0.60

Partnerships   **Hospital/Physician Group/MCO Alliances**

Hospital Executives

Importance vs. Preparedness

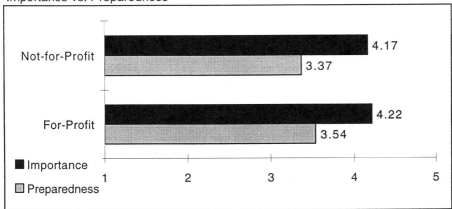

Rank	
Importance	2
Preparedness	3
Strategic Gap	1

Strategic Gap	
Not-for-profit	-0.80
For-profit	-0.68

Managed Care Executives

Importance vs. Preparedness

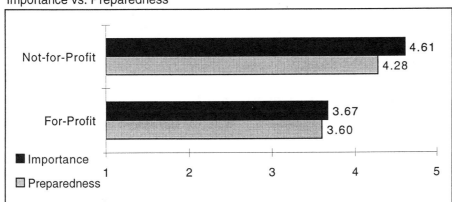

Rank	
Importance	2
Preparedness	2
Strategic Gap	1

Strategic Gap	
Not-for-profit	-0.33
For-profit	-0.07

Physician Group Practice Executives

Importance vs. Preparedness

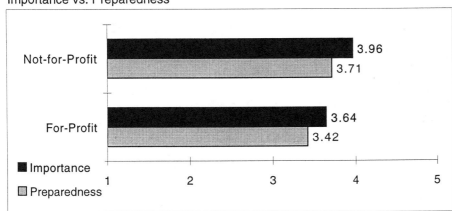

Rank	
Importance	3
Preparedness	3
Strategic Gap	1

Strategic Gap	
Not-for-profit	-0.25
For-profit	-0.22

Partnerships   **Strategic Position for Managed Care Contracting**

Hospitals vs. MCOs

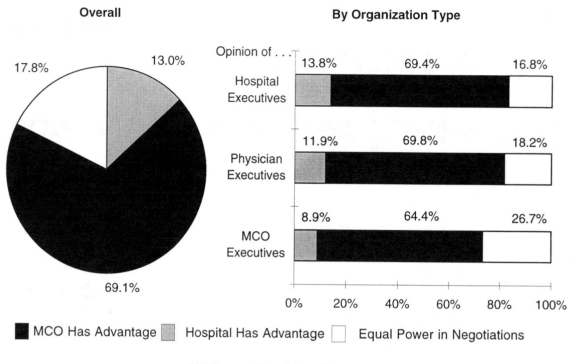

Overall

17.8% 13.0%

69.1%

By Organization Type

Opinion of . . .

Hospital Executives: 13.8% 69.4% 16.8%

Physician Executives: 11.9% 69.8% 18.2%

MCO Executives: 8.9% 64.4% 26.7%

0% 20% 40% 60% 80% 100%

■ MCO Has Advantage   ▨ Hospital Has Advantage   □ Equal Power in Negotiations

MCOs vs. Physician Groups

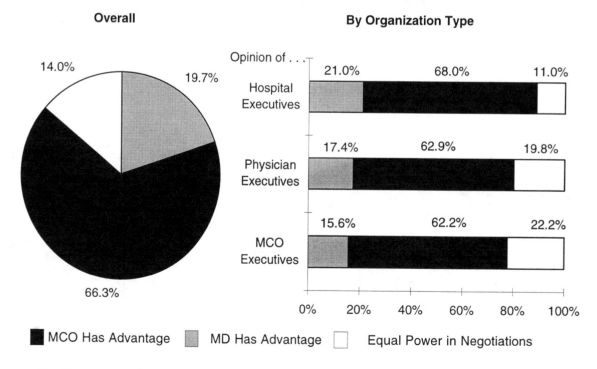

Overall

14.0% 19.7%

66.3%

By Organization Type

Opinion of . . .

Hospital Executives: 21.0% 68.0% 11.0%

Physician Executives: 17.4% 62.9% 19.8%

MCO Executives: 15.6% 62.2% 22.2%

0% 20% 40% 60% 80% 100%

■ MCO Has Advantage   ▨ MD Has Advantage   □ Equal Power in Negotiations

• Results may not total 100 percent due to rounding.

Partnerships   Strategic Position for Managed Care Contracting

Hospitals vs. Physician Groups

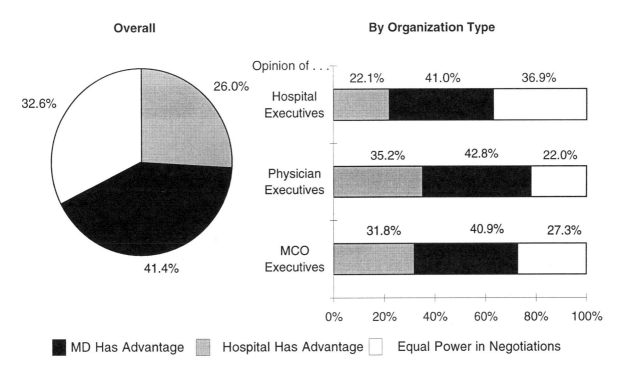

Overall

32.6%

26.0%

41.4%

By Organization Type

Opinion of . . .

| | 22.1% | 41.0% | 36.9% |

Hospital Executives

| 35.2% | 42.8% | 22.0% |

Physician Executives

| 31.8% | 40.9% | 27.3% |

MCO Executives

0%   20%   40%   60%   80%   100%

■ MD Has Advantage   ▨ Hospital Has Advantage   □ Equal Power in Negotiations

• Results may not total 100 percent due to rounding.

CHAPTER 4

Policy

Harris Meyer

Health care has been one of the most contentious issues in American political life during the 1990s, because people of different political views hold clashing visions of how the health care system should be organized and regulated.[1] Conservatives want it to be operated largely as a free-market system, while liberals favor a more regulatory approach that treats health care as a social good guaranteed to all. This fundamental disagreement threatens to produce ongoing policy turmoil. It finds its fullest expression in the fierce battle over the future of Medicare, for which a bipartisan commission appointed by the president and Congress will develop reform recommendations by 1999.[2] It remains to be seen if any consensus is possible.

In many ways, hospitals are the health care sector with the most to gain or lose from major policy changes, particularly in the area of financing. Policy makers fervently hope that legislative and market changes will push many hospitals to consolidate or close their doors entirely, thereby reducing the number of beds and lowering costs. Hospital executives are acutely conscious of this scenario, which is why they are far more likely to participate in legislative advocacy activities than are leaders of health plans or medical groups. According to the *Hospitals & Health Networks* Leadership Survey, about three-quarters of hospital leaders say they are involved in phoning, writing to, or meeting with lawmakers. Not-for-profit hospital leaders are somewhat more likely than their counterparts at for-profits to have engaged in legislative advocacy.

Managed care organizations (MCOs) stand at the center of the debate over the effects of the nation's shift from fee-for-service medicine to HMO-style care. As more Americans move into HMOs, preferred provider plans, point-of-service plans, and other variants, the clamor grows over the effects on quality and access and the percentage of health care premiums consumed by administrative costs and profits.[3] Not surprisingly, as health plans are becoming a major target of legislation and regulation, their trade associations are being forced to gear up their lobbying and public relations efforts. Still, managed care leaders are less active in legislative advocacy than are hospital executives. Less than half have phoned a legislator, and slightly less than two-thirds have written a letter or fax or attended a meeting with lawmakers. Leaders of not-for-profit plans are likelier than for-profit executives to have engaged in legislative advocacy.

Medical groups know they are directly affected by current changes in Medicare fee-for-service payment and have long been active in lobbying on that front. But they are increasingly recognizing that the overall shift of government health programs to managed care and the rules the government sets for managed care plans affect them, too. While medical practices are rapidly consolidating, many doctors still practice in small groups, so the amount of time they have to spend on advocacy, and their level of political sophistication, is limited. Plus, more than 40 percent of all physicians are now employees of large medical groups, hospital systems, or health plans, and employed doctors may see policy issues as less directly relevant than do private practitioners.[4] Traditionally, physicians have largely left policy matters to their many well-organized and powerful medical associations, which are organized by specialty as well as on a local, state, and national basis. Less than half the medical group leaders surveyed have phoned or met in person with lawmakers; almost two-thirds, however, have sent a fax or letter.

UNIVERSAL COVERAGE

The rising cost of health care, coupled with changes in the economy and the workforce, led to more Americans not having job-based health insurance. By 1997, the number of uninsured reached 41.4 million, or 16 percent of the working-age population.[5] Large businesses have steadily reduced the number of full-time positions, which usually come with employer-paid health benefits, and replaced them with part-time and contract posts, which often do not. Smaller firms, which have produced most of the new jobs in the past two decades, are significantly less likely to offer employees company-paid coverage and are more likely to require employees to pay a hefty share of the premium if they do offer such benefits.[6] Companies of all sizes have cut back on coverage of workers' dependents and hiked cost-sharing requirements. In addition, the growth of self-insurance by employers, and of insurers' setting premiums based on each group's claims history rather than on the community average, has sharply driven up rates for higher-risk individuals and groups.

The combination of soaring costs and falling rates of coverage led many state and federal elected officials in the late 1980s and early 1990s to call for government solutions. The health care reform issue hit the political main stage in 1988 when Democratic presidential nominee Michael Dukakis proposed that all employers be required to cover their workers. The issue became even hotter in 1992 when Democrat Bill Clinton was elected on a platform of universal coverage and cost control. The battle over President Clinton's health care reform plan—which featured a mandate on employers to cover their workers, a government-set health care budget, and regulated competition between private health plans—consumed Washington throughout 1993 and 1994. Along with several other comprehensive Democratic and Republican proposals, it went nowhere. By Clinton's own admission, the defeat of his plan—due in large part to withering attacks from Republicans, the health insurance industry, and the business community—led directly to the GOP takeover of Congress in the 1994 election.[7]

With the failure of political solutions, health care purchasers and providers moved full speed ahead with market-based restructuring. Private and public employers accelerated the shift of employees into managed care. While many claim that the managed care revolution has succeeded in controlling costs, it has done little to extend coverage to the nation's uninsured. As a result, health care is back on the political agenda. In 1996, Congress enacted the Health Insurance Portability and Accountability Act to make it easier for people to keep coverage when they change jobs or switch from group to individual coverage, and many states have passed even tougher measures. The political surprise in 1997 was that Congress approved a $24 billion, five-year program to expand coverage for the nation's 10 million uninsured children. But health care leaders appear to be pessimistic about the prospects for further coverage expansion.

Other than publicly funded clinics, hospitals are the only providers that are mandated by law to serve patients without health insurance, under a 1986 law that bars them from turning away emergency patients who require stabilization. In addition, many hospitals are located in communities with high rates of uninsured people, and they cannot easily avoid dealing with this problem. So hospitals have a strong interest in seeing that something is done about the nation's uninsured and that everyone who comes to their doors has some form of coverage. In the *Hospitals & Health Networks* Leadership Survey, 61 percent of hospital executives list indigent care as a pressing issue in their community—far more than chose any other issue. It's no surprise that hospitals, more than any other industry sector, have continued to push for state and federal coverage expansion since Clinton's universal coverage campaign died in 1994.

Hospital leaders are generally delighted with the child coverage expansion of 1997. They are hopeful about the effects but are concerned that the new law allows states to establish new and untested insurance programs for children. Many would prefer to see states use the money to expand Medicaid, the federal-state program for the poor and disabled, or to directly subsidize hospital programs that serve low-income children. But hospital leaders are not holding their breath waiting for action. They overwhelmingly say a federal system for ensuring universal coverage is unlikely by the year 2000, and only somewhat more likely by the year 2007.

Health plans theoretically have a strong interest in seeing the government help more Americans obtain health coverage, since they would be selling the policies. But up to now the health insurance industry, including the managed care sector, has not actively supported coverage expansion. During the 1997 congressional debate over expanding coverage to uninsured children, the industry warned that a new government program would undercut existing employer-based coverage and stated that it opposed a standard, comprehensive benefit package.[8] Managed care leaders doubt that a federal universal coverage system will be established by the year 2007. Still, almost two-thirds cite the uninsured as a pressing issue in their local community.

Doctors theoretically would benefit if every patient had insurance to pay for medical visits. But medical associations have been split on this issue, some backing government-guaranteed coverage and others ambivalent or opposed.[9] Many doctors are fearful that a government program would impose price controls and a new bureaucracy. And doctors are not as directly affected by the uninsured problem as hospitals, since they can legally turn away uninsured patients or set up shop in wealthier communities. Many doctors prefer policy approaches that encourage patients to pay for routine care on their own. Medical group leaders agree with their counterparts at hospitals and health plans that a federal universal coverage system is unlikely. While they rate indigent care as the top local health care issue, medical group leaders are much less likely to mention it than are hospital or health plan executives.

MEDICARE

In the late 1980s, politicians became preoccupied with cutting government spending and eliminating the huge federal budget deficit while simultaneously slashing taxes. That forced them to get serious about reining in the soaring costs of Medicare and Medicaid, which previously were seen as politically untouchable. In 1997, Congress and President Clinton reached agreement on a broad set of Medicare growth reductions and changes to save $115 billion through 2002 and extend the solvency of the Medicare Hospital Trust Fund until about 2007. An independent bipartisan commission will report back to Congress by early 1999 with recommendations on how to reform the program to address the huge costs associated with the retirement of the baby boomers starting in 2011. One possible recommendation is to shift more costs to beneficiaries, with protections for lower-income seniors. This policy won expectedly strong support in 1997 when the Senate voted to set the Medicare Part B premium (for physician, lab, and outpatient services) on a sliding scale based on income. This measure was ultimately rejected by President Clinton and the House.

Another likely reform, supported by both parties, is a major shift of beneficiaries into private managed care plans to control utilization and costs. The 1997 budget law aims to speed up that process by allowing managed care companies to offer plans that give patients greater choice of provider, including preferred provider and point-of-service options. It also boosts per capita payment rates in rural areas to spur managed care growth in places where few Medicare HMOs currently operate. And it eases the way for hospitals and medical groups to launch their own managed care plans, which will contract directly with Medicare to receive a per-member, per-month fee for all services, an arrangement known as capitation.

Hospitals generally support the growing political push to restructure Medicare. Two-thirds of hospitals leaders endorse in principle the concept of making wealthier beneficiaries pay higher premiums or reducing their benefits. They know that Medicare restructuring will lead to more managed care, and they believe that shifting their Medicare and Medicaid fee-for-service business to managed care is one of the most important challenges they face. In the *Hospitals & Health Networks* Leadership Survey, hospital executives rate Medicare/Medicaid managed care contracting as the policy issue most important to success. But they describe themselves as only moderately well prepared for the task. This is the policy issue that produced the largest strategic gap, that is, the biggest difference between the respondents' importance rating and self-described preparedness.

Some hospital leaders see provider-sponsored organizations (PSOs) as a panacea—allowing hospital systems to contract directly with Medicare to provide services efficiently, without managed care insurers taking a big cut off the top and dictating how services are delivered. But experts warn that some hospitals may not be up to the challenge of acting essentially as their own HMO and that policy makers will zoom in to tighten PSO regulation should financial collapses occur.[10]

Although they support managed care expansion, hospitals want to see the Medicare fee-for-service program remain financially viable for the time being. They believe that spending cuts for inpatient care and other services contained in the 1997 budget law will jeopardize hospitals' ability to serve Medicare fee-for-service patients. Hospitals face a major challenge in fending off further rate cuts, particularly if the industry as a whole continues to show comfortable profit margins on Medicare business.

Medicare is also an immediately pressing issue for health plans. The HMO industry has strongly supported efforts to transform Medicare into a managed care program. But only about 14 percent of seniors currently are in capitated plans, and many managed care companies still are in the early stages of developing Medicare products. Those with a significant presence in the Medicare market are concentrated in a few urban areas, mostly on the West Coast and in Florida. And no one has much experience offering Medicare plans other than straight HMOs, such as PPOs or point-of-service plans. The entire industry is going to have to rapidly increase its capacity to respond to the federal government's push to get far more seniors into managed care plans, to broaden the range of plan types, and to get seniors in nonurban markets into managed care. In the *Hospitals & Health Networks* Leadership Survey, plan executives rate Medicare/Medicaid contracting as one of the most important issues for success. Unlike hospital leaders, they feel better prepared for this policy challenge than for any other.

Shaping Medicare payment policy will be a political imperative for the managed care industry. The current formula pays plans 95 percent of the average local per capita cost of the Medicare fee-for-service program, with modest adjustments for age and sex. Government auditors say plans are significantly overpaid because they are enrolling seniors who are healthier than average and would cost Medicare less in the fee-for-service program, though the managed care industry sharply disputes that. There will be growing efforts to either adjust payments to reflect the true health status of managed care enrollees or to reduce payments across the board. The industry has already blocked one new government approach to rate setting—competitive bidding. The 1997 budget act includes a demonstration of competitive bidding, but it remains to be seen whether the industry will allow this activity to proceed. The law also will begin to level rates nationally, which will force plans in high-payment urban areas to cut costs or trim benefits. That could erode their present market advantage over the Medicare fee-for-service program. As for future Medicare restructuring, almost three-fifths of managed care executives favor means testing of premiums or benefits. One possible reason they are less likely to support that approach than leaders of hospitals or medical groups is that they are more familiar with the administrative difficulties of basing premiums or benefits on income.

Doctors are ambivalent about Medicare restructuring because many do not like managed care, and old-line Medicare represents their last big piece of fee-for-service business. But they favor the parts of Medicare reform that let them avoid insurance intermediaries and receive payment directly from patients, such as PSOs and medical savings account plans. They love the idea of means testing, with almost two-thirds of medical group leaders backing that approach.

Physician groups are at widely varying levels of readiness for Medicare and Medicaid managed care contracting. Surprisingly, medical group leaders do not rate this issue as important as do hospital and health plan leaders, nor do they list it as one of their top preparedness issues. The gap between its importance to them, and their preparedness for it, is much less than for hospital and health plan leaders. That suggests doctors could get blindsided by the rapid growth of managed care contracting in the near future.

Doctors are split by specialty on the merits of moving from separate fee-for-service payment systems for surgeons and nonsurgeons to one unified system. But the government is going that route anyway. Doctors are united in saying that the fee-for-service rate cuts already passed are excessive and that this will discourage doctors from accepting Medicare patients. Physician groups promise a major fight to temper upcoming Medicare rate squeezes resulting from the 1997 budget law, which pegs pay updates to the growth rate of the gross domestic product, with no adjustment for new technology. Medical lobbyists claim that formula will result in large fee cuts.

While physicians were successful in getting some Medicare changes in the 1997 budget law to give patients new plan options other than HMOs, it is unclear how viable those options are. Most observers doubt, for instance, that any but the largest medical groups will be able to operate PSOs without hospital or insurance partners.[11] If few patients or doctors are willing or able to choose the new non-HMO options, and if Medicare increasingly becomes the province of insurance-run managed care plans, then physician resistance to Medicare restructuring may stiffen.

MEDICAID

Congress also made far-reaching changes in Medicaid in 1997. But it retained the program as an entitlement based on income, age, and disability status rather than converting it into a block grant program in which states receive a fixed pot of money and spend it as they see fit (the model previously advocated by Republican leaders). At the same time, lawmakers reduced Medicaid net spending growth by $13 billion through 2002, mainly by cutting disproportionate share payments to hospitals that serve a large number of poor and elderly people.

Hospital leaders are worried about the cuts in disproportionate share payments, which will hit financially shaky inner-city and rural hospitals the hardest. Another concern is that Congress eliminated the so-called Boren rule requiring that states pay providers "reasonable and adequate" rates for serving Medicaid patients. In addition, it will be far easier for states to push recipients into mandatory managed care programs, since they will no longer have to get federal approval first. Governors argue that giving them increasing control over Medicaid will reduce costs while improving access and quality. Based on their own experience in dealing with state Medicaid programs, hospitals leaders do not necessarily buy this argument. When asked whether state administration of Medicaid would be more or less efficient than federal administration, they say it would make no difference.

The 1997 budget law provisions allowing states to move Medicaid recipients into managed care without federal approval would seem to be a bonanza for managed care plans. In addition, plans serving Medicaid patients no longer must have a certain percentage of commercial enrollees, making it much easier to participate in Medicaid. But plans may find Medicaid managed care expansion to be a mixed blessing, since Medicaid programs vary widely by state in terms of payment rates, program design, and administrative complexity. Health plan leaders may not yet fully appreciate this possibility. They are more likely than hospital executives to say that state administration of Medicaid would be more efficient than federal administration.

The complexity and political headaches for health plan leaders may grow as states increasingly shift their special-needs Medicaid populations—low-income seniors, disabled children and adults, AIDS patients, and the mentally ill—into managed care. Managed care plans have little experience serving these patients, who have advocacy groups looking out for them. A big question is whether health plans will choose to remain players in Medicaid if the political and financial issues become too troublesome.

Since the bulk of Medicaid care is delivered by a minority of doctors, physicians as a whole have not focused much on Medicaid as a policy issue. But those doctors whose practices consist heavily of Medicaid patients pay close attention. They are being strongly affected by the rapid shift to managed care. They will have to participate in, or form their own, Medicaid managed care plans. Otherwise they will have to pressure lawmakers to require Medicaid plans to contract with them and their hospitals and clinics. Still, most doctors probably have not thought deeply about this issue yet. As do health plan executives, medical group leaders say that state administration of Medicaid would be more efficient than federal administration. Mainstream medical group leaders have registered strong objections to one Medicaid provision in the 1997 budget law. It would let states pay doctors Medicaid rather than Medicare rates for poor and disabled seniors who qualify for both programs.

Medicaid could become a more salient issue for the broad physician community if state managed care initiatives disrupt the traditional safety-net provider network for Medicaid patients and the uninsured. If, for instance, inner-city hospitals and clinics are forced out of business as plans steer patients to other facilities, doctors who have not seen such patients in the past may face new pressure to care for them—at lower rates than they are used to, or without any compensation at all.

LONG-TERM CARE

A big part of Medicaid cost growth is due to increased spending on long-term care for the elderly and disabled. Medicaid will become even more of a long-term care program, because the 1996 welfare reform law will push more young women and children off the Medicaid rolls. It has become the de facto national nursing home payment system, even for the middle class, because nursing home care is too expensive for most families and few Americans currently have private long-term care insurance.[12]

Policy makers recently have moved to discourage middle-class families from seeking Medicaid nursing home coverage. New federal and state laws make it harder for people to hide their assets to qualify for the means-tested Medicaid benefits. Congress has even imposed criminal penalties on estate planning advisors who assist with asset transfers. At the same time, Congress encouraged more people to buy private long-term care insurance by providing new tax deductions for premiums. Experts caution, however, that private insurance may never be affordable for most Americans.[13]

Congress also sought to curb soaring Medicare nursing home and home health costs by directing Medicare administrators to develop prospective payment systems for skilled nursing facilities and home care agencies. This will be a tough challenge, both technically and politically, because reliable statistical tools to ensure that providers get paid appropriately based on a patient's condition have not been developed.[14] And serious tightening of the Medicare home care benefit—the cost of which has grown fivefold since 1990—could set off a popular revolt.

Hospitals have a heavy stake in long-term care since most operate nursing homes and home health care agencies and face strong pressure from payers to discharge patients quickly to long-term care facilities whenever possible. More than three-quarters of the hospital executives believe that patients and their families, not the government, will bear most of the increasing financial burden of these services. Still, more than half the executives worry that providers such as hospitals and nursing homes will have to eat some of the costs if neither patients nor the government are willing or able to pay.

As do health insurers in general, plans want to see Medicaid stop financing long-term care except for the poor.[15] They want to sell managed care products with nursing home and home health benefits to middle-class and affluent people. Health plan leaders agree with hospital leaders that patients and their families will increasingly have to ante up for long-term care. Still, in the near future, health plans are likely to find themselves increasingly mired in difficult issues of providing long-term care for Medicare and Medicaid patients. The reason is that they are signing up growing numbers of Medicare and Medicaid enrollees who eventually will need it. And soon plans will be serving disabled Medicaid recipients who require a great deal of chronic care. Studies show that Medicare HMOs offer drastically fewer home care visits than fee-for-service Medicare. Cost-saving efforts in this arena are likely to become a hot new area of controversy over managed care.[16]

Physicians generally have not shown a strong interest in long-term care, largely because most doctors are not heavily involved in home care and do not take care of patients in nursing homes. That is changing as the population ages and as managed care insurers push doctors to discharge patients sooner from the hospital and work with them in more cost-efficient settings such as the home or the nursing home. As with hospital and health plan leaders, medical group executives overwhelmingly expect that patients and their families will bear a growing burden for these costs.

Leaders of for-profit and not-for-profit organizations differ on this issue. Not-for-profit executives are much more likely to predict that individuals will bear an increasing burden for long-term care costs (79 percent versus 68 percent) and are also much likelier to say that institutional providers such as hospitals and nursing homes will take some of the hit (59 percent versus 43 percent). That view may reflect the fact that not-for-profit hospitals and long-term care facilities, particularly public institutions, currently provide more uncompensated care than do for-profits.

MANAGED CARE REGULATION

Angry at annual premium increases in double-digit percentages, business leaders in the late 1980s began moving their employees into prepaid managed care plans, for which they paid a flat fee per head for all covered services. Before that, most employers and unions offered indemnity coverage, where plans paid providers a fee for each service provided. By 1997, about three-quarters of all American workers were in some type of managed care plan. About 70 million were in HMOs, where enrollees must get their care from a limited panel of hospitals, doctors, and other providers.[17]

Government health programs such as Medicare, Medicaid, and the Department of Defense did the same with their beneficiaries. HMOs and other managed care plans saw enrollments soar and began offering a wider range of products to appeal to people who wanted more choice of provider. Hospitals and doctors banded together into larger networks to snare managed care contracts. Proprietary and not-for-profit chains raced to buy hospitals, medical practices, and outpatient facilities in order to build regional and national networks attractive to managed care insurers.

The shift to managed care has apparently borne fruit from a cost perspective. In 1995 and 1996, employer health care costs rose at about the same rate as general inflation. Government programs, which were still largely fee-for-service in 1997, are seeking similar reductions in spending growth and are trying to shift the bulk of their beneficiaries into managed care. The Balanced Budget Act of 1997 contains numerous changes in Medicare and Medicaid to speed this transition. Realizing that managed care cannot offer a complete solution right away, Congress also imposed new curbs on fee-for-service payments to hospitals and doctors and mandated new prospective payment systems for nursing homes, home health care, rehabilitation, and hospital outpatient services.

It is not completely clear that managed care is the magic bullet for all of health care. Some experts argue that employers and managed care plans have cut costs, not primarily by making care more efficient, but by slashing payments to providers and forcing employees to bear more of the costs.[18] They argue that costs will rise more rapidly in the next several years because savings from these sources have already been squeezed out.

Whether managed care has succeeded in controlling costs, its growth in both public and private health benefit programs has triggered a backlash among politicians and the public. Consumer complaints and news reports about problems such as coverage denials for potentially lifesaving services, new mothers whisked out of the hospital on the day of delivery, and HMO refusals to pay for reasonable emergency room visits have precipitated an angry flood of legislation and litigation.[19] Most states have passed laws to restrict what they consider abusive managed care practices. These new laws include bans on contracts that limit what doctors can tell patients, elimination of plan requirements that mastectomy be done as an outpatient procedure, and mandates that plans pay for emergency room visits when a "prudent layperson" would have deemed the visit necessary. Congress enacted similar provisions on physician "gag" clauses and emergency room visits for Medicare and Medicaid as part of the 1997 budget act.

President Clinton also appointed an independent commission in 1997 to make recommendations on health care quality and on managed care regulation in particular. The commission, due to report back in early 1998, was split between consumer advocates who backed an enforceable bill of rights for patients and industry representatives who advocated better quality measurement and reporting on a voluntary basis. Meanwhile, employers and the managed care industry are striving to develop voluntary quality assurance and accreditation mechanisms to fend off pressures for more government regulation, but the credibility and effectiveness of such efforts remain in question.

Meanwhile, different sectors of the health care industry are often battling fiercely over who will control the emerging managed care system. Hospitals and physicians are demanding the right to set up their own plans, organized under special rules, to contract directly with employers and government programs and bypass insurers. Managed care insurers vehemently oppose this plan, saying that it gives PSOs an unfair advantage and leaves consumers unprotected by the state insurance rules governing other health plans. In 1997, Congress moderately eased the way for providers to form PSOs to serve Medicare patients, but it is unclear how many providers can or will take advantage of the opportunity.

The fight over PSOs is part of a broader battle for control between the federal government and the states. States are demanding greater authority over Medicaid and even Medicare. The 1997 budget law expanded their powers, particularly over Medicaid. Some state leaders, backed by consumer and provider groups, also want more power to monitor self-insured employer and union plans and fold them into their state health care frameworks. Such plans currently are shielded from state regulation—and from many malpractice and other tort lawsuits—by the federal Employee Retirement Income Security Act, and powerful business and labor groups want to keep it that way. On the other hand, the federal government has begun trespassing onto insurance regulation turf traditionally held by the states. The Health Insurance Portability and Accountability Act of 1996 established some federal rules for the first time for private health insurers. Because of strong public support for greater consumer protections in health insurance, even congressional conservatives who generally espouse states' rights are now supporting some federal rules.

A large majority of hospital leaders expect the public backlash against managed care cost-control practices to continue. Nearly four-fifths of those surveyed expect a significant backlash against managed care insurers. But they also expect to catch some of the heat themselves; 58 percent say that consumers will aim their ire at hospitals. Only about two-fifths feel that physicians will be on the receiving end of this fury. As a result, more than two-thirds of hospital executives anticipate continued efforts by state and federal lawmakers to regulate managed care practices, by mandating standards for length of stay and treatment of particular medical conditions.

The managed care industry has been extremely defensive about the growing public criticism of health plans. The *Hospitals & Health Networks* Leadership Survey shows that while plan executives profess somewhat lower expectations than do hospital leaders that the backlash against cost control will continue, they see themselves as the main target. Almost 60 percent say cost controls will produce a significant consumer backlash against MCOs. Only about a third feel that hospitals or physicians will feel the sting. And two-thirds of plan executives expect further legislation to set minimum standards for coverage and treatment.

Doctors have taken the lead in criticizing managed care cost control practices. So it is not surprising that 80 percent of medical group leaders say that MCOs will face a consumer backlash on cost control. Almost half say that hospitals will also be targeted, while about two-fifths feel that doctors will face the public's wrath. Almost 70 percent of medical group leaders say legislative activity in this area will continue.

MEDICAL SAVINGS ACCOUNTS

Partly out of dissatisfaction with managed care, conservative political leaders are pressing to give consumers health insurance options in which they can deal directly with providers, without HMOs or employers as middlemen. The aim is to give consumers greater freedom to choose providers and benefit packages. In 1996, Congress, against the wishes of Clinton and most Democrats, established a four-year test of medical savings account plans (MSAs), with a cap of 750,000 policies. MSA holders can buy a high-deductible health insurance policy and deposit money in a special tax-sheltered savings account to cover out-of-pocket costs below the deductible. In 1997, Congress launched a test of MSAs for 390,000 Medicare beneficiaries. It also gave seniors the option to buy services from providers with their own money outside Medicare and to join private indemnity plans that cost more, ostensibly in return for greater clinical freedom. While proponents say these new plans open Medicare to greater market competition and will reduce overall health care costs, critics say they will cost Medicare more and hurt coverage for poorer and sicker seniors.

Conservatives are also clamoring to eliminate the tax advantage for employer-paid coverage and shift the incentives toward individual purchasing.[20] This stance is consistent with the desire of some parts of the business community to end employer responsibility for health benefits.

Hospital leaders are skeptical about MSAs and these other new Medicare plans because they require patients to pay a greater part of the bill out-of-pocket. Hospitals' experience is that trying to collect money directly from patients is difficult if not futile. Still, most hospital leaders say the federal tax break for MSAs probably will be extended to everyone following the current testing period.

Although smaller indemnity insurers like MSAs because they are basically indemnity products, managed care plans are less enthusiastic. They have a hard time seeing how a high deductible can be applied to an HMO or preferred provider product, which typically has a low or no deductible. Also, managed care plans encourage preventive care, while the aim of MSAs is to discourage subscribers from seeking care. Still, managed care plans are considering ways to marry MSAs with managed care, and some PPOs have begun offering MSA plans that give patients a discount if they use network providers. Plan executives are about as likely as hospital leaders to say that tax-sheltered MSAs will be extended after the current testing period.

Doctors are most enthusiastic about the new tax break for MSAs. Many see MSA plans as a way to preserve their fee-for-service practice and avoid managed care. But there is a split between primary care doctors, who worry that high-deductible plans will discourage patients from seeing them for routine care, and specialists, who figure that sicker patients will still have to come to them and that specialists will be able to set fees for MSA patients with no insurer oversight. Medical group leaders believe tax-sheltered MSAs are likely to continue after the current testing period.

FOR-PROFIT CONVERSION

A new and increasingly contentious policy arena is the conversion of not-for-profit hospitals and health plans to for-profit status, usually after a sale to a for-profit company. There has been a growing backlash against ownership by for-profit companies, particularly aggressive, publicly traded firms.[21] Critics charge that many for-profit acquisitions and conversions of not-for-profit hospitals and health plans have been arranged without input from the community, have involved conflicts of interest for executives and trustees, and have not compensated the community adequately for the loss of a valuable charitable asset. Since 1996, at least 25 states have considered or passed laws to more tightly regulate conversions of hospitals, and regulators in many states have modified or blocked such deals. Similarly, state regulators have scrutinized conversions of health plans and have forced converting plans in some cases to hand over more of the sales proceeds to charitable foundations dedicated to funding community health projects.

But with many communities having double the number of needed hospital beds, some experts fear that interfering with for-profit conversions and consolidations of hospitals and health plans will slow market-based efforts to squeeze out excess hospital capacity, diminish insurers' bargaining leverage, and thereby hamper cost containment. They also worry about the government's tampering with the market-consolidation process, by which the nation's surplus supply of medical schools and teaching hospitals is slowly being whittled down.

As managed care transforms health care into a more competitive industry and all health care organizations focus more on the bottom line, some community benefit functions formerly performed by charity-minded institutions are beginning to suffer. Some policy makers see the need for new ways of funding indigent care, medical education, research, infectious disease programs, and essential but money-losing services such as trauma care.[22] There is growing support for financing such activities through broad-based taxes, such as on insurance premiums and provider revenues. There are also moves in some states to require not-for-profit providers and health plans to deliver a certain level of these services as a condition of keeping their tax-exempt status.

The trend toward for-profit ownership has been encouraged by the prevailing political and economic view that health care should be run as a business like other industries. Health plan ownership has become largely for-profit, while hospitals are moving much more slowly in that direction. But health care leaders, particularly executives in the largely not-for-profit hospital industry, are ambivalent about this development. That is shown by the findings on what health care leaders expect for-profit conversions to accomplish, as well as by their views on ethical standards in the health care industry.

Hospital leaders expect for-profit ownership of hospitals to grow; the average response predicts that it will rise from the current 14 percent of the nation's facilities to 25 percent by 2007. But they are not enthusiastic about this trend. They believe that for-profit ownership will tend to decrease access, quality, and community health status, raise prices, and have little effect on controlling medical costs. On the other hand, they strongly believe that for-profit status will increase hospitals' access to capital.

Managed care leaders expect investor ownership of hospitals to grow slightly faster than do hospital executives; their average prediction is that for-profits will account for 29 percent of facilities by 2007. They also see for-profit hospital conversion in a somewhat more favorable light. They are considerably more likely to believe that change to investor-owned status will enhance access and quality and lower medical costs, less likely to worry that the new for-profit owners will raise prices, and even more optimistic than hospital leaders that conversions will expand access to capital.

Medical group leaders foresee the biggest increase in for-profit hospital ownership; their average prediction is that for-profits will comprise 31 percent of the nation's facilities by 2007. They sit midway between hospital and health plan leaders in how positively they view the likely impact of conversions.

Not surprisingly, investor-owned and not-for-profit organizations expressed significantly different expectations of the impact of for-profit hospital conversions. Leaders of for-profit organizations are considerably more likely than leaders of not-for-profits to say that conversions will enhance quality and access and improve community health and less likely to say that such transactions will raise prices to payers. The two groups express little difference of opinion about the effects on access to capital and health care costs.

LOCAL ISSUES

Health care leaders' perception of national policy issues is often shaped by what they see in their local community. Thus, questions about local issues can shed light on their broader policy views. Not surprisingly, indigent care is easily the most commonly cited local policy issue among all those surveyed, identified by 59 percent of respondents. After indigent care (61 percent), local policy problems most commonly cited by hospital leaders include the shortage of primary care physicians (50 percent) and the oversupply of hospital beds (39 percent). Health plan leaders most frequently name hospital overcapacity as a local problem (78 percent), followed by indigent care (65 percent), and the shortage of primary care doctors (39 percent). Medical group leaders most frequently identify indigent care as a local issue (55 percent), followed by hospital overcapacity (49 percent) and a shortage of primary care doctors (28 percent).

ANALYSIS

Health care leaders have a pragmatic view of policy developments. Even though hospital, health plan, and medical group leaders all consider indigent care one of their biggest problems, they are pessimistic about federal action on universal coverage. That is justified by the current political climate, which strongly proscribes the tax and spending hikes that would be needed to fund it. Nevertheless, President Clinton and some other political leaders see the new children's coverage initiative in the 1997 budget act as an incremental step toward further expansions. They hope to extend coverage next to the temporarily unemployed and the working poor, whose employers often do not provide health benefits. Proponents of coverage expansion take heart from surveys by the Kaiser Family Foundation and others, which consistently show that the public supports universal coverage as a national goal.

On Medicare, the major restructuring sought by political leaders will create conflicts between hospitals, plans, and medical groups as resources are reallocated. Hospitals and doctors still are focused on fee-for-service Medicare and thus have a sharply different perspective than health plans. This scenario could change as Medicare increasingly becomes a managed care program. As the three groups become more closely bound together in capitated systems, they will have more in common and may see more need to collaborate on policy issues.

In contrast to Medicare, hospitals, plans, and doctors probably will not find a convergence of interests on Medicaid as that program is restructured through managed care. Medicaid patients have long been segregated from the rest of the health care system. Traditional Medicaid providers want to protect the status quo because their financial survival depends on keeping these patients. Current attempts to mainstream Medicaid patients into commercial health plans and provider networks threaten the old providers. On the other hand, if policy makers do not continue their mainstreaming efforts, most providers and plans will have little interest in supporting the program politically or financially, and it could deteriorate.

The future of long-term care is tightly connected to the future of Medicaid, and many of the same intergroup dynamics apply. Most providers and plans do not deal much with long-term care patients; the only patients they seek are those who can afford to pay for their own care. But a public financing program will remain essential for the large number of Americans who cannot afford to pay for private insurance or for more than a brief nursing home stay. Providers and plans will have to work together to ensure that public funding remains adequate. Still, for-profit and not-for-profit organizations see their responsibilities on long-term care differently.

Hospitals, doctors, and health plans currently are at each others' throats over cost control practices and the issue of managed care regulation. But they are likely to develop more of a shared perspective on ensuring quality and patient and provider satisfaction as they form tighter integrated systems. They may be able to work out voluntary models of oversight and shared control. If that does not occur, however, health care could become even more adversarial, sparking greater regulation and litigation.

In reaction to managed care, interest is growing in MSA plans and other insurance options featuring greater patient financial responsibility. If such arrangements remain limited, they could provide an attractive and lucrative niche for some providers, insurers, and patients who are uncomfortable with managed care. But if they draw too many healthier and wealthier people away from conventional plans, they could cause havoc in the insurance market and would have to be more tightly regulated. In that case, policy schisms could develop between providers and plans that cater to the healthier and wealthier MSA market and those that serve the general market.

The future of for-profit conversions, and investor-owned health care in general, will probably be determined by how well for-profit organizations perform in the areas that health care leaders expressed concern about—access, quality, and cost. Leaders of for-profit and not-for-profit organizations already view the effects of conversions very differently. If for-profits fail to increase access and quality and demonstrate cost savings, opposition to further conversions will harden.

When asked to identify the major problems they face at the local level, leaders of hospitals, health plans, and medical groups agree on indigent care, hospital overcapacity, and the shortage of primary care physicians. But they are far from consensus on solutions. And there lies the nation's biggest health policy challenge.

References

1. Haynes Johnson and David S. Broder, *The System* (New York: Little Brown, 1996), p. x; Harris Meyer, "The Main Event," *Hospitals & Health Networks* (Oct. 5, 1996): 40.

2. Harris Meyer, "Medicare: Let the Games Begin . . . Again," *Hospitals & Health Networks* (Jan. 20, 1997): 32–38.

3. George Anders, *Health Against Wealth* (Boston: Houghton Mifflin, 1996), p. 13.

4. American Medical Association, *Socioeconomic Monitoring System, 1995–1996 Core Surveys* (Chicago: AMA).

5. *EBRI* [Employee Benefit Research Institute] *Notes* 18, no. 11 (Nov. 1997).

6. Jon R. Gabel, Paul B. Ginsburg, and Kelly A. Hunt, "Small Employers and Their Health Benefits, 1988–1996," *Health Affairs* 16, no. 5 (Sept./Oct. 1997): 103.

7. Johnson and Broder, p. 556.

8. *Health News Daily* (Nov. 13, 1996).

9. Harris Meyer, "Medicine at the Crossroads," *American Medical News* (Dec. 13, 1993): 1.

10. Terese Hudson, "The Great Debate," *Hospitals & Health Networks* (Jan. 20, 1996): 27.

11. Harris Meyer, "Door May Open Up for Provider Networks," *American Medical News* (Nov. 27, 1995): 3

12. Harris Meyer, "Egging People On," *Hospitals & Health Networks* 70, no. 20 (Oct. 20, 1996): 36.

13. Ibid., p. 38.

14. Harris Meyer, "Home (Care) Improvement," *Hospitals & Health Networks* 71, no. 8 (April 20, 1997): 40.

15. Meyer, "Egging People On," p. 38.

16. Robert E. Schlenker, Peter W. Shaughnessy, and David Hittle, "Patient-Level Costs of Home Health Care under Capitated and Fee-for-Service Payment," *Inquiry* 32, no. 3 (fall 1995): 252–70.

17. *The Interstudy Competitive Edge* 7, no. 2 (Sept. 1997).

18. Uwe E. Reinhardt, "Health System Change: Skirmish or Revolution?" *Health Affairs* 15, no. 4 (1996).

19. Anders, p. 216.

20. Meyer, "The Main Event," p. 44.

21. Harris Meyer and Terese Hudson, "Selling or Selling Out?" *Hospitals & Health Networks* 70, no. 11 (June 5, 1996): 22.

22. Gary Claxton, Judith Feder, David Shactman, and Stuart Altman, "Public Policy Issues in Nonprofit Conversions: An Overview," *Health Affairs* 16, no. 2 (March/Apr. 1997): 9.

Effect of Not-for-Profit Organizations Converting to For-Profit Status

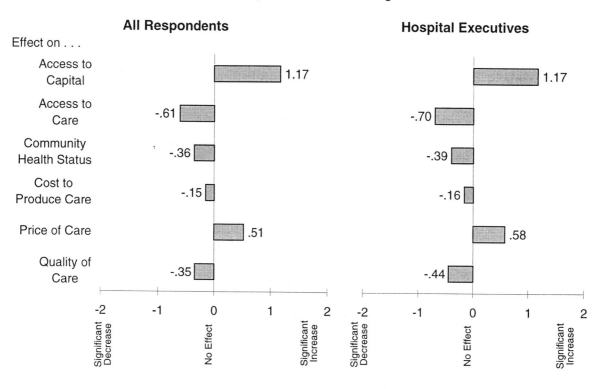

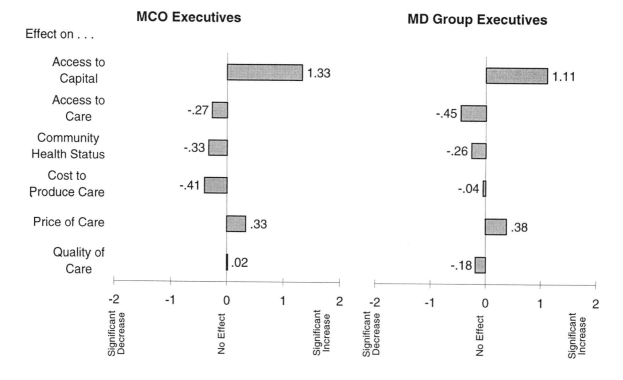

Political Actions Taken by All Respondents in the Last Year

Phoned Legislator

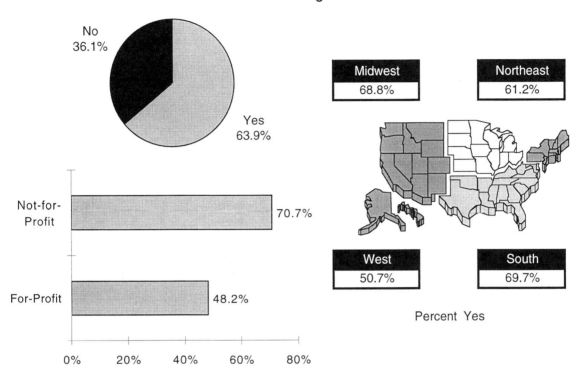

Met with Legislator

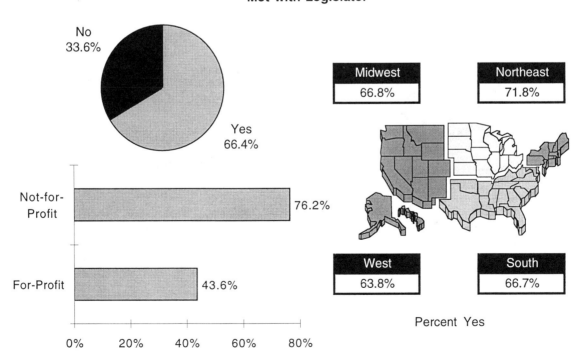

Political Actions Taken by All Respondents in the Last Year

Sent Faxes or Letters

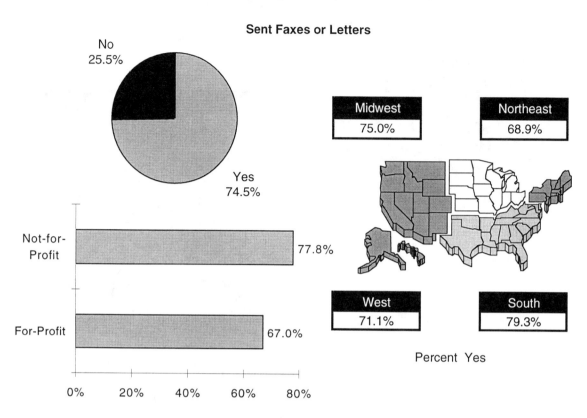

Volunteered Personal Time

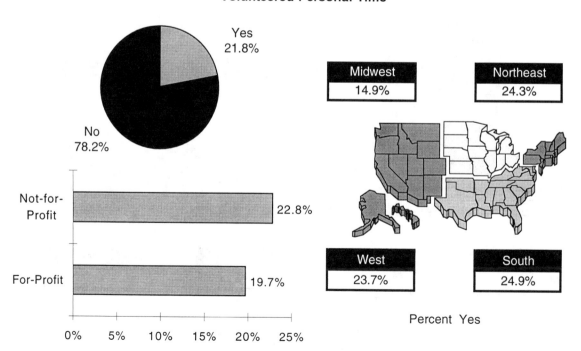

Political Actions Taken by Hospital Executives in the Last Year

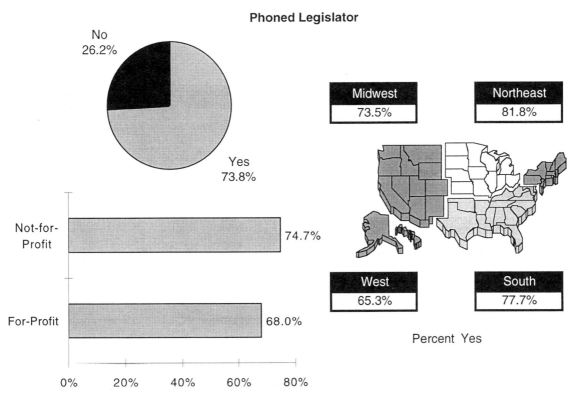

Phoned Legislator

No
26.2%

Yes
73.8%

Not-for-Profit 74.7%

For-Profit 68.0%

0%   20%   40%   60%   80%

Midwest
73.5%

Northeast
81.8%

West
65.3%

South
77.7%

Percent Yes

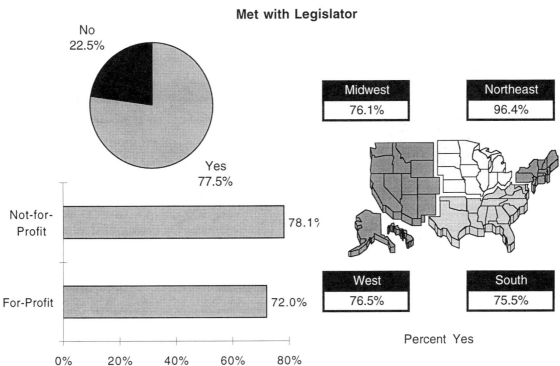

Met with Legislator

No
22.5%

Yes
77.5%

Not-for-Profit 78.1%

For-Profit 72.0%

0%   20%   40%   60%   80%

Midwest
76.1%

Northeast
96.4%

West
76.5%

South
75.5%

Percent Yes

Political Actions Taken by Hospital Executives in the Last Year

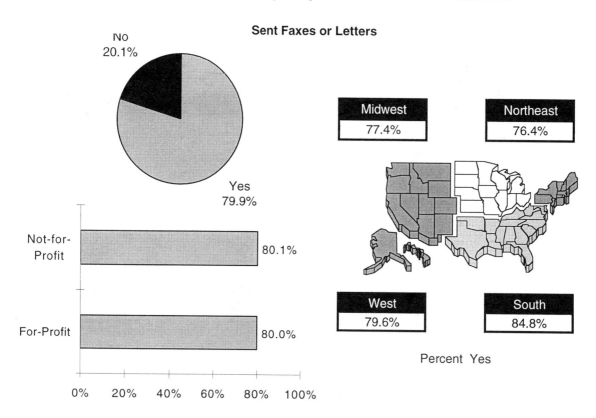

Sent Faxes or Letters

No 20.1%

Yes 79.9%

Not-for-Profit 80.1%

For-Profit 80.0%

Midwest 77.4%

Northeast 76.4%

West 79.6%

South 84.8%

Percent Yes

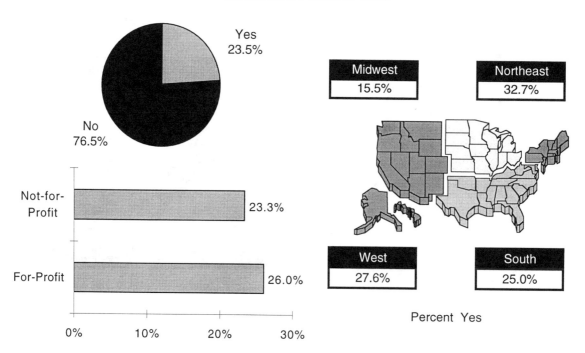

Volunteered Personal Time

Yes 23.5%

No 76.5%

Not-for-Profit 23.3%

For-Profit 26.0%

Midwest 15.5%

Northeast 32.7%

West 27.6%

South 25.0%

Percent Yes

Policy   Political Action

Political Actions Taken by Managed Care Executives in the Last Year

Phoned Legislator

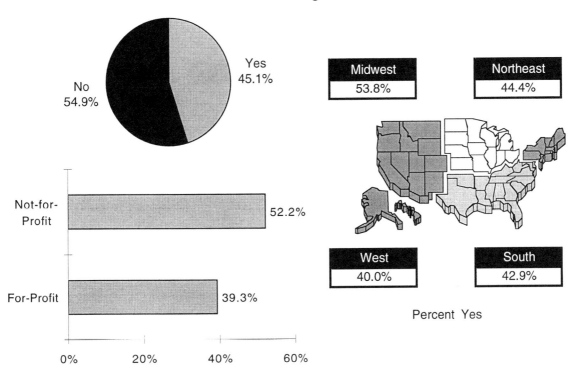

Midwest 53.8%	Northeast 44.4%
West 40.0%	South 42.9%

Percent Yes

Met with Legislator

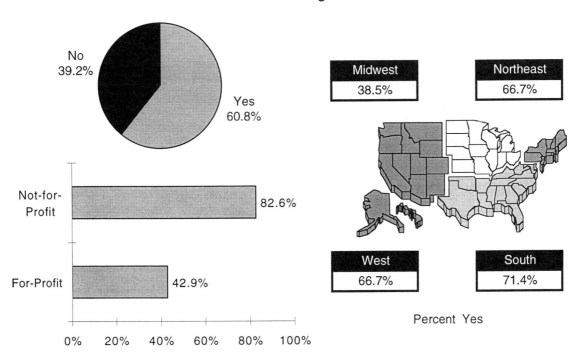

Midwest 38.5%	Northeast 66.7%
West 66.7%	South 71.4%

Percent Yes

Political Actions Taken by Managed Care Executives in the Last Year

Sent Faxes or Letters

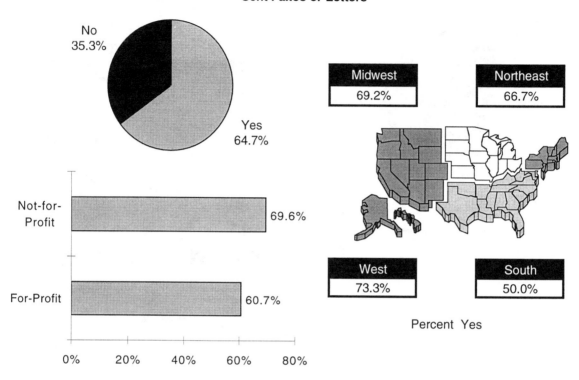

Volunteered Personal Time

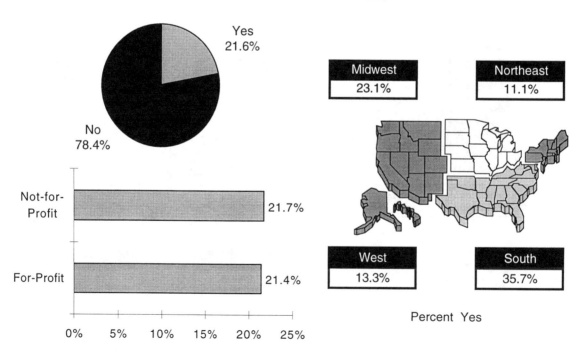

Political Actions Taken by Physician Group Executives in the Last Year

Phoned Legislator

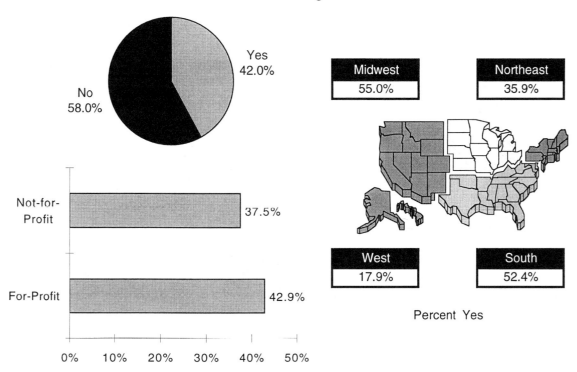

Met with Legislator

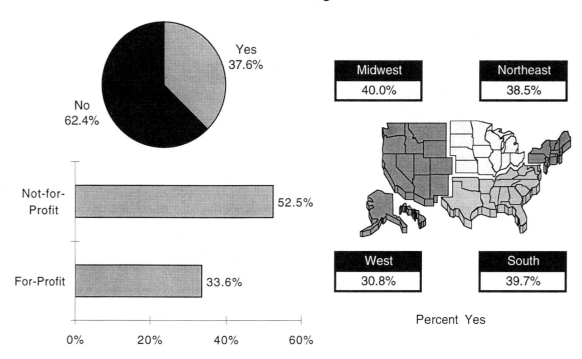

Policy   **Political Action**

Political Actions Taken by Physician Group Executives in the Last Year

Sent Faxes or Letters

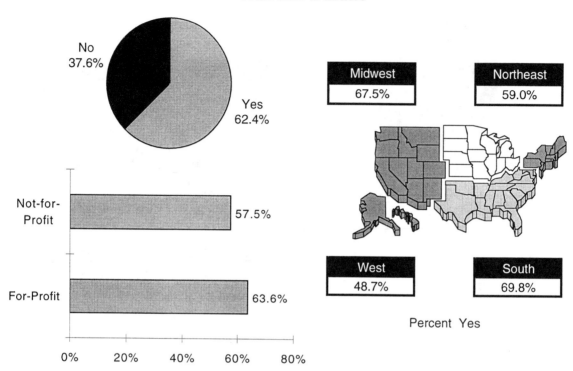

No
37.6%

Yes
62.4%

Midwest
67.5%

Northeast
59.0%

West
48.7%

South
69.8%

Not-for-Profit 57.5%

For-Profit 63.6%

Percent Yes

Volunteered Personal Time

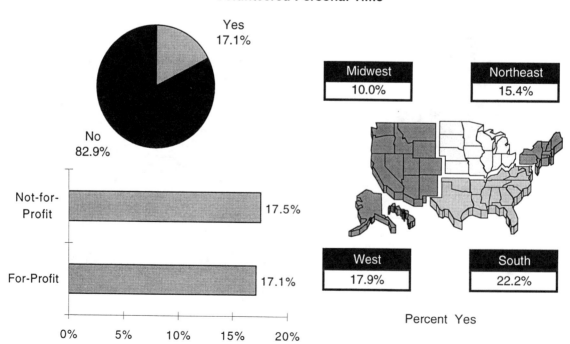

Yes
17.1%

No
82.9%

Midwest
10.0%

Northeast
15.4%

West
17.9%

South
22.2%

Not-for-Profit 17.5%

For-Profit 17.1%

Percent Yes

Would State Administered Block Grants Increase or Decrease Program Efficiency?

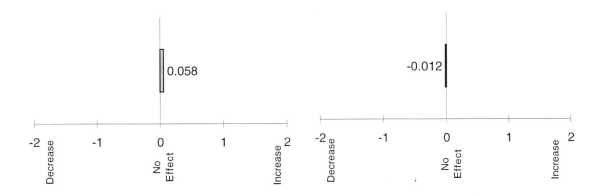

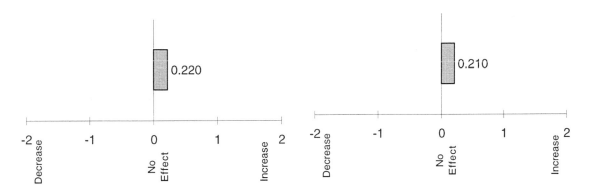

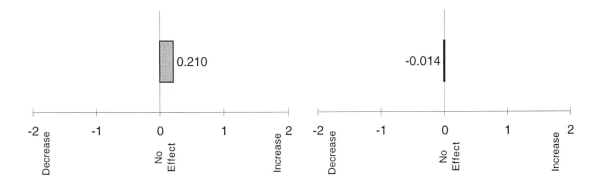

Who Will Pay for Increasing Costs of Long-Term Care and Home Care?

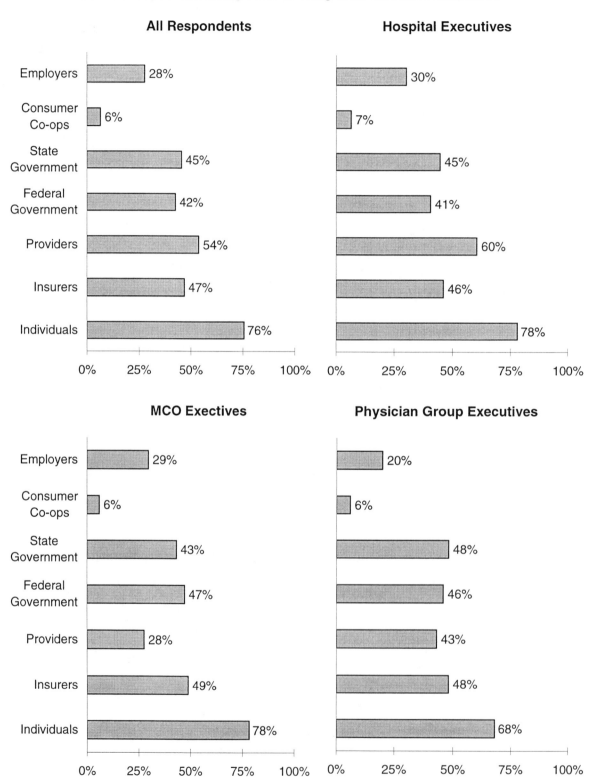

All Respondents

Employers	28%
Consumer Co-ops	6%
State Government	45%
Federal Government	42%
Providers	54%
Insurers	47%
Individuals	76%

Hospital Executives

Employers	30%
Consumer Co-ops	7%
State Government	45%
Federal Government	41%
Providers	60%
Insurers	46%
Individuals	78%

MCO Exectives

Employers	29%
Consumer Co-ops	6%
State Government	43%
Federal Government	47%
Providers	28%
Insurers	49%
Individuals	78%

Physician Group Executives

Employers	20%
Consumer Co-ops	6%
State Government	48%
Federal Government	46%
Providers	43%
Insurers	48%
Individuals	68%

• Percent of respondents identifying each area; multiple responses allowed.

Will a Focus on Cost Control Cause a Consumer Backlash Against . . .

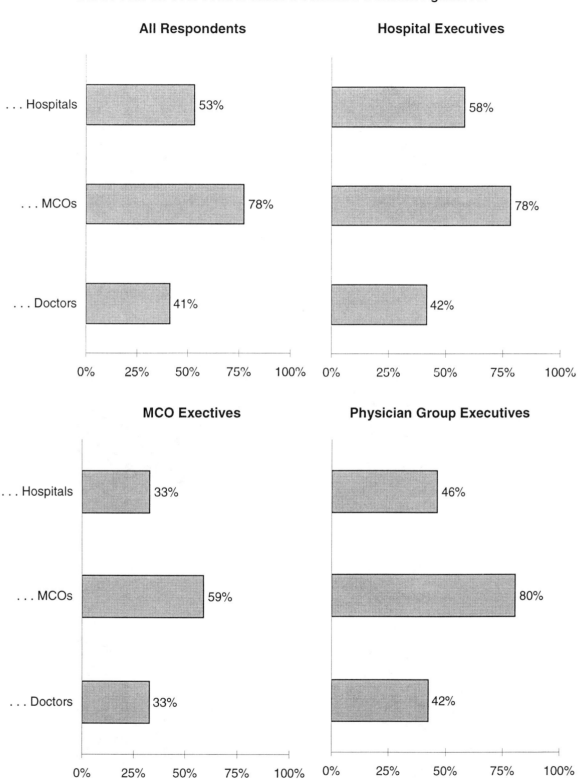

All Respondents

. . . Hospitals 53%

. . . MCOs 78%

. . . Doctors 41%

Hospital Executives

58%

78%

42%

MCO Exectives

. . . Hospitals 33%

. . . MCOs 59%

. . . Doctors 33%

Physician Group Executives

46%

80%

42%

• Percent of respondents identifying each area; multiple responses allowed.

Will There Be More Government Regulation of Specific Conditions and Procedures?

All Respondents

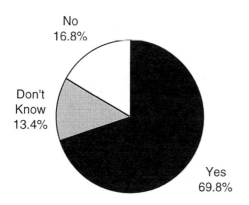

No
16.8%

Don't
Know
13.4%

Yes
69.8%

Hospital Executives

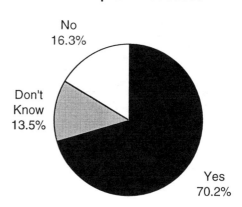

No
16.3%

Don't
Know
13.5%

Yes
70.2%

MCO Exectives

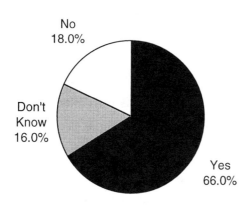

No
18.0%

Don't
Know
16.0%

Yes
66.0%

Physician Group Executives

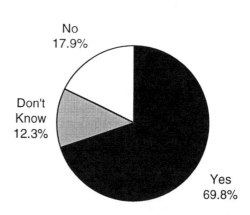

No
17.9%

Don't
Know
12.3%

Yes
69.8%

All For-Profit Executives

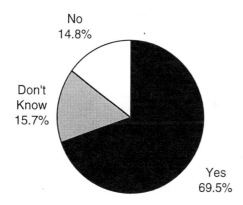

No
14.8%

Don't
Know
15.7%

Yes
69.5%

All Not-for-Profit Executives

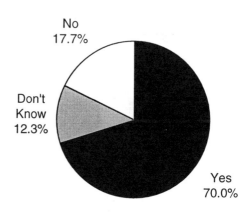

No
17.7%

Don't
Know
12.3%

Yes
70.0%

Do You Support Means Testing for Medicare?

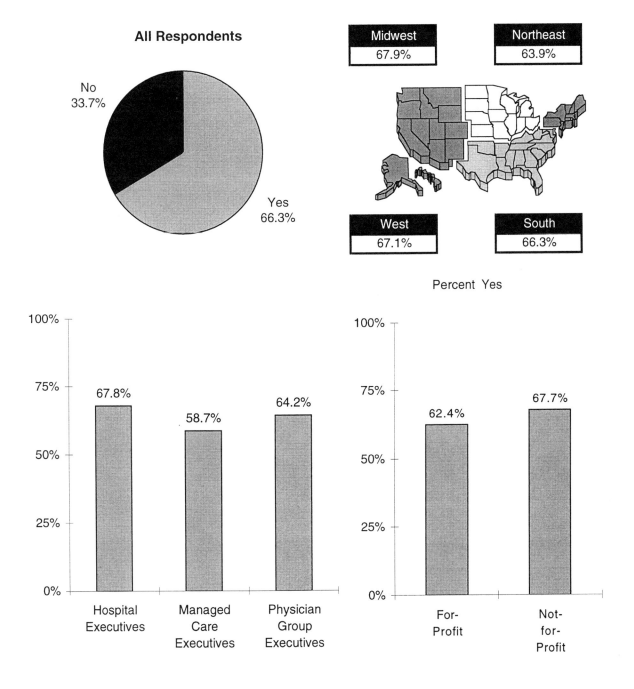

All Respondents

No 33.7%

Yes 66.3%

Midwest	Northeast
67.9%	63.9%

West	South
67.1%	66.3%

Percent Yes

Hospital Executives 67.8%
Managed Care Executives 58.7%
Physician Group Executives 64.2%

For-Profit 62.4%
Not-for-Profit 67.7%

5

Quality

Jan Greene

Quality has become the latest mantra of the health care industry. Quality, many executives believe, has the power to reshape the current imbalance between cost-cutting and appropriate patient care. Prompted by the perception that the country was spending too much on getting well, the quest for cost containment has come to dominate the actions of hospitals, health plans, and employers. So the marketplace was given the task of bringing spiraling health care inflation under control. As it turned out, HMOs managed to cut enough obvious fat from the system that the rate of increase in health insurance premiums slowed. But the law of unintended consequences kicked in, and many of their cost-cutting methods prompted questions from angry patients about whether quality was being cut at the same time. Suddenly, quality has become as important as cost-cutting, at least in public discourse.

There is another, deeper reason why quality has such resonance these days. Many influential health care thinkers contend that better care will actually cost less overall. When they examine practices of doctors and hospitals, researchers find that many have never been studied to see whether they actually work best. As a result, medical practices vary from region to region.[1] In addition, as much as 20 percent of what's done is inappropriate medically and could be both wasteful and harmful, according to Mark Chassin, a professor at Mount Sinai School of Medicine who specializes in evidence-based medicine, a movement to better study the scientific underpinnings of medical care.[2] By choosing the remedies with the best outcomes, the system could provide better care and avoid wasting resources.

Marketing is yet another reason that quality has become such a rallying cry in health care. As the marketplace gets more competitive, both among insurers and providers, it becomes more important for an organization to prove its worth. Consumers, employers, and managed care organizations (MCOs) are all asking for hard data on whether the care being provided is worth the money they are paying.

Quality is also a key component of the latest marketplace development, the call for *value*. Boiled to its essence, that's what purchasers want, be they patients or employers. There are two components to value, price and quality, and the market requires both lower costs and higher quality. Both these objectives will have to be met if the health care system is to get back in the good graces of the American public, who have grave doubts about whether they are getting a good deal for the billions of dollars spent each year.

Slowly, report cards on hospitals and health plans are becoming more common as employers band together in large markets and use their clout to get better deals. Along the way, accrediting agencies have sprung up for every part of the health care system. The venerable hospital accreditor, the Joint Commission on Accreditation of Healthcare Organizations, inspects institutions once every three years and focuses on processes. Its accreditation has become a requirement of participation in Medicare and many health plans. But critics of the Joint Commission say its standards have not kept up with the times and point to a potential conflict of interest when the Joint Commission reviews a hospital that is paying a big fee for that accreditation review.[3]

Employers and managed care companies spearheaded the National Committee for Quality Assurance (NCQA) to develop ways to measure the quality of MCOs. This effort resulted in the widely used Health Plan Employer Data and Information Set (HEDIS), a set of HMO measures. An alternative organization, the Foundation for Accountability (FAACT), sprang up later with a stated focus on providing quality information from a consumer point of view. It has developed its own set of indicators, which some employers prefer.[4]

Doctors have recently joined the game. Although specialty societies have long offered board certification as a means of ensuring a doctor's knowledge of the field, the American Medical Association has developed an accreditation program it says is more wide ranging, including a site visit to the physician's office to ensure the practice is run according to quality standards identified by the American Medical Accreditation Program.

While all of these organizations, and others, are developing ways to measure performance and outcomes, they certainly have not perfected them yet, and a fair amount of controversy remains over the way measurement ought to be done.

ISSUES FOR HOSPITAL EXECUTIVES

Most hospital leaders say they report quality of care to constituents in some fashion. By constituents, they could mean employers, payers, patients, or the community. Although 30 percent of hospital leaders said they do not report quality to their constituents, that percentage is likely to decrease during the next several years as the marketplace demands more detailed information about quality, including measures such as success rates for certain procedures, the rate of hospital-acquired infections, and the training level of nurses and technicians.

Hospitals that do report quality were most likely to provide information through printed material or information sheets (See table 5-1). Many hospitals print brochures that are used at health fairs or in direct mail campaigns. The

Table 5-1. Top Quality—Reporting Tools by Organization

Tool	Hospitals	MCOs	Medical Groups
Printed information sheets	59%	71%	43%
Advertising	37%	31%	18%
Report cards	18%	39%	13%
Internet	11%	14%	12%

next most likely communication form is advertising, such as hospital ads commonly seen on billboards and in newspapers. The Internet remains a tool in limited use by hospitals for quality reporting.

The most common quality measurement tool used by hospitals is the patient satisfaction survey. Ninety-four percent of hospital executives say their organization uses such surveys to gauge quality. Joint Commission standards are another common type of quality measurement tool used by hospitals. Nearly 77 percent of hospital leaders say they use them, which is close to the proportion of hospitals the Joint Commission accredits. Seventy percent of hospitals also use internally developed standards to gauge quality. The *Hospitals &Health Networks* Leadership Survey also asked respondents to rate the quality of care provided by their own organization, from extremely high to extremely low. The average response for hospitals fell just above "somewhat high," 4.2 on a scale of 1 to 5. By contrast, hospital leaders give lower ratings for the quality of care provided by their competitors. That rating falls below "somewhat high," with a mean response of 3.8. They feel a little more charitable about the region in which they operate, which they rate a 3.9, but the overall health care industry fares the worst among hospital leaders, getting a 3.7 rating. Overall, hospital leaders feel the best about the care being provided by their organization, but not as good about their competitors or about the industry in general.

The leaders were also asked about the importance of various issues to the strategic success of their organization. On a list of 21 different strategic, policy, and personnel issues, hospital executives rated "measuring quality/outcomes" as sixth, behind information technology and having an educated board.

Asked about the potential impact of various market trends on quality of care, hospital executives reserve their strongest opinions for capitation, the per-member, per-month prepaid payment method pioneered by HMOs. Forty percent of hospital leaders say that capitation has resulted in reduced quality of care. This figure is striking, considering how common capitation has become in many advanced managed care markets. Another 52 percent of hospital executives, however, say they do not think capitation has made a difference in quality. A minority are also worried about global case rates, which lump together a number of medical services into one payment; 18 percent of hospital executives say case rates have reduced quality.

Hospital leaders are supportive of clinical pathways, which help standardize the care of patients with certain common disorders. Seventy-one percent of the hospital executives say that clinical pathways have improved quality, while 27 percent say they have made no difference.

ISSUES FOR MANAGED CARE EXECUTIVES

MCOs, owing to their reliance on data to carry out the basic tasks of running an HMO, may be in the best position to collect quality information and distribute it. And most report doing so; just 18 percent of MCOs report that they do not report quality of care to their constituents. Seventy-one percent of MCOs surveyed said their organizations provide printed material or information sheets on their quality of care. The next most likely way of communicating is through report cards, a format that has become popular for HMOs to promote the rates of preventive care provided to their members (39 percent report using them). But MCOs also advertise; 31 percent report doing so. Just 14 percent are using a Web site on the Internet to provide quality information.

MCOs are fans of the patient satisfaction survey; 84 percent say they use them. But HEDIS, the measurement tool devised by the NCQA, has become quite popular as well: 75 percent of the managed care survey respondents report using it. With the advent of HEDIS 3.0, an expanded set of measures meant to provide more information on the actual outcomes of medical care, more payers are requiring that participating health plans use this reporting tool. About two-thirds of health plans report using their own internally developed benchmarks to assess quality, and another 26 percent say they use some other type of quality measurement tool. Although the Joint Commission is typically thought of as the accreditor for hospitals, 37 percent of the managed care respondents say they use Joint Commission standards. Those respondents could be using the network accreditation now offered by the Joint Commission, or else they might be vertically integrated systems that include both hospital and managed care functions.

Managed care executives give their own organization's quality of care a relatively high rating, a mean of 4.2 on a scale of 1 to 5. But they grade their competitors, along with the entire managed care industry, somewhat lower. Managed care executives give both their industry and their competitors a 3.6 rating, somewhat higher than neutral. (See figures 5-1 and 5-2.) Asked about the strategic importance of measuring quality and outcomes to the success of their organizations, managed care executives ranked the issue fairly high, at 5th of 21 issues. At the same time, though, they do not feel nearly as prepared to handle the challenges it presents. They rank measuring quality as 2d among the issues they feel least confident about resolving.

When asked about the impact of various market trends on quality of care, MCOs expressed their strong support for clinical pathways. These standardization tools have helped improve care, say 82 percent of managed care executives. This strong response is consistent with managed care's basic reliance on guidelines that make medical care more predictable and uniform, both important to "managing" care.[5]

Capitation is one of the most criticized developments of the managed care revolution because, critics say, it gives doctors and hospitals an incentive to curtail care. Of course, managed care executives would disagree with the critics. Fifty-four percent of the managed care executives feel the per-member, per-month prepayment method has made no difference in quality, and 29 percent say it has actually improved quality. Leaders of managed care see this financial incentive as a useful way to make providers accountable for what they do. Managed care executives also say global case rates have a positive influence on quality. Twenty-eight percent of managed care leaders say global case rates improve quality, while 63 percent said they make no real difference.

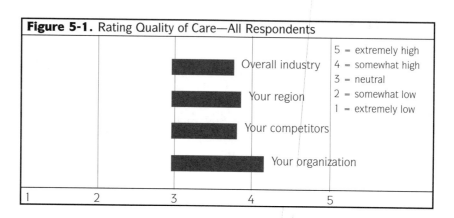

Figure 5-1. Rating Quality of Care—All Respondents

Overall industry
Your region
Your competitors
Your organization

5 = extremely high
4 = somewhat high
3 = neutral
2 = somewhat low
1 = extremely low

ISSUES FOR GROUP PRACTICE EXECUTIVES

Medical group practices are the most likely of the three groups not to report quality to their constituents. Forty-five percent of physician groups do not report quality versus 30 percent of hospitals and 18 percent of MCOs. One reason could be that the science of measuring quality is the least evolved for physicians.

Still, 43 percent of physician groups provide some kind of printed material or information sheets to their constituents. Another 18 percent say they advertise, and 12 percent use a Web site on the Internet. And just because physician groups may not have yet perfected a set of quality indicators to provide the public, most still assess themselves internally: 85 percent of physician group executives surveyed say they conduct patient satisfaction surveys. In addition, 60 percent use internally developed benchmarks to keep track of quality, 25 percent use HEDIS measures, and 24 percent use Joint Commission standards. Physician groups rate their own quality of care a 4.5 on a scale of 5. They see their competitors as less competent, rating them a 3.9 and the entire medical community a 3.8.

Strategically, physician groups see measuring quality of care and outcomes as one of their top goals. At the same time, they list it as one of the greatest challenges they face and as an issue about which they don't feel altogether prepared.

When asked about the impact of certain market trends on the overall quality of health care in America, physician groups were fairly critical of capitation. Nearly half of them say per-member, per-month payment for health care has reduced quality. This view is consistent with the views so vehemently expressed by many medical associations about the negative impact of managed care payment systems on the doctor-patient relationship.

Physician groups are fairly skeptical about how much clinical pathways have helped quality. MCOs and hospitals have turned to these methods of standardizing care to ensure that patients with certain common conditions are cared for in a systematic fashion. But 44 percent of physician groups surveyed say they do not think clinical pathways make any difference in quality. About half think pathways do yield an increase in quality. About half of physician groups think that the advent of physician groups has served to improve quality of care, presumably because the physicians in the group can help one another in making medical decisions.

KEY COMPARISONS

There is wide variation in the way that the health care sectors assess and report the quality of care they provide. For instance, MCOs are much more likely to

Figure 5-2. Rating Quality of Care at Your Organization—by Respondent Groups

report quality to their constituents than are medical groups—18 percent of MCOs do not report quality versus 49 percent of medical groups. And managed care is more likely to produce report cards with comparative information on quality. This statistic is consistent with a simple fact about the market: MCOs sell themselves directly to employers and need data to back up their marketing claims. They also face more direct scrutiny from the employers, who demand information about HMOs. However, patient satisfaction surveys are more consistently and widely used by all types of health care organizations, with at least 84 percent of them reporting their use. These are relatively easy tools to administer compared with the complex task of identifying performance measures or measuring outcomes. Few respondents are using Web sites on the Internet to provide consumers with quality information.

In self-assessments of quality, doctor groups have the best self-image, perhaps because doctors need a surfeit of confidence to do their job. Medical group administrators are the most likely to rate their quality of care as "extremely high"—with more than half doing so—but just 27 percent of hospital leaders and 24 percent of managed care executives did the same. Instead, most hospital and managed care executives described their quality as "somewhat high." But in sizing up the competition, everyone was less charitable; they were all more likely to consider the quality of their rivals as "neutral."

The executives part company in their perspectives on how certain market trends have affected quality of care. Hospital and physician group managers see capitation as reducing quality of care, while managed care leaders either think it makes no difference or believe it actually improves quality of care. (See figure 5-3) Those in managed care also are more likely to think that global case rates are good for quality, while few physician group or hospital people share that view.

Managed care leaders are also more enthusiastic about clinical pathways; a majority believe that the standardized paths of care improve quality. Many physician group leaders think that they did not make much of a difference.

There are also significant differences of opinion on the impact of vertical integration on quality. MCOs see the alliances between providers and managed care as a good thing, improving quality. But both hospitals and physician groups are less persuaded, seeing the linkup of two organizations as having negligible impact on quality. Experience with these arrangements has shown that the natural conflicts involved are difficult, if not impossible, to resolve.[6]

For-profits differ from not-for-profits on the relationship between quality and capitation. For-profit hospitals are more likely to say that capitation has hurt quality than are not-for-profit hospitals (54 percent versus 39 percent). But the opposite is true for managed care, where 23 percent of tax-exempt HMO leaders say capitation has lowered quality, while 12 percent of for-profit managed care executives think so.

IMPLICATIONS

Throughout the industry there is uncertainty about how quality should be measured and how that information should be communicated. Even as health care organizations are feeling more pressure from the marketplace to provide such information, they run into roadblocks when trying to condense complex data into meaningful information consumers can use. The range of uses for quality measures accounts for some of the difficulty: Information may be needed for process improvement; policy making; community health assessment; and consumer selection of hospitals, health plans, and physicians.

Hospitals and physician groups seem to be focusing internally, hoping that once measurement is perfected on the inside it can be shared with the outside world. The market, however, may not wait that long. And if these organizations decide to enter the marketplace with their own health plan, they will face the same kind of pressure to produce quality measures faced by managed care.

Of course, there are political reasons for the lack of progress in quality measurement. Saying you want to measure quality both to better compete in the marketplace and to better serve your patients or members is easy, but it is quite a different matter to accept the criticism if the resulting numbers are not flattering. When the NCQA was developing its HEDIS set of quality indicators, it was relatively simple to get health plans to agree to count preventive measures, such as the number of elderly receiving flu immunizations, because that is where health plans excel. But it has been much harder to get agreement on measuring outcomes, even the most basic, such as how many elderly plan members actually came down with the flu that year.

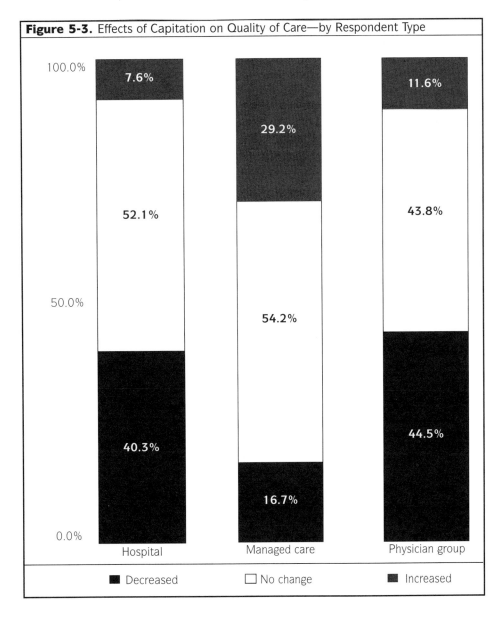

Figure 5-3. Effects of Capitation on Quality of Care—by Respondent Type

Some observers are skeptical about whether real, useful quality measures will ever become available in the United States. Others see market forces as pushing inevitably in that direction. Policy makers have increasingly relied on the marketplace to change the health care system for the better; and, theoretically, in the marketplace what the consumer wants, the consumer gets. Of course, since most Americans get their health insurance through an employer-sponsored plan, the employer is the real buyer. Employers will have to push hardest for quality information. Recent surveys of employers indicate that while an increasing number of large companies are demanding quality data from health plans and providers, the vast majority still see price as the most important factor.[7] Until that changes, or until the government mandates consumer protections that incorporate quality reporting, it is unlikely that the toughest questions in the science of health care quality measurement will get answered.

Meanwhile, in the marketplace, the financial side of health care continues to develop ways to improve value by cutting costs. This push has clearly created anxiety among doctors and hospitals, whose leaders indicate that they find such tools as capitation antithetical to medical quality. These financial tools will probably become less controversial when they can be balanced by solid information on outcomes, and when evidence-based medicine is able to provide clear guidelines for the best, safest, and most cost-effective ways of providing medical care. Until then, the debate over quality will remain more of a political battle than a scientific one.

References

1. *The Dartmouth Atlas of Health Care* (Chicago: American Hospital Publishing, 1996).

2. Mark Chassin, "Medical Ethics in the New Medical Marketplace" (paper presented at the Agency for Health Care Policy and Research conference, Washington, D.C., July 1997).

3. Mari Edlin, "One Thumb Down for Reviewers," *Hospitals & Health Networks* 71, no. 16 (Aug. 20, 1997): 49–50.

4. *Redesigning Health Care for the New Millennium: An Assessment of the Health Care Environment in the United States* (Irving, Tex.: VHA Inc., 1997): 53.

5. Peter MacPherson, "Measure by Measures," *Hospitals & Health Networks* 70, no. 6 (March 20, 1996): 53–56.

6. Gloria Shur Bilchik, "Can Rivals Play Nice?" *Hospitals & Health Networks* 71, no. 8 (Apr. 20, 1997): 24–28.

7. *Partnering for Value: The Second Annual Washington Business Group on Health/Watson Wyatt Worldwide Study on Value in Health Care* (Washington, D.C.: Watson Wyatt, 1997).

Quality **Measurement**

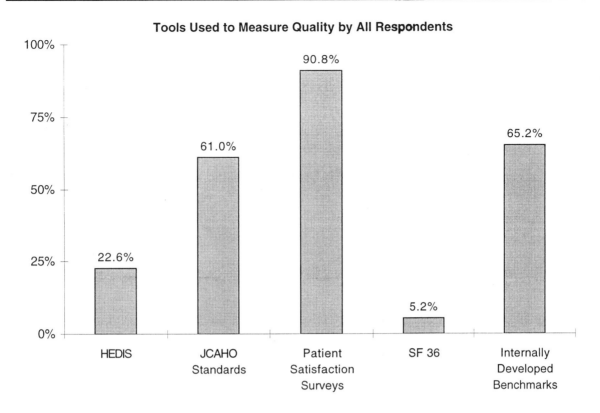

Tools Used to Measure Quality by All Respondents

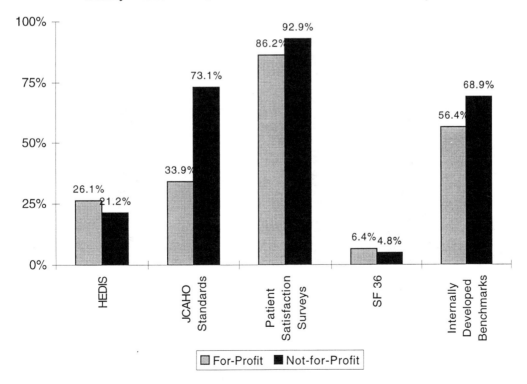

Quality Measurement--For-Profit and Not-for-Profit All Respondents

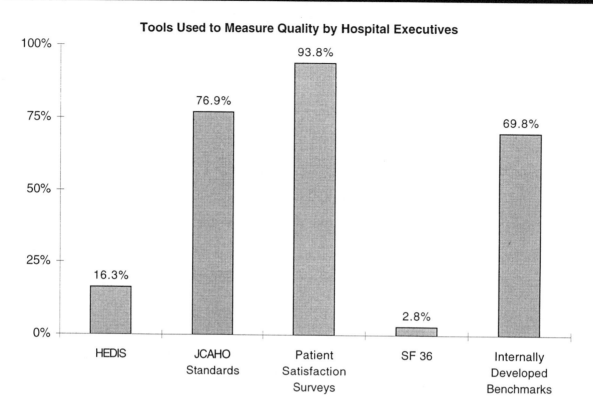

Tools Used to Measure Quality by Hospital Executives

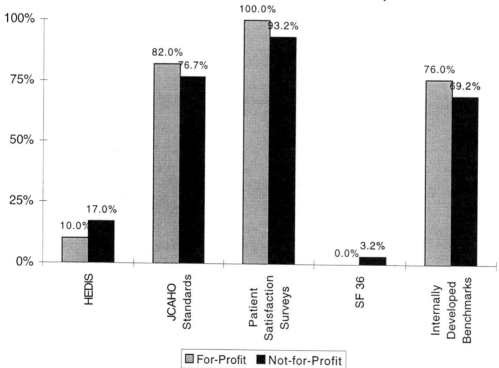

Quality Measurement--For-Profit and Not-for-Profit Hospital Executives

Tools Used to Measure Quality by Managed Care Executives

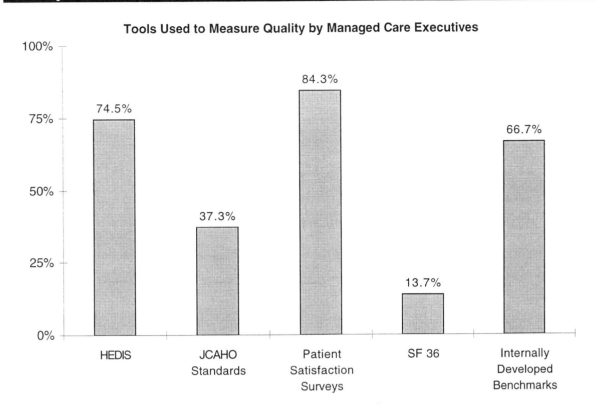

Quality Measurement--For-Profit and Not-for-Profit Managed Care Executives

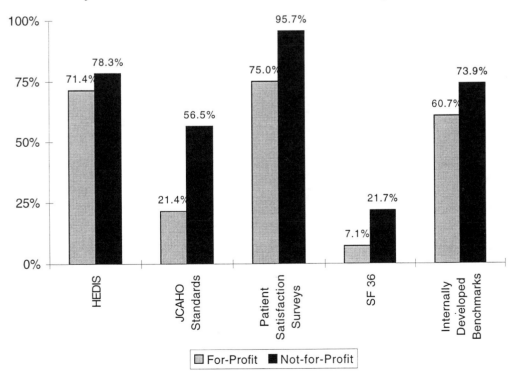

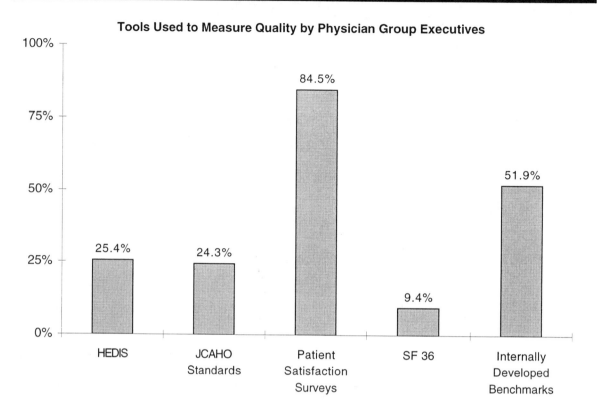

Tools Used to Measure Quality by Physician Group Executives

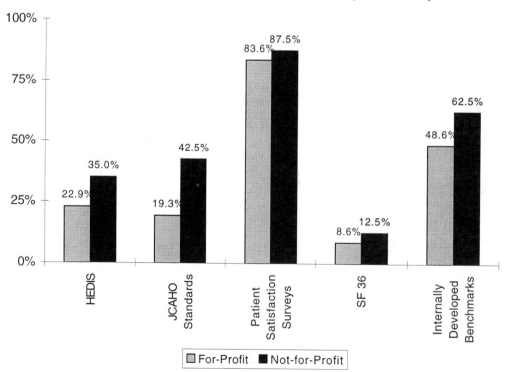

Quality Measurement--For-Profit and Not-for-Profit Physician Group Executives

☐ For-Profit ■ Not-for-Profit

Quality   Reporting

Do You Report Quality to Your Constituents?

All Respondents   **Not-For-Profit**   **For-Profit**

Methods Used to Report Quality to Constituents

All Respondents

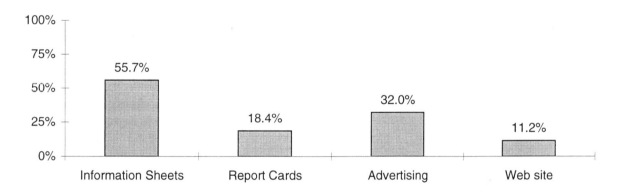

For-Profit vs. Not-for-Profit Respondents

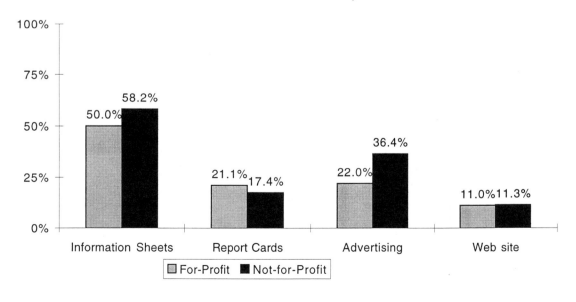

Do You Report Quality to Your Constituents?

Methods Used to Report Quality to Constituents

Hospital Executives

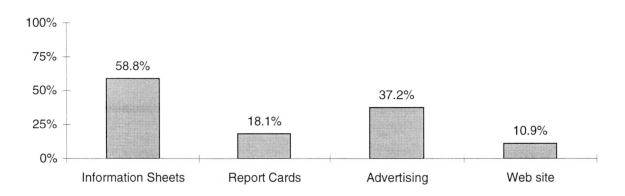

For-Profit vs. Not-for-Profit Hospital Executives

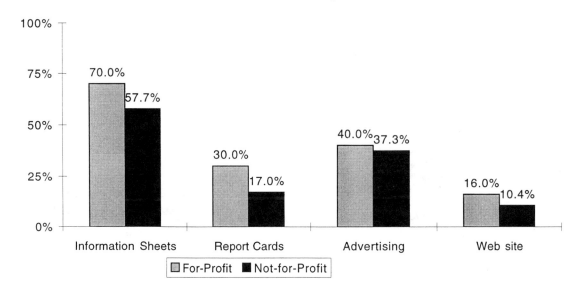

Quality   Reporting

Do You Report Quality to Your Constituents?

All Respondents

No
17.6%

Yes
82.4%

Not-For-Profit

No
8.7%

Yes
91.3%

For-Profit

No
25.0%

Yes
75.0%

Methods Used to Report Quality to Constituents

Managed Care Executives

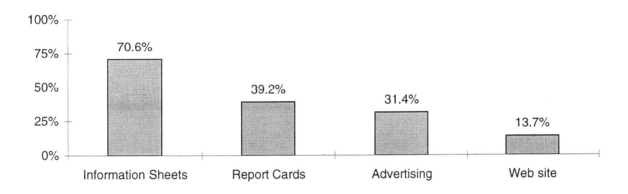

For-Profit vs. Not-for-Profit Managed Care Executives

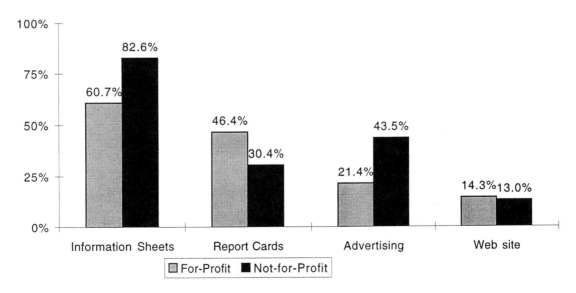

Do You Report Quality to Your Constituents?

All Respondents   Not-For-Profit   For-Profit

Methods Used to Report Quality to Constituents

Physician Group Executives

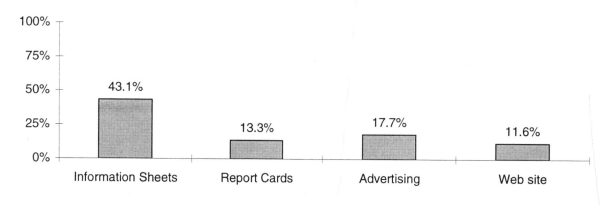

For-Profit vs. Not-for-Profit Physician Group Executives

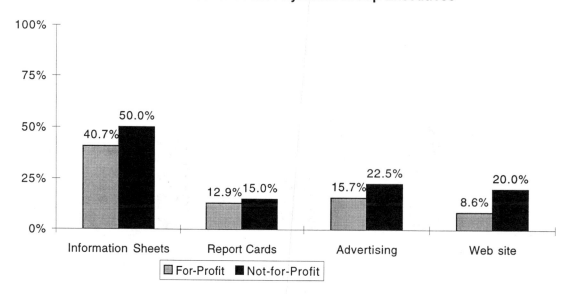

Quality   **Capitation**

The Effect of Capitation on Quality

All Respondents

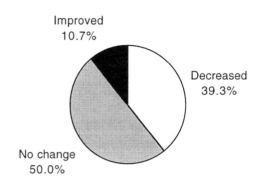

	Decreased	No Change	Improved
Northeast	27.2%	64.2%	8.6%
Midwest	39.2%	53.1%	7.7%
South	45.1%	47.3%	7.6%
West	38.5%	41.8%	19.7%
For-Profit	43.7%	43.1%	13.2%
Not-for-Profit	37.4%	53.1%	9.5%

Hospital Executives

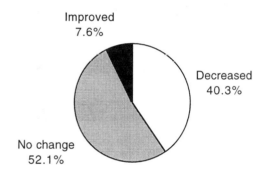

	Decreased	No Change	Improved
Northeast	25.0%	70.5%	4.5%
Midwest	39.6%	53.5%	6.9%
South	45.4%	49.6%	5.0%
West	41.7%	44.4%	13.9%
For-Profit	54.3%	40.0%	5.7%
Not-for-Profit	38.9%	53.1%	7.9%

MCO Executives

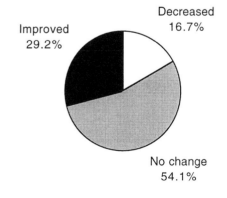

	Decreased	No Change	Improved
Northeast	0.0%	75.0%	25.0%
Midwest	0.0%	69.2%	30.8%
South	28.6%	50.0%	21.4%
West	30.8%	30.8%	38.5%
For-Profit	11.5%	53.8%	34.6%
Not-for-Profit	22.7%	54.5%	22.7%

• Results may not total 100 percent due to rounding.

The Effect of Capitation on Quality

Physician Group Executives

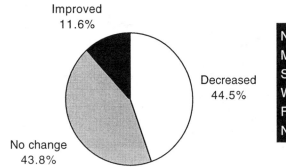

	Decreased	No Change	Improved
Northeast	37.9%	51.7%	10.3%
Midwest	55.2%	44.8%	0.0%
South	49.0%	41.2%	9.8%
West	35.1%	40.5%	24.3%
For-Profit	47.8%	41.6%	10.6%
Not-for-Profit	33.3%	51.5%	15.2%

Comparison of Respondents

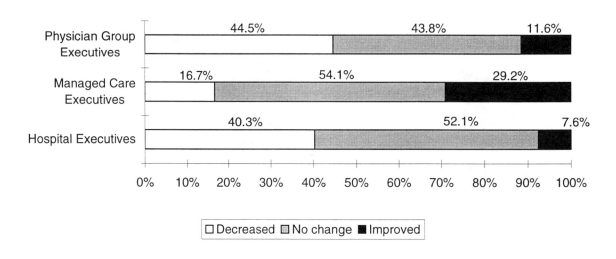

• Results may not total 100 percent due to rounding.

Quality   Discounted Fee-for-Service

The Effect of Discounted Fee-for-Service on Quality

All Respondents

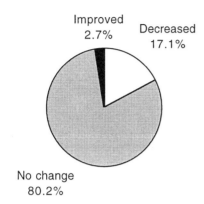

Improved 2.7%
Decreased 17.1%
No change 80.2%

	Decreased	No Change	Improved
Northeast	20.8%	76.0%	3.1%
Midwest	14.4%	82.6%	3.0%
South	19.4%	78.6%	2.0%
West	13.6%	83.0%	3.4%
For-Profit	16.8%	81.3%	1.9%
Not-for-Profit	17.4%	79.5%	3.1%

Hospital Executives

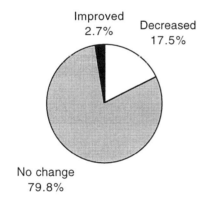

Improved 2.7%
Decreased 17.5%
No change 79.8%

	Decreased	No Change	Improved
Northeast	18.0%	78.0%	4.0%
Midwest	13.3%	83.3%	3.3%
South	20.5%	77.3%	2.3%
West	17.0%	80.9%	2.1%
For-Profit	14.9%	83.0%	2.1%
Not-for-Profit	17.9%	79.2%	2.8%

MCO Executives

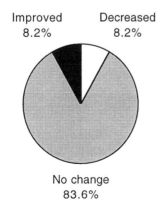

Improved 8.2%
Decreased 8.2%
No change 83.6%

	Decreased	No Change	Improved
Northeast	11.1%	77.8%	11.1%
Midwest	0.0%	92.3%	7.7%
South	15.4%	84.6%	0.0%
West	7.1%	78.6%	14.3%
For-Profit	10.7%	82.1%	7.1%
Not-for-Profit	4.8%	85.7%	9.5%

• Results may not total 100 percent due to rounding.

Quality   Discounted Fee-for-Service

The Effect of Discounted Fee-for-Service on Quality

Physician Group Executives

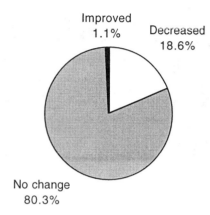

Improved
1.1%

Decreased
18.6%

No change
80.3%

	Decreased	No Change	Improved
Northeast	27.0%	73.0%	0.0%
Midwest	23.7%	76.3%	0.0%
South	17.5%	81.0%	1.6%
West	7.7%	89.7%	2.6%
For-Profit	18.7%	80.6%	0.7%
Not-for-Profit	18.9%	78.4%	2.7%

Comparison of Respondents

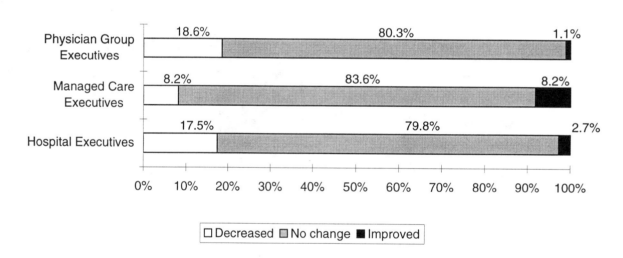

Physician Group Executives — 18.6% 80.3% 1.1%

Managed Care Executives — 8.2% 83.6% 8.2%

Hospital Executives — 17.5% 79.8% 2.7%

0% 10% 20% 30% 40% 50% 60% 70% 80% 90% 100%

☐ Decreased ▨ No change ■ Improved

• Results may not total 100 percent due to rounding.

The Effect of Global Case Rates on Quality

All Respondents

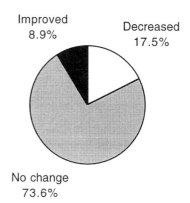

	Decreased	No Change	Improved
Northeast	19.7%	69.7%	10.5%
Midwest	19.3%	74.0%	6.7%
South	14.9%	77.9%	7.2%
West	18.6%	67.8%	13.6%
For-Profit	16.0%	74.3%	9.7%
Not-for-Profit	18.3%	73.3%	8.4%

Hospital Executives

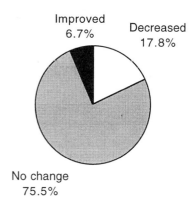

	Decreased	No Change	Improved
Northeast	16.7%	71.4%	11.9%
Midwest	17.8%	77.6%	4.7%
South	15.4%	79.4%	5.1%
West	23.6%	66.7%	9.7%
For-Profit	11.9%	85.7%	2.4%
Not-for-Profit	18.6%	74.2%	7.2%

MCO Executives

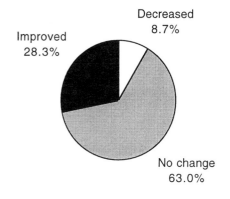

	Decreased	No Change	Improved
Northeast	0.0%	71.4%	28.6%
Midwest	0.0%	84.6%	15.4%
South	7.7%	69.2%	23.1%
West	23.1%	30.8%	46.2%
For-Profit	3.8%	69.2%	26.9%
Not-for-Profit	15.0%	55.0%	30.0%

• Results may not total 100 percent due to rounding.

Quality   **Global Case Rates**

The Effect of Global Case Rates on Quality

Physician Group Executives

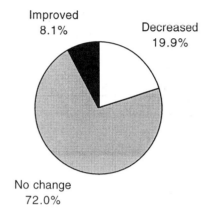

	Decreased	No Change	Improved
Northeast	29.6%	66.7%	3.7%
Midwest	33.3%	56.7%	10.0%
South	15.2%	76.1%	8.7%
West	6.1%	84.8%	9.1%
For-Profit	20.6%	71.0%	8.4%
Not-for-Profit	17.2%	75.9%	6.9%

Comparison of Respondents

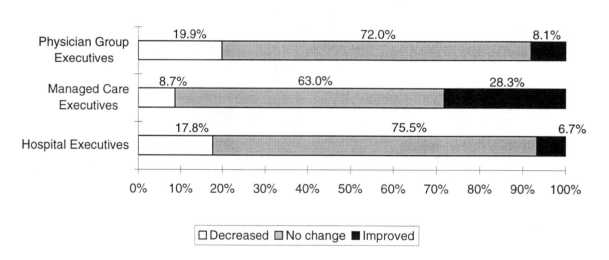

• Results may not total 100 percent due to rounding.

| Quality | Clinical Paths |

The Effect of Clinical Paths on Quality

All Respondents

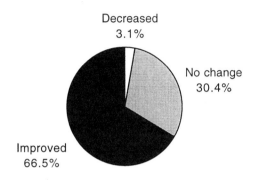

Decreased
3.1%

No change
30.4%

Improved
66.5%

	Decreased	No Change	Improved
Northeast	6.7%	28.9%	64.4%
Midwest	2.7%	31.9%	65.4%
South	2.1%	29.1%	68.8%
West	3.1%	30.2%	66.7%
For-Profit	4.2%	38.2%	57.6%
Not-for-Profit	2.7%	27.2%	70.2%

Hospital Executives

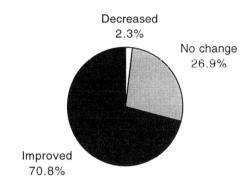

Decreased
2.3%

No change
26.9%

Improved
70.8%

	Decreased	No Change	Improved
Northeast	4.0%	16.0%	80.0%
Midwest	1.5%	31.4%	67.2%
South	1.8%	26.5%	71.7%
West	3.5%	24.7%	71.8%
For-Profit	0.0%	25.0%	75.0%
Not-for-Profit	2.5%	27.3%	70.2%

MCO Executives

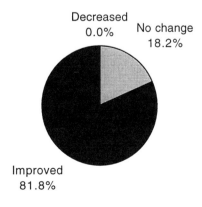

Decreased
0.0%

No change
18.2%

Improved
81.8%

	Decreased	No Change	Improved
Northeast	0.0%	50.0%	50.0%
Midwest	0.0%	15.4%	84.6%
South	0.0%	23.1%	76.9%
West	0.0%	0.0%	100.0%
For-Profit	0.0%	17.4%	82.6%
Not-for-Profit	0.0%	19.0%	81.0%

• Results may not total 100 percent due to rounding.

The Effect of Clinical Paths on Quality

Physician Group Executives

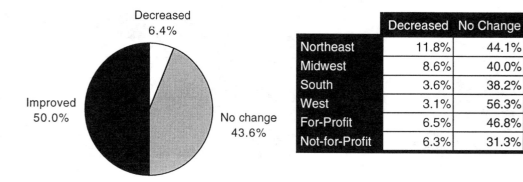

	Decreased	No Change	Improved
Northeast	11.8%	44.1%	44.1%
Midwest	8.6%	40.0%	51.4%
South	3.6%	38.2%	58.2%
West	3.1%	56.3%	40.6%
For-Profit	6.5%	46.8%	46.8%
Not-for-Profit	6.3%	31.3%	62.5%

Comparison of Respondents

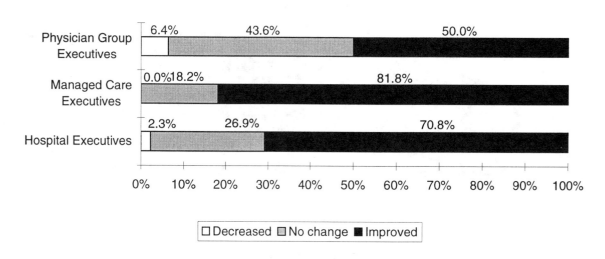

• Results may not total 100 percent due to rounding.

Quality   Self Assessment

How Do You Rate the Quality of Care . . .

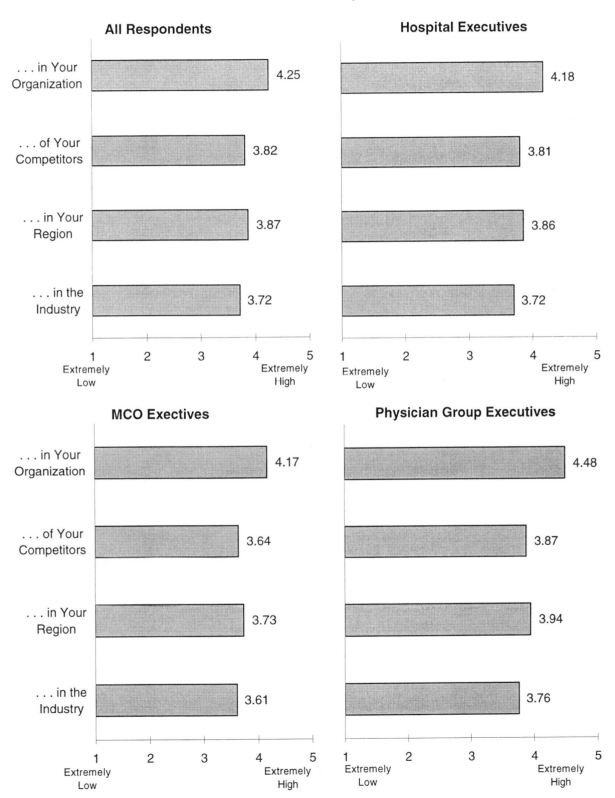

All Respondents

. . . in Your Organization	4.25
. . . of Your Competitors	3.82
. . . in Your Region	3.87
. . . in the Industry	3.72

1 — Extremely Low
5 — Extremely High

Hospital Executives

. . . in Your Organization	4.18
. . . of Your Competitors	3.81
. . . in Your Region	3.86
. . . in the Industry	3.72

1 — Extremely Low
5 — Extremely High

MCO Exectives

. . . in Your Organization	4.17
. . . of Your Competitors	3.64
. . . in Your Region	3.73
. . . in the Industry	3.61

1 — Extremely Low
5 — Extremely High

Physician Group Executives

. . . in Your Organization	4.48
. . . of Your Competitors	3.87
. . . in Your Region	3.94
. . . in the Industry	3.76

1 — Extremely Low
5 — Extremely High

How Will Managed Care/Provider Alliances Influence Quality?

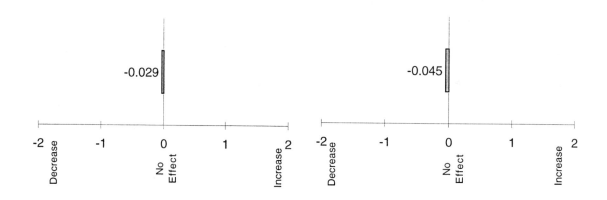

All Respondents

Hospital Executives

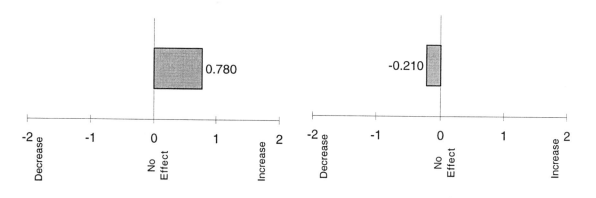

MCO Exectives

Physician Group Executives

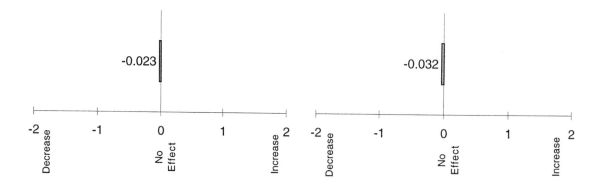

For-Profit Respondents

Not-for-Profit Respondents

CHAPTER 6

Physician Relations

Jon Asplund

To hear doctors tell it, managed care has gagged them, tied their hands, and cut the cash right out of their wallets. From their point of view, working with managed care companies has been more of a mugging than a relationship. But there are two sides to every story. For the institutions contracting with physicians, doctors often appear to be obstinate, frivolous, and naive. Hospital executives and physicians have historically operated under a cloud of suspicion and mistrust.[1]

Both hospital and managed care executives realize the importance of physicians in care delivery, but they have struggled with doctors on the often fractious issue of cost control. Hospital and managed care executives say that to remain competitive they have to alter the ingrained behavior of physicians. They blame the escalating health care costs of the 1970s and 1980s on the excesses and impracticalities of physicians, who in their eagerness to provide the best care available neglected the financial consequences.

Many doctors continue to see themselves as part scientist, part artist.[2] The concept of business entrepreneur is still foreign, if not distasteful, to them. But the role of physicians in the American health care system is undergoing radical change. Physicians face new opportunities, such as practicing in large groups, contracting directly with employers, and reinventing themselves as physician executives and entrepreneurs. And they must select from a variety of practice options, such as employment by a hospital, joining a group practice, or affiliating with a practice management company.

As the pressure mounts to cut costs and improve quality, physicians must work more closely with hospital, managed care, and group practice executives. Many are breaking the old stereotype, pursuing graduate business degrees and becoming health care executives themselves. Others join or organize doctors unions in a quest for managed care negotiating leverage and other collective bargaining advantages.

PAYMENT

Of all the changes facing physicians and their relationships with patients, insurers, and other providers, payment issues seem to be causing the most consternation.

Capitation

Hospital leaders clearly see capitation as the payment mechanism most detrimental to the doctor-patient relationship. A large number of hospital respondents say capitation interferes with the physician-patient relationship. A mere 7.5 percent say capitation helps the relationship between patients and their doctors. Although the data suggest that hospitals feel under siege by capitation, in 1996 only 34.9 percent of hospital HMO contracts were reimbursed through capitation, according to data collected by SMG Marketing Group.[3] The data also show that capitated contracts between hospitals and preferred provider organizations were almost nonexistent, 0.2 percent.

Sixty-three percent of the leaders at group practices say capitation has interfered with the relationship between patient and physician, and a mere 4 percent see capitation as improving the relationship. By and large, respondents say that other payment options neither interfere with nor improve physician-patient relations. A total of 76.5 percent of group practice leaders see discounted fee-for-service as having no effect on the relationship. Global case rates matter little for 64.2 percent of practice leadership.

Managed care in the United States uses the widest variety of payment methods and has pioneered new ones, including capitation. (See table 6-1.) Almost 48 percent of managed care leaders say capitation has interfered with the relationship between physicians and their patients. And 41.3 percent think it has no bearing on any changes in the relationship, while 10.9 percent think that capitation has had a positive effect on that relationship.

Less than half the leaders in managed care say capitation has hurt the physician-patient relationship, but close to two-thirds of hospitals and group practices feel that way. The numbers back up what has been seen in the marketplace. Both hospitals and doctors say that capitation can provide the wrong incentives by making it profitable to limit care. Managed care argues that fee-for-service arrangements offer equally perverse incentives—namely, that physicians are encouraged to overtreat patients, racking up unnecessary costs for insurers and the government.

Fee-for-Service

Hospital executives are most familiar with discounted fee-for-service, the traditional form of payment. (See table 6-2.) And their comfort level with that form

Table 6-1. Primary Care Physician Capitated Contracts—by Age of Plan

Age of Plan	Average Percent of Contracts
<5 years	69.4
5–9 years	75.5
10–14 years	75.0
>14 years	75.0
All HMOs	74.2

Source: Hoechst Marion Roussel, *HMO/PPO Digest 1996.* Managed Care Digest Series. (Kansas City, MO: Hoechst Marion Roussel, 1996).

of payment is evident. Nearly 70 percent of hospital leaders say that discounted fees have had no effect on the physician-patient relationship. Still, a large plurality disagrees. Almost 25 percent of hospital respondents say discounted fee-for-service has interfered with the physician-patient relationship. Physician group leaders follow suit; 22.3 percent say discounted fee-for-service has interfered with the relationship.

In effect, managed care leaders also defend discounted fee-for-service payments; 85.1 percent say the practice has no effect on the physician-patient relationship. Only 12.8 percent say discounting fees interferes with the physician-patient relationship, slightly more than half the percentage of hospital leaders who say it interferes with the physician-patient bond.

Global Case Rates

Among hospital leaders, the view of global case rates falls somewhere between capitation and fee-for-service. The majority of respondents, 55.2 percent, say global rates—in which hospitals and doctors are paid a set price for particular services or types of cases and diseases—cause no change in the physician-patient relationship. Yet 39 percent of hospital executives disagree, saying global case rates hurt the physician-patient bond. It is notable, then, that 5.8 percent of hospital leaders and 3.7 percent of group practice officials say that global rates improve the patient's bond with the doctor. The practice of applying global case rates might be too new to yield reliable opinions either way.

Although the majority of managed care officials say global rates do not change the relationship between physicians and patients, the issue is not without its partisans. Twenty percent say global rates improve the physician-patient relationship, and 24.4 percent say it interferes with the relationship. The split convictions of these segments indicate a basic difference in the perceptions about global case rates and their applications. The practice may be seen as helpful to patients because it works to standardize treatment by having one price for one type of case. On the other hand, it is just that kind of standardization that may be viewed as detrimental to individual relationships between doctors and patients.

While there are some indications that capitation as we know it is not long for this world, in 1996 capitation was in use for physician reimbursement in three-fourths of all HMO contracts, according to Hoechst Marion Roussel's Managed Care Digest.[4] But traditional reimbursement was still popular. Some form of fee-for-service payment to doctors was in use in 69.3 percent of HMO contracts, the digest showed. Managed care leaders are adamant that a discounted fee-for-service arrangement does little to the physician-patient relationship. Among managed care respondents, 85.1 say discounting regular fees does not change the relationship.

Table 6-2. Fee-for-Service Physician Reimbursement— by Age of Plan	
Age of Plan	Percent of HMOs
<5 years	75.0
5–9 years	74.6
10–14 years	70.3
>14 years	55.7
All HMOs	69.3

Source: Hoechst Marion Roussel, *HMO/PPO Digest 1996.* Managed Care Digest Series. (Kansas City, MO: Hoechst Marion Roussel, 1996).

PUBLIC OPINION

Hospitals and doctors blame managed care for the consumer backlash against health care. Eighty percent of physician practice respondents believe a backlash will hit managed care organizations (MCOs). Seventy-eight percent of hospital leaders predict that managed care will bear the brunt of consumer antagonism. These figures may not come as any surprise since managed care is the segment driving the squeeze on costs. On the other hand, only 59 percent of managed care leaders think their organization will be the focus of a backlash.

PHYSICIAN GROUP PRACTICES

The perception of clout can help determine the outcome of any negotiated agreement. Hospitals and physicians negotiate payment mechanisms, common portions of managed care contracts, hospital policy, hospital privileges for doctors, and more. In negotiations with physicians, hospitals confess to a lack of self-confidence. Forty-one percent of hospital leaders say physician groups are in a stronger position to negotiate with hospitals; only 22 percent give the edge to hospitals. Hospitals also indicate they are neither interested nor ready to deal with physician practice management companies.

Managed care sees group practices as a double-edged sword. In order to maintain a network, MCOs need physicians to be grouped in some fashion. But group practices have given doctors strength. With the rise of large, corporate physician practice management companies, managed care is seeing a tougher negotiator on the other side of the table. Almost 44 percent of managed care respondents say group practices have had no influence on the physician-patient relationship. And almost the same number say groups have improved the relationship between doctor and patient.

MCOs still believe they have the upper hand when negotiating with physicians. Sixty-two percent of managed care leaders say they have the stronger position. But managed care leaders are actually more modest about their negotiating position than might be predicted by the assessment of hospitals and physician groups, 68 percent of whom say MCOs have the upper hand when dealing with doctors. Even physician group leaders give MCOs more credit than managed care leaders give themselves; 63 percent say MCOs have a stronger position in negotiating with physicians.

By and large, group practice leaders think group practices have not interfered with the physician-patient relationship. Respondents are roughly split between those judging group practices as neutral to the physician-patient bond and those saying they improve the relationship. Only 5.2 percent of group practice leaders say group practices are detrimental to the physician-patient relationship. It is hard to imagine different results. If doctors thought coming together in a group practice severely affected patients' attitudes, the independent physician practice would not be on the endangered species list.

MANAGEMENT

All three groups, hospitals, MCOs, and group practices, want their physician managers to concentrate on strategy and policy. Only MCOs reported overwhelming increases in physicians taking on operational duties. Governance remains the least likely place to see an enlarged role for physicians.

Doctors are being invited into hospital management, especially in areas where the physician perspective is needed. In the area of strategic planning, the physician role in management has increased in the last two years, according to nearly 72 percent of hospital leaders. But doctors are not getting as involved in day-to-day management. Less than half of hospital leaders say the role of physicians in operations management has increased. The physician perspective is becoming more important to hospitals when it comes to policy. The presence of physician-managers in matters of policy has increased at nearly 60 percent of the hospitals whose leaders were surveyed. Just over half of the hospital leaders say that over the last two years physicians have gotten more involved in governance at their facilities.

The results are not terribly surprising. Doctors might be as hesitant to get their hands in day-to-day operations as hospital administrators are to give untested managers operational duties. Much of the vision needed in strategic planning has to do with the core processes of the hospital and how they will change with advances in medicine, technology, and payment methods. Doctors are seen as fit diagnosticians of the future of medicine and, for that matter, managed care and physician reimbursement issues. In terms of governance, more than half of the hospitals have increased the physician role on boards of directors.

MCOs seem to be making a concerted effort to bring more doctors into management ranks. And unlike hospitals, health plans are involving doctors in operational matters; 71.4 percent report doing so. Close to 80 percent are bringing doctors into strategic roles, and more doctors have also begun handling policy issues at health plans; 67.3 percent of surveyed MCOs had done so in the last two years. Governance, meanwhile, lags behind these areas. Physician leadership in governance has increased in only half of all MCOs.

Managed care plans are taking decisive steps to develop physician leaders. More than three-quarters have moved doctors directly into positions of leadership. About half use education to develop physician leadership. Slightly more than half of all group practices are also increasing the role of doctors in management. As with hospitals, group practices are most likely to have involved doctors in strategy development during the last two years.

Doctors continue to hold leadership positions in group practices. At the same time, about 10 percent say physician management of day-to-day operations has decreased in the past two years. Apparently, physician leaders at some group practices are pulling back from operational duties and passing those responsibilities to nonphysician administrators, as their groups grow and require more management expertise.

Nearly half of all respondents say they are moving doctors directly into management posts. Educational programs are also popular, with about 45 percent taking that route. All three groups say education is one of the key ways they develop physicians as leaders. MCOs and group practices tend to skip the educational stage more often than hospitals. Nearly two-thirds of hospitals favor educational programs in bringing physician leaders up to speed for management. Even before doctors get the management training, they get the title and the duties, according to 45.7 percent of hospital leaders. At the same time, nearly a quarter are not actively developing their doctors as leaders at all, and the same amount signal no change in physicians moving into management roles.

The presence of physician leadership in group practices depends on whether they are designed to be led by doctors or set up as corporate physician management companies, which deliberately leave doctors out of the management function. No major push for new physician leaders is evident in the responses from group practice managers.

CLINICAL PATHS

The *Hospitals & Health Networks* Leadership Survey reveals much less anxiety among leaders when questions about the physician-patient relationship move away from payment issues. Hospital leaders are sanguine about the use of clinical paths. These condition-specific guidelines improve the physician-patient bond according to more than a third of hospitals. Only 16.7 percent say pathways hurt the relationship. Hospitals support clinical paths, which provide physicians, nurses, and other clinicians with a more standardized way to care for patients, thereby weeding out costly and inefficient variations and physician practice patterns. But the results indicate that clinical paths have not had as significant an effect on patient relations as some have hoped; 45.7 percent of hospital leaders surveyed say they have no effect.

Managed care leaders definitely support clinical paths. More than 43 percent say they have improved relations between doctors and patients. Now more than ever, health plans shun excessive involvement in day-to-day medical decisions. The furor over utilization review and limits on hospital stays is evident in many federal and state laws requiring health plans to pay for certain types of care. As physicians increase their use of clinical paths, managed care plans may see utilization figures slowing or even decreasing, with variations in care following suit. Clinical paths may not require managed care interference in specific cases, because clear guidelines are meant to standardize all cases. Utilization review requires interference in individual patients' cases.

While MCOs are the most supportive of clinical paths, all three groups say pathways play only a small role in the physician-patient relationship. Not surprisingly, group practices give themselves credit for better relations with patients; 41 percent say groups improve the relationship. Hospitals are not as convinced; only 33 percent say group practices improve the relationship between doctors and patients.

Group practice officials remain somewhat ambivalent about the use of clinical paths. Almost half of those surveyed say protocols have no effect on the physician-patient relationship; about one-third credit pathways for improved relations; and one-sixth say they have interfered. If it were undisputed that pathways improve health care delivery, perhaps more physician groups would get behind them. But many doctors regard clinical paths as a managerial attempt to usurp their judgment and a measure driven more by cost savings than by clinical improvement.

IMPLICATIONS

The interests of medicine and management do not always coincide, but the willingness of hospitals, managed care plans, and group practices to bring more physicians to the management table indicates that there are ways to find common ground. The *Hospitals & Health Networks* Leadership Survey supports other evidence that the role of physicians is changing. For example, as part of the strategy to integrate four hospitals and academic partner Washington University School of Medicine, St. Louis–based BJC Health System in January 1996 named nine physicians to its board of directors.[5] Physician movement into the ranks of management could have profound effects.

Physicians are not only representing their own kind; they are now being asked to provide strategic vision. Just as the growth of group practices consolidates physician power, the move to physician leadership can increase the

Table 6-3. Representative Physician Leadership Programs

Sponsor	History	Duration	Cost	Delivered
American College of Medical Executives	20 years	Three 4.5-day seminars	$1,200/seminar	Centrally
Advisory Board	2 years	Two days	$32,000–$65,000/hospital	Locally
Massachusetts Medical Society	4 years	Two modules for 70 hours	$495/module	Locally
VHA and College of William & Mary	2 years	Four 1.5-day seminars	$75,000 per hospital	Locally
Wharton School	3 years	Four days	$3,100 (incl. room and board)	Centrally
Dartmouth	2 years	Three to four academic quarters	$20,000	Locally

Source: VHA, 1996

power base of doctors. But the current wisdom is that a more powerful medical staff serves the interests of hospitals and managed care. Bringing physician leaders on board helps align the incentives of administration and doctor. The rapid pace of change also requires physician leaders to champion new ideas. These doctors help their colleagues accept necessary changes, whether in technology, clinical paths, or payment systems.

The respondents agree that education is necessary to bring physician leaders along. Years of initial training and continuing education have made American physicians exemplary clinicians, but they have not had much training in managing people or balancing a budget. Nearly two-thirds of hospitals are looking to educational programs for help. A majority of managed care respondents also use education as a main component of moving doctors into leadership roles. For 20 years, the American College of Physician Executives has provided such education. (See table 6-3.) A 1996 VHA Inc. study points out a number of major colleges and universities that have created physician management programs in recent years.[6]

It is also clear that both hospitals and physicians fear capitation is eroding the public trust. MCOs also recognize capitation as problematic to that relationship, although to a lesser extent. In markets that managed care has penetrated heavily, many of its tactics face fierce opposition. That may well limit its growth elsewhere.

References

1. K. Lumsdon, "Why Doctors Don't Trust You," *Hospitals & Health Networks* 70, no. 6 (March 20, 1996): 26–32.

2. Timothy J. Hoff and David P. McCaffrey, "Adapting, Resisting, Negotiating," *Work and Occupations* (May 1996).

3. Hoechst Marion Roussel, *HMO/PPO Digest 1996*. Managed Care Digest Series. (Kansas City, MO: Hoechst Marion Roussel, 1996).

4. Ibid.

5. Wayne M. Lerner, ed., *Anatomy of a Merger: BJC Health System* (Chicago: Health Administration Press, 1997), p. 66.

6. VHA Inc. and Deloitte & Touche LLP, *1997 Environmental Assessment: Redesigning Health Care for the Millennium* (Irving, Tex: VHA Inc., 1997), p. 102.

Physician Relations   **Capitation**

The Effect of Capitation on Physician Relations

All Respondents

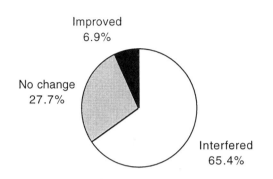

	Interfered	No Change	Improved
Northeast	60.5%	31.4%	8.1%
Midwest	65.6%	27.8%	6.6%
South	67.0%	26.6%	6.4%
West	65.9%	26.8%	7.3%
For-Profit	63.9%	30.6%	5.5%
Not-for-Profit	65.9%	26.5%	7.6%

Hospital Executives

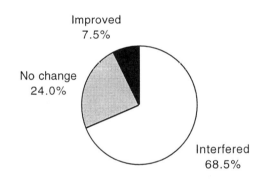

	Interfered	No Change	Improved
Northeast	67.4%	23.9%	8.7%
Midwest	66.4%	25.2%	8.4%
South	69.5%	24.8%	5.7%
West	70.3%	20.3%	9.5%
For-Profit	68.2%	27.3%	4.5%
Not-for-Profit	68.3%	23.7%	8.0%

MCO Executives

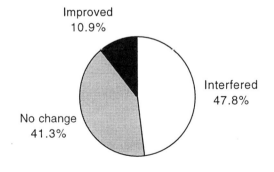

	Interfered	No Change	Improved
Northeast	50.0%	37.5%	12.5%
Midwest	46.2%	46.2%	7.7%
South	30.8%	53.8%	15.4%
West	66.7%	25.0%	8.3%
For-Profit	44.0%	44.0%	12.0%
Not-for-Profit	52.4%	38.1%	9.5%

• Results may not total 100 percent due to rounding.

Physician Relations   **Capitation**

The Effect of Capitation on Physician Relations

Physician Group Executives

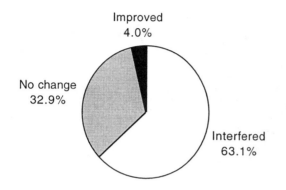

	Interfered	No Change	Improved
Northeast	53.1%	40.6%	6.3%
Midwest	71.0%	29.0%	0.0%
South	69.4%	24.5%	6.1%
West	56.8%	40.5%	2.7%
For-Profit	66.7%	28.9%	4.4%
Not-for-Profit	51.4%	45.7%	2.9%

Comparison of Respondents

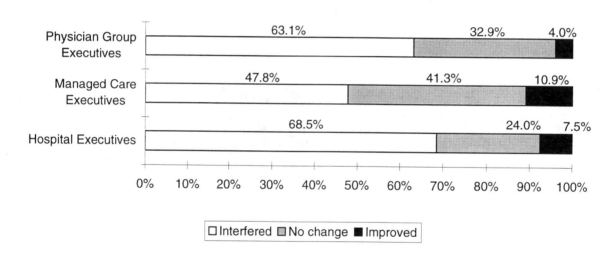

• Results may not total 100 percent due to rounding.

Physician Relations   **Discounted Fee-for-Service**

The Effect of Discounted Fee-for-Service on Physician Relations

All Respondents

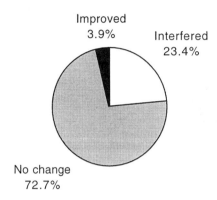

	Interfered	No Change	Improved
Northeast	24.5%	72.3%	3.2%
Midwest	23.5%	73.5%	3.1%
South	26.3%	69.3%	4.4%
West	17.7%	78.2%	4.1%
For-Profit	21.9%	74.9%	3.3%
Not-for-Profit	23.9%	71.8%	4.2%

Hospital Executives

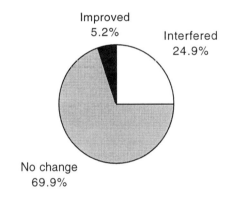

	Interfered	No Change	Improved
Northeast	23.4%	72.3%	4.3%
Midwest	23.4%	72.4%	4.1%
South	29.0%	65.3%	5.7%
West	20.2%	74.5%	5.3%
For-Profit	22.9%	66.7%	10.4%
Not-for-Profit	25.1%	70.3%	4.6%

MCO Executives

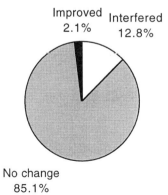

	Interfered	No Change	Improved
Northeast	11.1%	88.9%	0.0%
Midwest	8.3%	91.7%	0.0%
South	16.7%	83.3%	0.0%
West	14.3%	78.6%	7.1%
For-Profit	14.8%	85.2%	0.0%
Not-for-Profit	10.0%	85.0%	5.0%

• Results may not total 100 percent due to rounding.

Physician Relations   Discounted Fee-for-Service

The Effect of Discounted Fee-for-Service on Physician Relations

Physician Group Executives

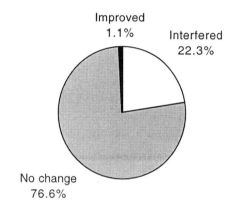

	Interfered	No Change	Improved
Northeast	28.9%	68.4%	2.6%
Midwest	28.2%	71.8%	0.0%
South	20.6%	77.8%	1.6%
West	12.8%	87.2%	0.0%
For-Profit	22.9%	75.7%	1.4%
Not-for-Profit	18.4%	81.6%	0.0%

Comparison of Respondents

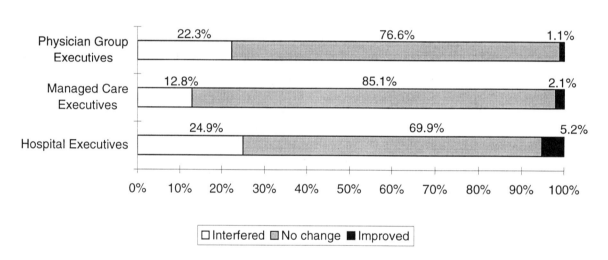

□ Interfered   ▨ No change   ■ Improved

• Results may not total 100 percent due to rounding.

Physician Relations   Global Case Rates

The Effect of Global Case Rates on Physician Relations

All Respondents

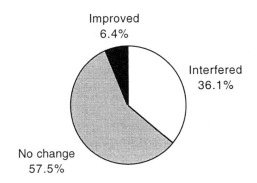

Improved
6.4%

Interfered
36.1%

No change
57.5%

	Interfered	No Change	Improved
Northeast	44.7%	44.7%	10.5%
Midwest	38.6%	55.2%	6.2%
South	33.7%	61.4%	5.0%
West	32.8%	61.2%	6.0%
For-Profit	33.3%	60.2%	6.4%
Not-for-Profit	37.4%	56.2%	6.5%

Hospital Executives

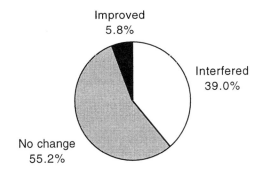

Improved
5.8%

Interfered
39.0%

No change
55.2%

	Interfered	No Change	Improved
Northeast	53.8%	33.3%	12.8%
Midwest	40.0%	55.2%	4.8%
South	35.6%	60.3%	4.1%
West	38.6%	55.7%	5.7%
For-Profit	33.3%	64.3%	2.4%
Not-for-Profit	39.8%	54.0%	6.2%

MCO Executives

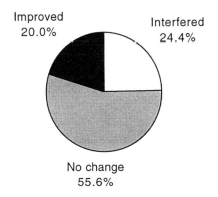

Improved
20.0%

Interfered
24.4%

No change
55.6%

	Interfered	No Change	Improved
Northeast	25.0%	50.0%	25.0%
Midwest	25.0%	58.3%	16.7%
South	7.7%	69.2%	23.1%
West	41.7%	41.7%	16.7%
For-Profit	20.0%	56.0%	24.0%
Not-for-Profit	30.0%	55.0%	15.0%

• Results may not total 100 percent due to rounding.

Physician Relations   **Global Case Rates**

The Effect of Global Case Rates on Physician Relations

Physician Group Executives

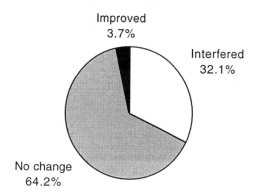

Improved
3.7%

Interfered
32.1%

No change
64.2%

	Interfered	No Change	Improved
Northeast	37.9%	58.6%	3.4%
Midwest	39.3%	53.6%	7.1%
South	34.9%	62.8%	2.3%
West	17.6%	79.4%	2.9%
For-Profit	36.5%	59.6%	3.8%
Not-for-Profit	16.7%	80.0%	3.3%

Comparison of Respondents

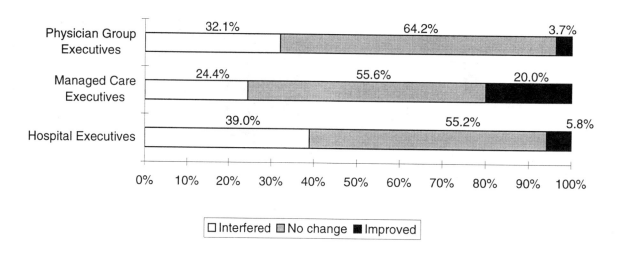

Physician Group Executives: 32.1% / 64.2% / 3.7%
Managed Care Executives: 24.4% / 55.6% / 20.0%
Hospital Executives: 39.0% / 55.2% / 5.8%

□ Interfered ▨ No change ■ Improved

• Results may not total 100 percent due to rounding.

Physician Relations　　　　　　　　　　　　　　　　**Clinical Paths**

The Effect of Clinical Paths on Physician Relations

All Respondents

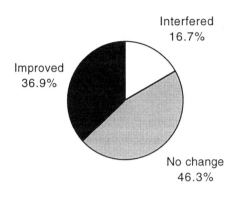

	Interfered	No Change	Improved
Northeast	16.3%	43.0%	40.7%
Midwest	16.8%	46.9%	36.3%
South	19.3%	48.9%	31.8%
West	12.7%	42.1%	45.2%
For-Profit	16.1%	47.4%	36.5%
Not-for-Profit	17.1%	45.9%	37.1%

Hospital Executives

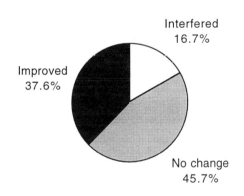

	Interfered	No Change	Improved
Northeast	14.9%	42.6%	42.6%
Midwest	14.4%	49.2%	36.4%
South	22.0%	47.0%	31.0%
West	11.3%	37.5%	51.3%
For-Profit	17.4%	41.3%	41.3%
Not-for-Profit	16.7%	46.2%	37.1%

MCO Executives

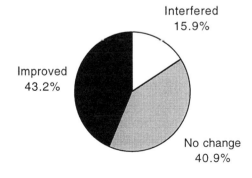

	Interfered	No Change	Improved
Northeast	16.7%	50.0%	33.3%
Midwest	16.7%	25.0%	58.3%
South	15.4%	53.8%	30.8%
West	15.4%	38.5%	46.2%
For-Profit	16.7%	37.5%	45.8%
Not-for-Profit	15.0%	45.0%	40.0%

• Results may not total 100 percent due to rounding.

Physician Relations   **Clinical Paths**

The Effect of Clinical Paths on Physician Relations

Physician Group Executives

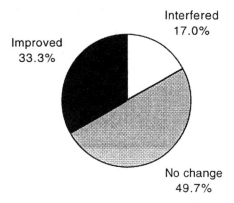

Interfered
17.0%

Improved
33.3%

No change
49.7%

	Interfered	No Change	Improved
Northeast	18.2%	42.4%	39.4%
Midwest	25.7%	45.7%	28.6%
South	11.5%	53.8%	34.6%
West	15.2%	54.5%	30.3%
For-Profit	15.6%	51.6%	32.8%
Not-for-Profit	22.6%	41.9%	35.5%

Comparison of Respondents

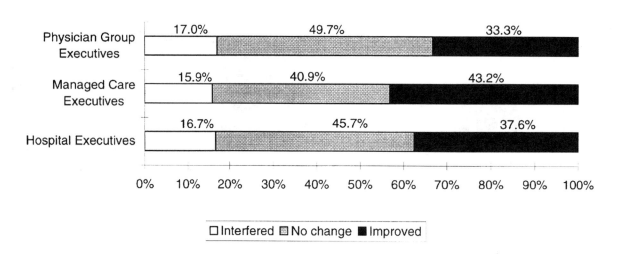

Physician Group Executives: 17.0% | 49.7% | 33.3%
Managed Care Executives: 15.9% | 40.9% | 43.2%
Hospital Executives: 16.7% | 45.7% | 37.6%

0% 10% 20% 30% 40% 50% 60% 70% 80% 90% 100%

□ Interfered ▨ No change ■ Improved

• Results may not total 100 percent due to rounding.

Physician Relations **Group Practice**

The Effect of Group Practice on Physician Relations

All Respondents

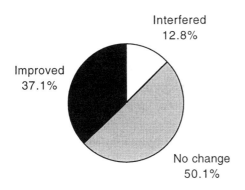

Interfered 12.8%
Improved 37.1%
No change 50.1%

	Interfered	No Change	Improved
Northeast	14.4%	44.4%	41.1%
Midwest	11.8%	53.2%	34.9%
South	14.5%	52.3%	33.2%
West	9.4%	45.7%	44.9%
For-Profit	6.8%	45.9%	47.3%
Not-for-Profit	15.4%	52.3%	32.3%

Hospital Executives

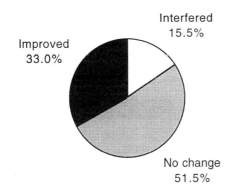

Interfered 15.5%
Improved 33.0%
No change 51.5%

	Interfered	No Change	Improved
Northeast	21.7%	41.3%	37.0%
Midwest	13.9%	54.0%	32.1%
South	16.9%	54.2%	28.9%
West	11.4%	47.7%	40.9%
For-Profit	8.9%	53.3%	37.8%
Not-for-Profit	16.1%	51.8%	32.1%

MCO Executives

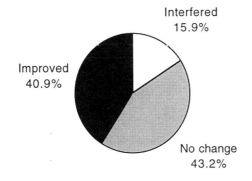

Interfered 15.9%
Improved 40.9%
No change 43.2%

	Interfered	No Change	Improved
Northeast	14.3%	42.9%	42.9%
Midwest	0.0%	36.4%	63.6%
South	23.1%	69.2%	7.7%
West	23.1%	23.1%	53.8%
For-Profit	16.7%	37.5%	45.8%
Not-for-Profit	15.0%	50.0%	35.0%

• Results may not total 100 percent due to rounding.

Physician Relations   **Group Practice**

The Effect of Group Practice on Physician Relations

Physician Group Executives

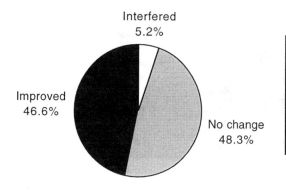

	Interfered	No Change	Improved
Northeast	5.4%	48.6%	45.9%
Midwest	7.9%	55.3%	36.8%
South	6.5%	43.5%	50.0%
West	0.0%	48.6%	51.4%
For-Profit	4.4%	44.9%	50.7%
Not-for-Profit	8.1%	59.5%	32.4%

Comparison of Respondents

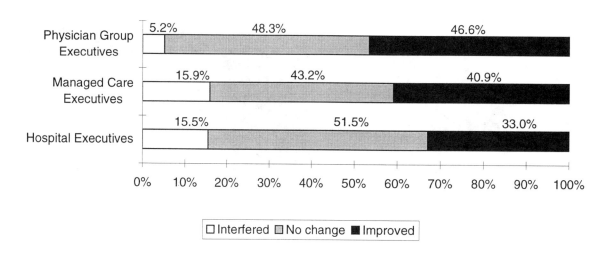

• Results may not total 100 percent due to rounding.

Physician Relations | Operations

How the Physician Role in Operations Has Changed in the Last Two Years

All Respondents

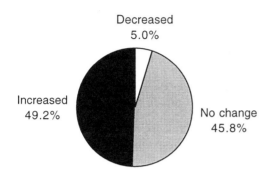

	Decreased	No Change	Increased
Northeast	5.0%	42.0%	53.0%
Midwest	2.0%	49.0%	49.0%
South	6.6%	44.4%	49.0%
West	6.7%	46.0%	47.3%
For-Profit	9.3%	44.4%	46.3%
Not-for-Profit	3.2%	46.2%	50.5%

Hospital Executives

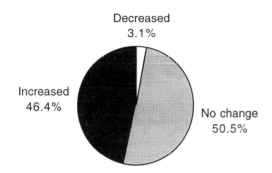

	Decreased	No Change	Increased
Northeast	0.0%	49.1%	50.9%
Midwest	1.3%	51.0%	47.7%
South	5.5%	51.6%	42.9%
West	3.1%	48.0%	49.0%
For-Profit	0.0%	57.1%	42.9%
Not-for-Profit	3.5%	49.5%	47.0%

MCO Executives

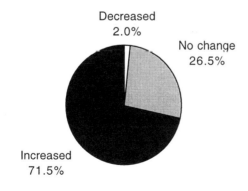

	Decreased	No Change	Increased
Northeast	0.0%	55.6%	44.4%
Midwest	0.0%	30.8%	69.2%
South	7.1%	7.1%	85.7%
West	0.0%	23.1%	76.9%
For-Profit	3.7%	29.6%	66.7%
Not-for-Profit	0.0%	22.7%	77.3%

• Results may not total 100 percent due to rounding.

Physician Relations   **Operations**

How the Physician Role in Operations Has Changed in the Last Two Years

Physician Group Executives

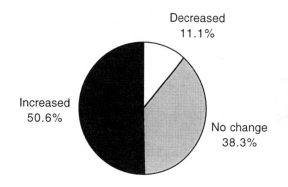

Decreased
11.1%

Increased
50.6%

No change
38.3%

	Decreased	No Change	Increased
Northeast	13.2%	28.9%	57.9%
Midwest	5.0%	47.5%	47.5%
South	9.5%	31.7%	58.7%
West	17.9%	48.7%	3.3%
For-Profit	13.6%	42.9%	43.6%
Not-for-Profit	2.6%	23.1%	74.4%

Comparison of Respondents

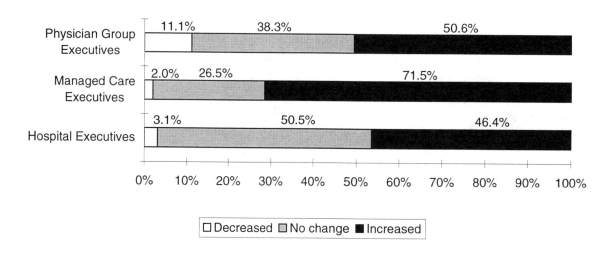

☐ Decreased ▨ No change ■ Increased

• Results may not total 100 percent due to rounding.

Physician Relations   Strategy

How the Physician Role in Strategy Has Changed in the Last Two Years

All Respondents

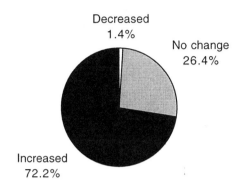

	Decreased	No Change	Increased
Northeast	2.0%	18.0%	80.0%
Midwest	1.0%	25.7%	73.3%
South	1.5%	29.7%	68.7%
West	1.3%	27.3%	71.3%
For-Profit	0.9%	29.2%	69.9%
Not-for-Profit	1.6%	25.1%	73.3%

Hospital Executives

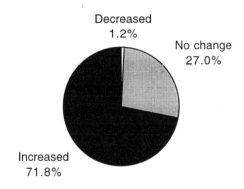

	Decreased	No Change	Increased
Northeast	0.0%	11.3%	88.7%
Midwest	0.7%	26.8%	72.5%
South	2.2%	31.9%	65.9%
West	1.0%	26.5%	72.4%
For-Profit	0.0%	36.7%	63.3%
Not-for-Profit	1.4%	25.6%	73.0%

MCO Executives

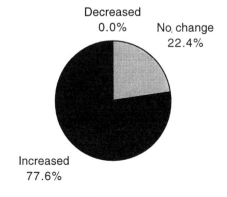

	Decreased	No Change	Increased
Northeast	0.0%	33.3%	66.7%
Midwest	0.0%	23.1%	76.9%
South	0.0%	21.4%	78.6%
West	0.0%	15.4%	84.6%
For-Profit	0.0%	25.9%	74.1%
Not-for-Profit	0.0%	18.2%	81.8%

• Results may not total 100 percent due to rounding.

How the Physician Role in Strategy Has Changed in the Last Two Years

Physician Group Executives

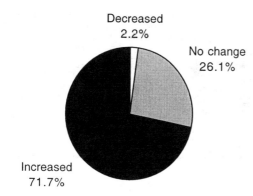

Decreased
2.2%

No change
26.1%

Increased
71.7%

	Decreased	No Change	Increased
Northeast	5.3%	23.7%	71.1%
Midwest	2.5%	22.5%	75.0%
South	0.0%	25.4%	74.6%
West	2.6%	33.3%	64.1%
For-Profit	1.4%	27.1%	71.4%
Not-for-Profit	5.1%	23.1%	71.8%

Comparison of Respondents

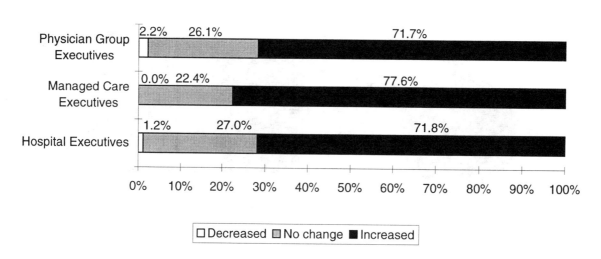

□ Decreased ▨ No change ■ Increased

• Results may not total 100 percent due to rounding.

Physician Relations   **Governance**

How the Physician Role in Governance Has Changed in the Last Two Years

All Respondents

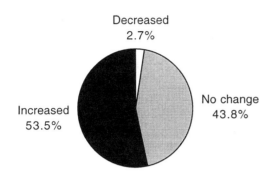

Decreased
2.7%

Increased
53.5%

No change
43.8%

	Decreased	No Change	Increased
Northeast	3.0%	38.0%	59.0%
Midwest	2.0%	40.6%	57.4%
South	3.5%	46.3%	50.2%
West	2.0%	47.3%	50.7%
For-Profit	2.8%	44.7%	52.6%
Not-for-Profit	2.6%	43.0%	54.4%

Hospital Executives

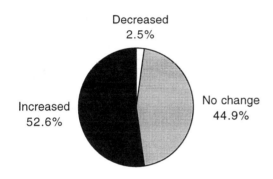

Decreased
2.5%

Increased
52.6%

No change
44.9%

	Decreased	No Change	Increased
Northeast	1.9%	26.4%	71.7%
Midwest	2.0%	42.3%	55.7%
South	3.9%	49.2%	47.0%
West	1.0%	51.0%	48.0%
For-Profit	0.0%	55.1%	44.9%
Not-for-Profit	2.8%	43.3%	53.9%

MCO Executives

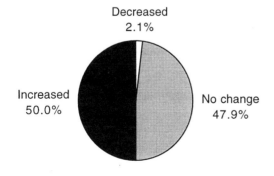

Decreased
2.1%

Increased
50.0%

No change
47.9%

	Decreased	No Change	Increased
Northeast	0.0%	66.7%	33.3%
Midwest	0.0%	61.5%	38.5%
South	0.0%	30.8%	69.2%
West	7.7%	38.5%	53.8%
For-Profit	3.8%	61.5%	34.6%
Not-for-Profit	0.0%	31.8%	68.2%

• Results may not total 100 percent due to rounding.

Physician Relations   Governance

How the Physician Role in Governance Has Changed in the Last Two Years

Physician Group Executives

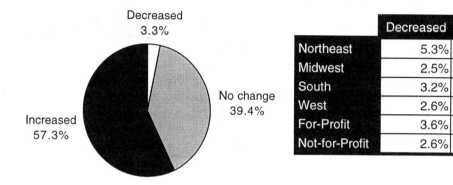

	Decreased	No Change	Increased
Northeast	5.3%	47.4%	47.4%
Midwest	2.5%	27.5%	70.0%
South	3.2%	41.3%	55.6%
West	2.6%	41.0%	56.4%
For-Profit	3.6%	37.9%	58.6%
Not-for-Profit	2.6%	46.2%	51.3%

Comparison of Respondents

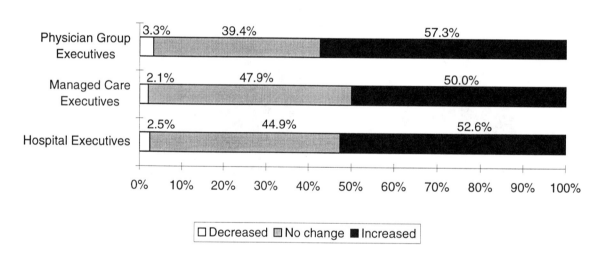

• Results may not total 100 percent due to rounding.

Physician Relations   **Policy**

How the Physician Role in Policy Has Changed in the Last Two Years

All Respondents

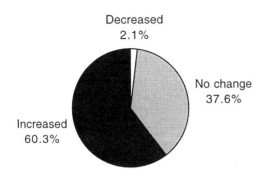

Decreased
2.1%

No change
37.6%

Increased
60.3%

	Decreased	No Change	Increased
Northeast	3.0%	32.0%	65.0%
Midwest	1.0%	36.8%	62.2%
South	3.5%	36.8%	59.7%
West	0.7%	44.3%	55.0%
For-Profit	3.2%	37.0%	59.7%
Not-for-Profit	1.6%	37.5%	60.9%

Hospital Executives

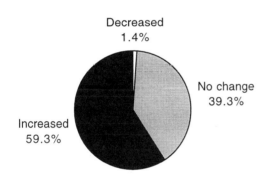

Decreased
1.4%

No change
39.3%

Increased
59.3%

	Decreased	No Change	Increased
Northeast	1.9%	30.2%	67.9%
Midwest	0.7%	39.2%	60.1%
South	2.8%	39.8%	57.5%
West	0.0%	44.3%	55.7%
For-Profit	0.0%	44.9%	55.1%
Not-for-Profit	1.6%	38.1%	60.2%

MCO Executives

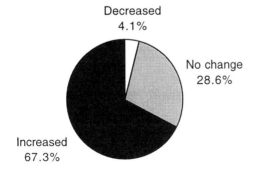

Decreased
4.1%

No change
28.6%

Increased
67.3%

	Decreased	No Change	Increased
Northeast	0.0%	44.4%	55.6%
Midwest	0.0%	30.8%	69.2%
South	7.1%	21.4%	71.4%
West	7.7%	23.1%	69.2%
For-Profit	7.4%	33.3%	59.3%
Not-for-Profit	0.0%	22.7%	77.3%

• Results may not total 100 percent due to rounding.

Physician Relations   **Policy**

How the Physician Role in Policy Has Changed in the Last Two Years

Physician Group Executives

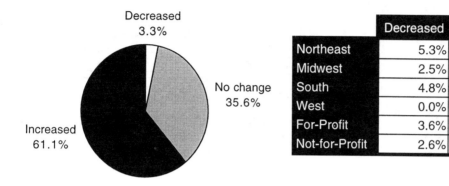

	Decreased	No Change	Increased
Northeast	5.3%	31.6%	63.2%
Midwest	2.5%	30.0%	67.5%
South	4.8%	31.7%	63.5%
West	0.0%	51.3%	48.7%
For-Profit	3.6%	35.0%	61.4%
Not-for-Profit	2.6%	38.5%	59.0%

Comparison of Respondents

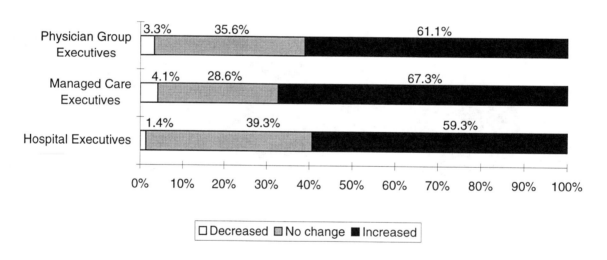

• Results may not total 100 percent due to rounding.

7

Information Technology

Christopher Serb

Only a few years ago, health care information technology was confined to the basements of large hospitals, where technicians crunched numbers on mammoth mainframe computers. Who would have imagined then that operating room scheduling could be done with the click of a mouse button, or that doctors could update charts by talking right into their computers, or that the King of Jordan's x-rays could be electronically beamed to an oncologist half a world away? Anyone who described these advances as imminent was more likely to be called a crackpot than a visionary.

It turns out that the crackpots were, indeed, visionaries. Applications that promise to deliver cost savings, improved patient care, and top-flight management information are emerging at an astounding pace. As technology has evolved, it has also become more user-friendly. Mainframes have been replaced by decentralized client-server systems. Enterprise-wide solutions are consolidating individual, incompatible departmental systems. Software programs have moved beyond accounting and billing and into doctors' offices, imaging centers, and even marketing departments.

By its very nature, information technology is expensive and complex, a combination that causes many chief executives to hesitate. To get a clearer picture of their concerns, *Hospitals & Health Networks* asked senior executives to rank the importance of information technology and their readiness to address it; to rate four specific information technology issues: electronic medical records, standard patient identification numbers, telemedicine, and the World Wide Web; and to forecast their future spending.

STRATEGIC READINESS

Health care executives are caught in a difficult situation: They want and need the benefits of information technology, but they are not prepared to deal with it. Survey respondents were asked to rank the importance of 21 key health care issues on a scale of 1 to 5, with 5 indicating "most important." As a group they gave information technology an average rating of 4.5, making it the number two issue on health care executives' minds (after "commitment to mission").

When asked how they would rate their readiness for information technology planning, leaders responded with an average score of 3.5, just above "neutral." (See figure 7-1.) Executives recognize a considerable gap between the importance of information technology and their ability to actually use it. Statistically, the gap measures a full point; but the survey cannot measure how many wasted dollars, months of delays, and aborted efforts that gap represents.

The survey reveals that the importance of information technology varies according to the type of organization the respondents belong to. Executives from managed care organizations (MCOs) and group practices name information technology as their top strategic goal, giving it an average ranking of 4.7 and 4.5, respectively. Thus, information technology is more important than commitment to mission to these executives, while hospital executives rank information technology second. Because most hospitals are still not-for-profit, it makes sense that they would place more importance on mission.

Tax status has no impact on how health care leaders rate the importance of information technology; executives from both for-profit and not-for-profit organizations give information technology the same rating. However, for-prof-

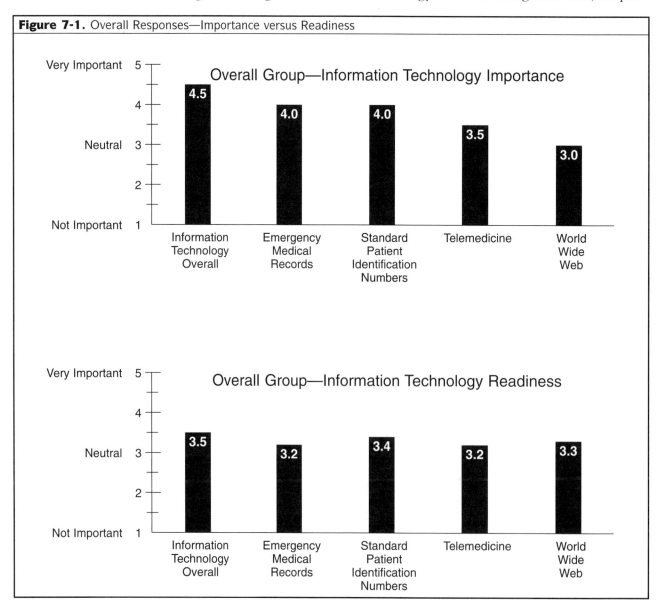

Figure 7-1. Overall Responses—Importance versus Readiness

its feel much more prepared than not-for-profits to handle information technology, probably because for-profits such as Columbia/HCA have easier access to the huge amounts of capital necessary to run a good information network.[1]

The importance ranking stands in stark contrast to health care executives' self-assessment of readiness. None of the groups surveyed feel confident in their ability to deal with the new technologies; information technology is identified across the board as the largest strategic gap organizations face. MCOs feel the most prepared (3.7), followed closely by group practices (3.6), while hospitals lag further behind (3.4). Hospitals and group practices that are not-for-profit feel least prepared to take on information technology, while, surprisingly, not-for-profit MCOs feel just as ready as any group in the for-profit sector. The reason for this confidence may be that the large not-for-profit health plans that have survived the takeover-and-conversion frenzy of recent years and the larger plans—namely, Kaiser Permanente and some of the Blue Cross plans—can meet the capital requirements of information technology planning.

In line with this lack of strategic readiness, none of the executives surveyed consider themselves ready to deal with the costs, staffing requirements, or organizational commitment required for today's advanced information systems. Hospital and managed care executives both ranked their readiness for information technology 12th, while group practices ranked it 7th. Leaders are more ready and willing to deal with the thorny issues of pricing, credentialing, and contracting with Medicare and Medicaid managed care than to deal with information.

That leaves a significant gap, the largest single strategic gap for each group. Health care leaders have a long way to go—and a lot of dollars to spend—before systemwide computerized scheduling or a virtual doctor's visit with the King of Jordan is an actual piece of strategy.

ELECTRONIC MEDICAL RECORDS

Organizations are seeking a better system than paper records, which consume a lot of clerical time and physicial space, are not easily updated, and often require a large staff to maintain. As Andersen Consulting observed, "The physical structure of the traditional medical record is a major obstacle to smooth, efficient health care."[2] On the most basic level, electronic medical records involve shifting a patient's paper medical record into a central, easily accessible computer database. More advanced records can store digitized x-rays and other images. Computerized records increase efficiency by providing instant information to doctors and reducing the space taken up by medical records rooms and the staff required to maintain them. With computerized systems, the records room may become a thing of the past. One site, the Arizona Medical Clinic in Peoria, Arizona, reported a 60 percent reduction in chart pulls—that is, consultations of paper files—during its first six months with an electronic system.[3]

Eventually, a good electronic record system can be used for outcomes research. For example, doctors can compare general health and the number of follow-up visits needed by patients who received different treatments for the same disease by searching the electronic database.

All three groups of health care leaders recognize the importance of electronic medical records, which will help organizations save time, money, and energy that is currently spent sorting through layers of paperwork. Leaders rank computerized records and standard patient identification numbers as the most important of the four specific technologies *Hospitals & Health Networks* enumerated in the survey. Group practices place electronic medical records first, while hospitals and MCOs rank the records a close second.

Just as health care organizations are not confident of their overall ability to use technology, their leaders also feel unprepared to deal with the individual technologies. Electronic medical records are a case in point: Although they tied as the most important information technology area, they also tied with telemedicine as the area that leaders are least ready to address. Part of the problem is cost. A large health care system may have to spend $10 million to computerize its patient records.[4] Such an investment should save money in the long term, but its benefits may not be immediately apparent; doctors often struggle to make the switch from paper records, and the health system might have to keep its file room staff or hire transcriptionists to enter the paper charts into the electronic system. But security is a larger concern: Many executives will not invest in computerized records until vendors can guarantee that hackers will not be able to break into them and snoop through confidential information. In addition, few organizations even agree on what an electronic record should include.[5]

Group practices are most confident in their ability to deal with the issue of computerized records. This confidence may not last long; many industry experts think that physician groups have been slow to adopt electronic medical records.[6] In fact, 43 percent of all respondents to the *1997 HIMSS/HP* [Healthcare Information and Management Systems Society/Hewlett-Packard] *Leadership Survey* identify doctors' offices as a part of the health care system in dire need of computerization.[7]

STANDARD PATIENT IDENTIFICATION NUMBERS

Health care organizations generally have patient information scattered throughout their various systems. Billing departments may identify patients by invoice number; claims departments may use Social Security numbers; doctors may use a patient's last name and first initial. This loose approach may have worked in small, pre–managed care systems, before capitation and the recent wave of mergers and acquisitions. But as organizations grow and payment systems become more complicated, health care executives are trying to find a standard way of identifying each patient, which will then serve as the "glue" of an information department.[8] Right now, most information specialists contend that a modified form of the Social Security number is the best identifier.[9]

Patient identifiers are closely related to patient records, so it makes sense that health care leaders emphasize the importance of both. Standard patient identifiers and computerized medical records each receive a rating of 4.0 to tie as the most important individual technology. Hospitals and MCOs both rank identifiers as their most important individual information technology issue, while group practices rank them second. Health care executives are clearly saying that these two interrelated technologies are key issues for all types of organizations. As C. Peter Waegemann, executive director of the Medical Records Institute, notes, "Hospitals, health maintenance organizations, clinics, physician offices and many other providers are recognizing that . . . electronic patient record systems should be the next major goal of computerization."[10]

Health care leaders are not fully confident of their ability to deal with patient identification systems, but they are more ready for this application than for the other technologies. The overall survey group ranks patient identifiers as the issue they are most prepared to tackle; hospitals and group practices rank this technology first, while MCOs rank it second. The reason for this relative confidence may be that an identification system can be applied in stages; organizations can use computer technology to give each patient a number but can also assign those numbers manually to paper patient records or billing records until the electronic versions are fully operational.

TELEMEDICINE

In some regions of the country, sophisticated medicine is not available because small hospitals cannot afford expensive specialists. Procedures such as hip replacement surgery may require three or four trips to a large hospital for diagnosis, treatment, and follow-up. Telemedicine can eliminate some of those costly visits; the small hospital or clinic can take an x-ray or CAT scan and beam it to a large hospital for expert analysis. Telemedicine shows the most promise in rural areas: The state of Oklahoma has built the nation's largest telemedicine network, linking 40 hospitals and several clinics.[11] While it is hard to assess clinical savings at this point, one network in Montana estimates that telemedicine saved its members almost $1 million in travel expenses alone in 1996.[12]

Of the four key technologies, telemedicine ranks third in importance, with a score of 3.5. Hospital leaders think very highly of telemedicine, ranking it only slightly below patient identifiers and computerized records. (See figures 7-2 and 7-3.) The most publicized forms of advanced telemedicine, such as teleradiology, promise to help rural hospitals provide better, more sophisticated care to remote and less mobile populations. Telemedicine increases a facility's ability to get multiple consultations from experts across the nation or around the world. Effective, low-tech telemedicine applications, such as home-based blood analyzers that use telephone links to send information to physician offices, are also emerging.

In the minds of group practice executives, telemedicine ties with the Web as the least important technology. MCO executives put it in last place, giving it a neutral rating. The low rating from the group practice respondents reflects how physicians view the technology. They see it in terms of its most

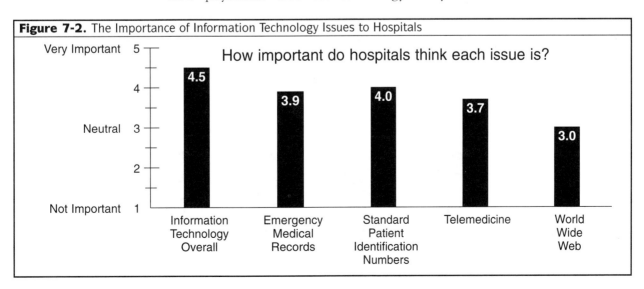

Figure 7-2. The Importance of Information Technology Issues to Hospitals

How important do hospitals think each issue is?

4.5	3.9	4.0	3.7	3.0
Information Technology Overall	Emergency Medical Records	Standard Patient Identification Numbers	Telemedicine	World Wide Web

Very Important 5 — Neutral 3 — Not Important 1

sophisticated, high-tech, and publicized forms, which, because of their high cost, are currently available only to hospital-based specialists. Group practice leaders have no vested interest in these technologies, but that may change as low-tech telemedicine takes hold. The managed care attitude toward telemedicine is consistent with a payer role: Managed care executives hope to encourage increases in quality but want to discourage increases in cost. Their ambivalence may represent the conflicting nature of this technology: It promises to improve quality, but its associated costs are often prohibitive. Again, that may change as low-tech telemedicine evolves.

Because group practice and managed care leaders do not consider telemedicine an important issue, they have not prepared for it, as their readiness scores attest. For the overall group, telemedicine ties with electronic medical records for the area that executives are least prepared to address. But hospitals—the only group that rates the technology highly—have invested more heavily in telemedicine, and they are much more ready to deal with the issue. Hospital executives give telemedicine a readiness score of 3.4, making it a tie with patient identifiers as areas they are most ready to address.

THE WORLD WIDE WEB

Several years ago, few people knew about the Web. Today, more and more businesses are creating home pages, and health care organizations are no exception. Recently, some organizations have used certain Web technologies to create "intranets," closed networks that allow doctors, caregivers, billing departments, and others to share information within an organization.

Despite the hype, health care leaders are not too impressed by the Web; survey respondents rank it last in importance, giving it a neutral score. Nevertheless, members of every part of the health care industry, including hospitals, insurers, supply management companies, and purchasing groups, already have colorful home pages, and many organizations embraced the Web long before they set up electronic records or purchased cost-information programs. While health care companies are investing large sums in their Internet presence, however, they do not see much return in the Web yet. According to a 1997 Ernst & Young survey, fewer than 35 percent of health care providers have developed an Internet strategy.[13]

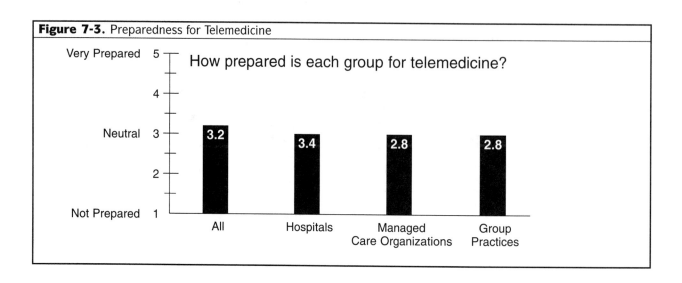

Figure 7-3. Preparedness for Telemedicine

How prepared is each group for telemedicine?

	All	Hospitals	Managed Care Organizations	Group Practices
Score	3.2	3.4	2.8	2.8

(Scale: Very Prepared 5, 4, Neutral 3, 2, Not Prepared 1)

MCOs were the only group to rank the Web above neutral in importance, perhaps because health plans can use the Web to mass-market their services to Internet-savvy consumers. Meanwhile, hospitals and group practices are more likely to market their services to health plans, where a general Web approach would not be particularly effective. In addition, managed care companies can use the Internet to improve member services. Many of the big health plans allow customers to request more information or ask questions directly through their Web sites; Aetna U.S. Healthcare, for example, allows members to switch their primary care physician on line, and other plans are expected to follow suit.[14]

The survey group ranks the Web second overall in terms of their readiness to use it, demonstrating relatively high confidence. In fact, the Web is the only technology to yield a positive strategic gap, meaning that organizations think their ability to deal with it is greater than its actual importance. This statistic does not imply that health care organizations are Web masters, however; Internet readiness may rank second overall, but its score, 3.3, is still barely above neutral.

IMPLICATIONS

As more and more industries take to the information superhighway, health care seems to be stuck in the breakdown lane. Health care executives believe information technology is vital to the future of their organization, but they are not ready to handle it yet. That leaves leaders with a critical strategic gap. Closing this gap must be a top priority for health care leaders in the coming years.

Paul Ginsberg, Ph.D., sees a bright future for information technology in health care. Ginsberg, president of the Center for Studying Health System Change, foresees the potential for HMOs to evolve into organizations that control and manage the information infrastructure. "HMOs may develop the information systems and rent them to providers," he says.[15] Clearly, he thinks the winners will not just be those organizations that jump on the information technology bandwagon; they will be the ones taking the reins.

Because information technology is evolving so quickly, however, many organizations are cautious about taking risks; information technology's promise may appear to be boundless, but so does the opportunity for failure. But many organizations have implemented information technology plans and thrived. Kaiser Permanente of Ohio invested $10 million in developing an electronic medical record system that now saves the organization $2.6 million a year in reduced staffing and overhead.[16] One researcher who studied a Massachusetts physician's office reports that electronic records will allow each doctor to see an average of 13 more patients a week simply by reducing time spent on paperwork.[17] And the Veterans Health Administration has been able to provide advanced care at its remote hospitals and clinics by beaming images to specialists at larger hospitals.[18]

So far, however, innovative information projects seem to be the exception rather than the rule. Health care already lags far behind other industries in information technology; now those health care organizations that don't adopt information technology plans will be left behind their own industry's leaders.[19] The first question every health care executive must ask is, Can we afford to invest in information technology? The most obvious answer is yet another question: Can we afford not to?

References

1. Fred Bazzoli, "Anticipating Explosive Growth," *Health Data Management* 5, no. 7 (July 1997): 46–48.

2. Gwendolyn B. Moore, David A. Rey, and John D. Rollins, *Prescription for the Future: How the Technology Revolution Is Changing the Pulse of Global Health Care* (Santa Monica, Cal.: Knowledge Exchange, 1996), p. 17.

3. Damon Braly, "Assess Your Current Processes before Selecting CPR Vendors," *Health Management Technology* 17, no. 8 (July 1996): 40.

4. Chuck Appleby, "Payoff@InfoTech.Now," *Hospitals & Health Networks* 71, no. 19 (Oct. 5, 1997): 58

5. Trudy Rice Thompson, "Easier Said Than Done," *Hospitals & Health Networks* 70, no. 13 (July 5, 1996): 29

6. Alan Bingham, "Computerized Patient Records Benefit Physician Offices," *Healthcare Financial Management* (Sept. 1997): 68–70.

7. *1997 HIMSS/HP Leadership Survey* (Chicago: Healthcare Information and Management Systems Society, 1997).

8. Lynn Kuehn, *Health Information Management: Medical Records in Group Practice* (Englewood Colo.: Center for Research in Ambulatory Health Care Administration, 1997), p. 101.

9. "Modified Social Security Number Called Best Patient ID Option," *Health Data Management* (Jan. 1997).

10. C. Peter Waegemann, "When Will Complete Medical Record Systems Exist?" *Health Management Technology* 17, no. 3 (Mar. 1996): 66.

11. Chuck Appleby, "Oklahoma's Highway to Health," *Hospitals & Health Networks* 71, no. 6 (Mar. 20, 1997): 88.

12. William McCall, "The Doctor Will See You Now—on TV," *Los Angeles Times,* May 12, 1997, p. D-9.

13. *The Role of the Internet in Health Care: Current State* (New York: Ernst & Young, 1997).

14. Ibid.

15. Alden Solovy, "Backlash to the Future: Is an HMO an HMO an HMO?" *Hospitals & Health Networks* 70, no. 8 (Apr. 20, 1996): 42.

16. Allan Khoury, "Finding Value in EMRs," *Health Management Technology* (July 1997): 34–36.

17. Alan Bingham, "Computerized Patient Records Benefit Physician Offices," *Healthcare Financial Management* (Sept. 1997): 68–70.

18. Chris Serb, "The New VA," *Hospitals & Health Networks* 71, no. 12 (June 20, 1997): 56–58.

19. Saad J. Allawi, "Five Irresistible Forces," *Healthcare Forum Journal* 40, no. 1 (Jan./Feb. 1997): 48–51.

Information Technology — Rankings

Ranking by All Respondents

1. Electronic Medical Records

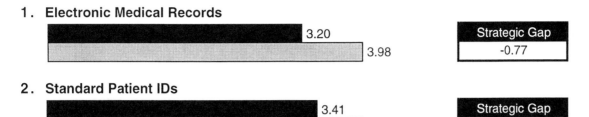

3.20
3.98

Strategic Gap
-0.77

2. Standard Patient IDs

3.41
3.99

Strategic Gap
-0.58

3. Telemedicine

3.19
3.48

Strategic Gap
-0.29

4. Internet/World Wide Web

3.25
3.00

Strategic Gap
0.25

Ranking by Hospital Executives

1. Electronic Medical Records

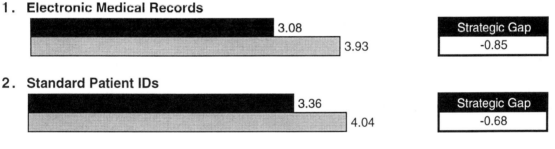

3.08
3.93

Strategic Gap
-0.85

2. Standard Patient IDs

3.36
4.04

Strategic Gap
-0.68

3. Telemedicine

3.36
3.69

Strategic Gap
-0.33

4. Internet/World Wide Web

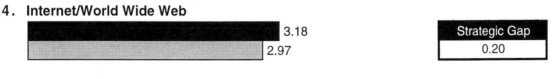

3.18
2.97

Strategic Gap
0.20

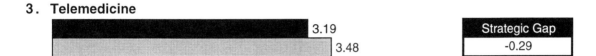

■ Preparedness　▨ Importance

- Respondents ranked the importance of four partnership combinations for developing their strategies.
- Respondents also ranked their preparedness for dealing with these partnership combinations.
- Combinations are ranked from largest to smallest strategic gap.
- Small discrepancies between the strategic gap and the rankings may occur due to rounding.

Information Technology   Rankings

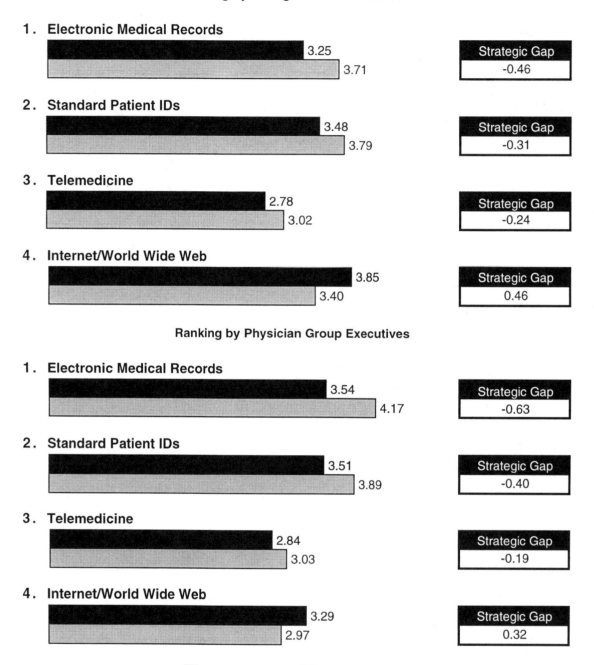

Ranking by Managed Care Executives

1. Electronic Medical Records

3.25
3.71

Strategic Gap
-0.46

2. Standard Patient IDs

3.48
3.79

Strategic Gap
-0.31

3. Telemedicine

2.78
3.02

Strategic Gap
-0.24

4. Internet/World Wide Web

3.85
3.40

Strategic Gap
0.46

Ranking by Physician Group Executives

1. Electronic Medical Records

3.54
4.17

Strategic Gap
-0.63

2. Standard Patient IDs

3.51
3.89

Strategic Gap
-0.40

3. Telemedicine

2.84
3.03

Strategic Gap
-0.19

4. Internet/World Wide Web

3.29
2.97

Strategic Gap
0.32

■ Preparedness   ▨ Importance

• Respondents ranked the importance of four partnership combinations for developing their strategies.
• Respondents also ranked their preparedness for dealing with these partnership combinations.
• Combinations are ranked from largest to smallest strategic gap.
• Small discrepancies between the strategic gap and the rankings may occur due to rounding.

Information Technology   Electronic Medical Records

Overall Results

Importance vs. Preparedness

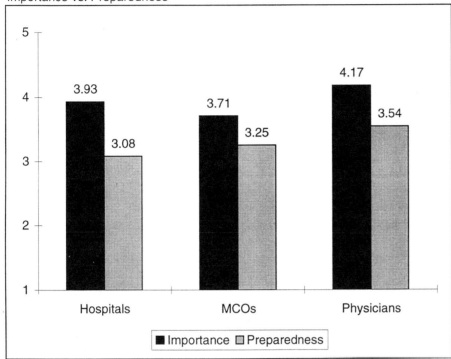

Strategic Gap	
Hospitals	-0.85
MCOs	-0.46
Physicians	-0.63

Rank	
Importance	2
Preparedness	3
Strategic Gap	1

• The higher the importance ranking, the more important the technology is to respondents.
• The higher the readiness ranking, the better the respondents view the preparedness of their institutions.
• "Strategic gap" refers to the difference between importance and preparedness.
• The rank refers to the rank of the technologies out of the 4 included in the survey. Ranks are given for importance, readiness, and strategic gap. The highest rank is 1; the lowest rank is 4.

Regional Results

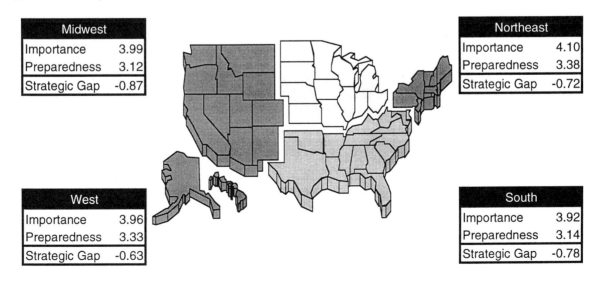

Midwest	
Importance	3.99
Preparedness	3.12
Strategic Gap	-0.87

Northeast	
Importance	4.10
Preparedness	3.38
Strategic Gap	-0.72

West	
Importance	3.96
Preparedness	3.33
Strategic Gap	-0.63

South	
Importance	3.92
Preparedness	3.14
Strategic Gap	-0.78

Information Technology   Electronic Medical Records

Hospital Executives

Importance vs. Preparedness

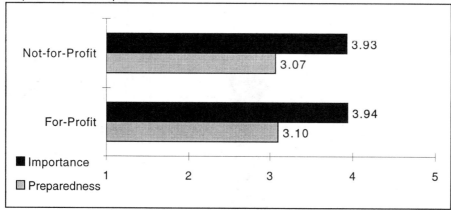

Rank	
Importance	2
Preparedness	4
Strategic Gap	1

Strategic Gap	
Not-for-profit	-0.86
For-profit	-0.84

Managed Care Executives

Importance vs. Preparedness

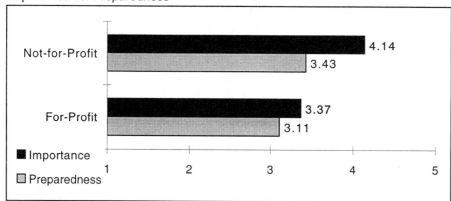

Rank	
Importance	2
Preparedness	3
Strategic Gap	1

Strategic Gap	
Not-for-profit	-0.71
For-profit	-0.26

Physician Group Practice Executives

Importance vs. Preparedness

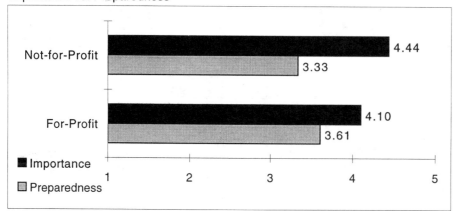

Rank	
Importance	1
Preparedness	1
Strategic Gap	1

Strategic Gap	
Not-for-profit	-1.10
For-profit	-0.49

Information Technology | Telemedicine

Overall Results

Importance vs. Preparedness

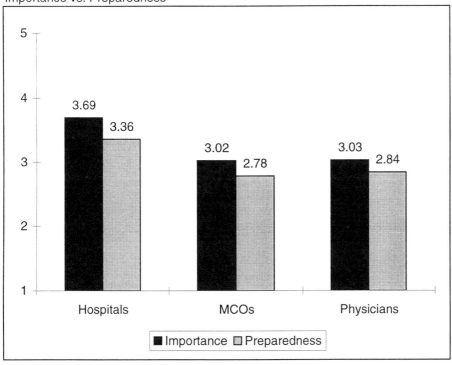

Strategic Gap	
Hospitals	-0.33
MCOs	-0.24
Physicians	-0.19

Rank	
Importance	3
Preparedness	4
Strategic Gap	3

- The higher the importance ranking, the more important the technology is to respondents.
- The higher the readiness ranking, the better the respondents view the preparedness of their institutions.
- "Strategic gap" refers to the difference between importance and preparedness.
- The rank refers to the rank of the technologies out of the 4 included in the survey. Ranks are given for importance, readiness, and strategic gap. The highest rank is 1; the lowest rank is 4.

Regional Results

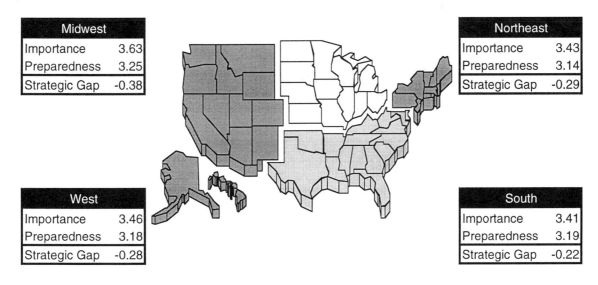

Midwest	
Importance	3.63
Preparedness	3.25
Strategic Gap	-0.38

Northeast	
Importance	3.43
Preparedness	3.14
Strategic Gap	-0.29

West	
Importance	3.46
Preparedness	3.18
Strategic Gap	-0.28

South	
Importance	3.41
Preparedness	3.19
Strategic Gap	-0.22

Information Technology | Telemedicine

Hospital Executives
Importance vs. Preparedness

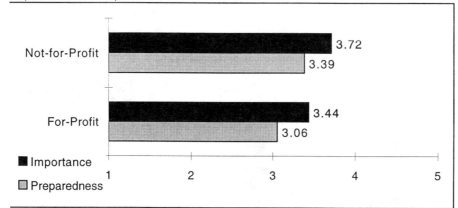

Rank	
Importance	3
Preparedness	2
Strategic Gap	3

Strategic Gap	
Not-for-profit	-0.33
For-profit	-0.38

Managed Care Executives
Importance vs. Preparedness

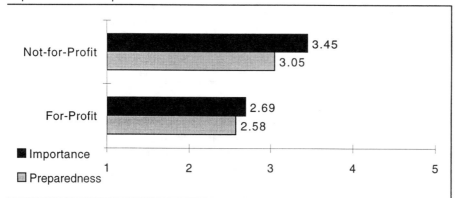

Rank	
Importance	4
Preparedness	4
Strategic Gap	3

Strategic Gap	
Not-for-profit	-0.40
For-profit	-0.12

Physician Group Practice Executives
Importance vs. Preparedness

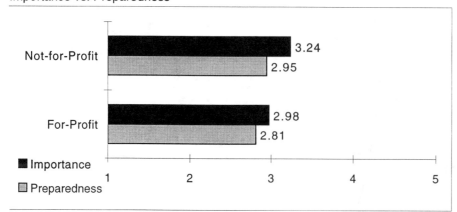

Rank	
Importance	3
Preparedness	4
Strategic Gap	3

Strategic Gap	
Not-for-profit	-0.29
For-profit	-0.16

Information Technology

Standard Patient IDs

Overall Results

Importance vs. Preparedness

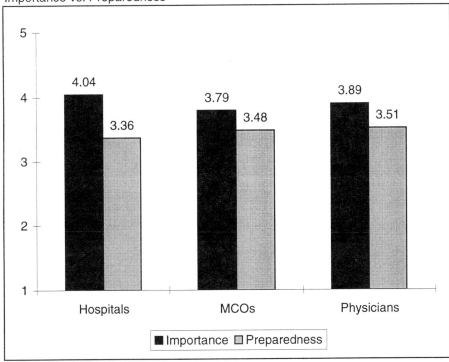

Strategic Gap	
Hospitals	-0.68
MCOs	-0.31
Physicians	-0.40

Rank	
Importance	1
Preparedness	1
Strategic Gap	2

- The higher the importance ranking, the more important the technology is to respondents.
- The higher the readiness ranking, the better the respondents view the preparedness of their institutions.
- "Strategic gap" refers to the difference between importance and preparedness.
- The rank refers to the rank of the technologies out of the 4 included in the survey. Ranks are given for importance, readiness, and strategic gap. The highest rank is 1; the lowest rank is 4.

Regional Results

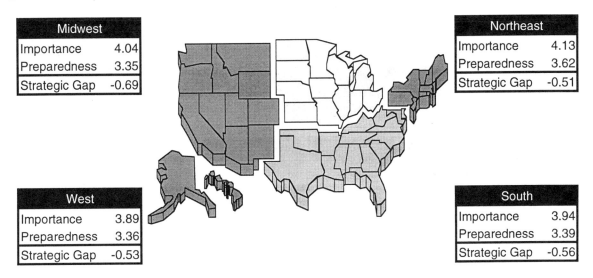

Midwest	
Importance	4.04
Preparedness	3.35
Strategic Gap	-0.69

Northeast	
Importance	4.13
Preparedness	3.62
Strategic Gap	-0.51

West	
Importance	3.89
Preparedness	3.36
Strategic Gap	-0.53

South	
Importance	3.94
Preparedness	3.39
Strategic Gap	-0.56

Information Technology	Standard Patient IDs

Hospital Executives

Importance vs. Preparedness

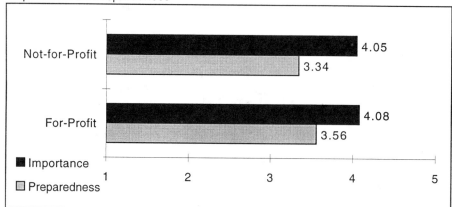

Rank	
Importance	1
Preparedness	1
Strategic Gap	2

Strategic Gap	
Not-for-profit	-0.70
For-profit	-0.52

Managed Care Executives

Importance vs. Preparedness

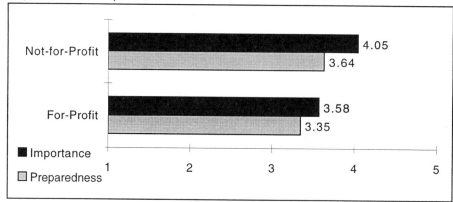

Rank	
Importance	1
Preparedness	2
Strategic Gap	2

Strategic Gap	
Not-for-profit	-0.41
For-profit	-0.23

Physician Group Practice Executives

Importance vs. Preparedness

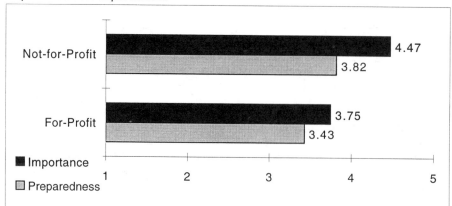

Rank	
Importance	2
Preparedness	2
Strategic Gap	2

Strategic Gap	
Not-for-profit	-0.66
For-profit	-0.32

Information Technology | Internet/World Wide Web

Overall Results

Importance vs. Preparedness

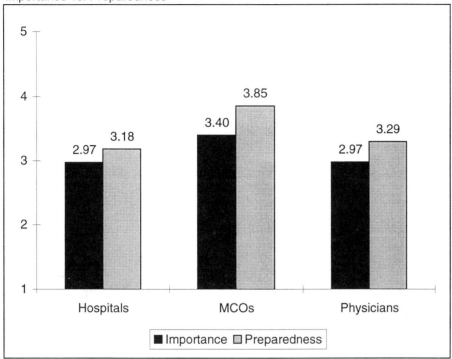

Strategic Gap	
Hospitals	0.20
MCOs	0.46
Physicians	0.32

Rank	
Importance	4
Preparedness	2
Strategic Gap	4

• The higher the importance ranking, the more important the technology is to respondents.
• The higher the readiness ranking, the better the respondents view the preparedness of their institutions.
• "Strategic gap" refers to the difference between importance and preparedness.
• The rank refers to the rank of the technologies out of the 4 included in the survey. Ranks are given for importance, readiness, and strategic gap. The highest rank is 1; the lowest rank is 4.

Regional Results

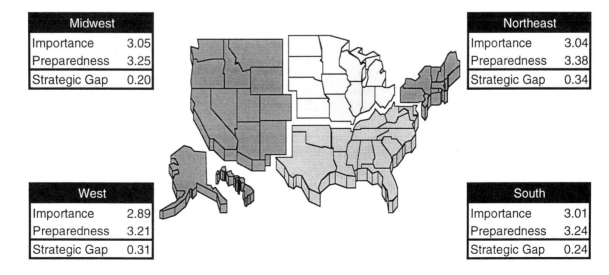

Midwest	
Importance	3.05
Preparedness	3.25
Strategic Gap	0.20

Northeast	
Importance	3.04
Preparedness	3.38
Strategic Gap	0.34

West	
Importance	2.89
Preparedness	3.21
Strategic Gap	0.31

South	
Importance	3.01
Preparedness	3.24
Strategic Gap	0.24

Information Technology **Internet/World Wide Web**

Hospital Executives

Importance vs. Preparedness

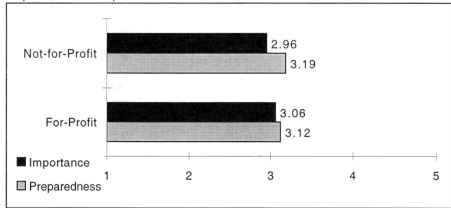

Rank	
Importance	4
Preparedness	3
Strategic Gap	4

Strategic Gap	
Not-for-profit	0.23
For-profit	0.06

Managed Care Executives

Importance vs. Preparedness

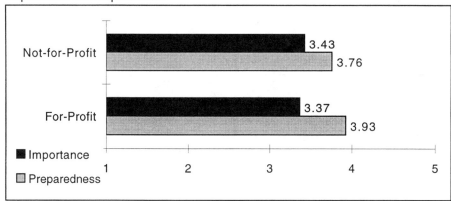

Rank	
Importance	3
Preparedness	1
Strategic Gap	4

Strategic Gap	
Not-for-profit	0.33
For-profit	0.56

Physician Group Practice Executives

Importance vs. Preparedness

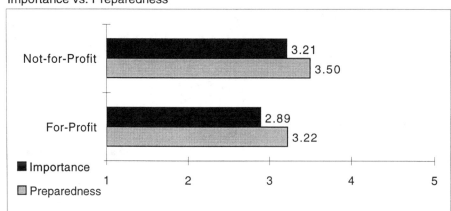

Rank	
Importance	4
Preparedness	3
Strategic Gap	4

Strategic Gap	
Not-for-profit	0.29
For-profit	0.33

CHAPTER 8

Business Ethics

Margaret F. Schulte

According to the early Greek philosophers, the application of ethical principles in commerce was essential to sucess. This is also true in health care. Yet the founding ethic of health care—the Hippocratic oath, a set of codes with roots in Greek philosophy—appears to be in jeopardy these days, besieged by both market-driven reform and scientific advancement. Moreover, health care's ethical quandary has not escaped the American public. At a recent national forum, Sister Mary Jean Ryan of SSM Health Care System of St. Louis lamented, "Somewhere along the line, . . . in our drive to remain financially viable, the public's trust was lost."[1]

Managed care brought a new dimension to ethics in health care, but it is not itself to blame for the current crisis in confidence. As Mark Waymack, president of the Chicago Clinical Ethics Program, notes, managed care is "sometimes defined as a payment mechanism in which a provider receives a fixed amount per enrollee, and sometimes it means the delivery system. There is nothing intrinsically unethical about either of these."[2] Yet managed care has heightened the awareness of ethical challenges; it has solved some old problems and created altogether new ones. The managed care movement has overcast the physician's environment with gatekeeper and managed care approval mechanisms that potentially lead to underutilization of services or postponement of care.

In the shift from fee-for-service to managed care, the people served are no longer "patients" but rather "covered lives." According to this new worldview, patients are not assets but liabilities. Nevertheless, patients still see themselves in their human, pained context. They have a different set of expectations for the health care system, namely, timely access to the best care in the world.

This divergence of expectations generates ethical conflict; for it is in relationships with others—customers, constituents, and stakeholders—that ethical issues emerge for any business. And in the business of health care, provider organizations are the "Times Square" of human interaction. People of diverse cultures and experience, people with different expectations and different financial resources, intermingle in health care facilities. In addition, unlike most other businesses, the interactions in health care are those in which one person seeks help from another in an unequal balance of power. The one is hurt; the other can ease suffering and, potentially, cure. The one is vulnerable; the other powerful. In light of this imbalance, it is vitally important that ethical reasoning and values be at the foundation of decisions made by health executives. That is the only way to restore the faith of the American public.

The foundation of faith is trust, and trust flows directly from the integrity that guides behavior. Yet as writer Chuck Appleby concluded in a recent *Hospitals & Health Networks* story on how ethics has influenced decisions in health care delivery and payment systems, integrity is an "embattled virtue." He suggests that "incorporating ethics into business decisions has stymied health care executives across the country."[3] As part of the *Hospitals & Health Networks* Leadership Survey, we wanted to find out what health care leaders are doing about fostering both medical and business ethics. We asked specifically about the adoption of codes of ethics and the value of formal ethics training.

CODES OF ETHICS

In facing ethical dilemmas, a number of health care systems have moved to formally adopt codes of ethics and ethical guidelines to instruct their decisions. Just as the clinical and business aspects of medical care delivery are distinct, so are the codes of ethics that guide behavior in each of these realms. A medical code of ethics addresses clinical activities, and a business code addresses the business functions. Some organizations have even moved to create separate codes to address the specific organizational behavior in the complicated world of managed care. The "Ethics Guidelines for Managed Care Contracting" developed by the Shared Corporate Ethics Committee of the Eastern Mercy Health System and Mercy Health System in June of 1995 have become an oft-quoted example of how health systems can create their path through the maze of ethical issues raised under managed care. The guidelines are based on three fundamental premises:

- Respect for the dignity of humans
- That dignity can only be protected and realized in community
- Special responsibility for the poor

Health care providers are not consistent in their adoption of codes of ethics and some have a long way to go to put values-oriented guidelines for behavior into place. Only 69 percent of hospitals have adopted a code of ethics to guide their business decisions, and only 64 percent have adopted a medical code of ethics. The good news is that roughly two-thirds of health care organizations have codes of ethics; the bad news is that one-third do not. For-profit hospitals have a statistically higher track record than not-for-profit hospitals in adopting codes of ethics. This effort may be a response to the intense scrutiny to which some for-profit organization's business practices have been subjected by federal investigators. For example, Tenet, as part of its 1994 settlement with the Department of Justice and Department of Health and Human Services, specifically committed to implementing oversight procedures and ethics training.[4] Eighty-eight percent of for-profits have a business code of ethics, compared with 67 percent among not-for-profit organizations. Seventy-seven percent of for-profits have a medical code of ethics, while 62 percent of not-for-profits have one.

Physician groups are even less likely to have adopted a formal code of ethics. Less than half (41 percent) of physician practices say that they have a code of medical ethics. The reason may be that the medical arts are already governed by a code—the Hippocratic oath. In contrast to hospitals, not-for-profit practices are significantly ahead of for-profit practices in adopting ethical guidelines. Sixty percent of the former have adopted a code of ethics, while 36 percent of the latter have one. Regarding business ethics, overall only 36 percent of physician practices have adopted a code. Of these, the rate of adoption in not-for-profit organizations is 58 percent. Only 30 percent of for-profit group practices have adopted a code of business ethics.

Managed care organizations (MCOs) respond differently to questions on codes of ethics. Managed care is defined by many to be a movement away from a medical professionalism to a managerial professionalism—to the corporatization of medical care. Managed care's unique ethical issues arise in this transition. Certainly, extreme adherence to financial motives corrupts medical ideals. For example, strong incentives to refuse or postpone services ultimately backfire when the quality of care deteriorates to the point where users and purchasers take notice.

So what have managed care plans done to assure that individuals in their ranks have the guidance they need to make ethical decisions and create ethical policies? Sixty percent of MCOs have adopted codes of business ethics. In contrast to the hospital findings, however, for-profit entities lag behind not-for-profits. Among for-profit managed care entities, 57 percent have adopted these codes, while among not-for-profits, 67 percent have done so.

MCOs have not done very much to formulate codes of medical ethics. Only 44 percent say that they have such a code. Of these, the for-profits again significantly lag behind not-for-profit organizations. Thirty percent of the former have codes of medical ethics, compared with 57 percent of the latter.

ETHICS EDUCATION

Ethics researchers, including James R. Rest, Linda Trevino, and Lawrence Kohlberg, have emphasized the relationship between ethics education and ethical decision making. However, results of the *Hospitals & Health Networks* Leadership Survey suggest that, in practice, education is not a priority among our hospitals. Only 28 percent of hospitals report that they require education in business ethics for their senior managers. Even fewer, 23 percent, require education in medical ethics. The Greek philosophers would have winced at such disregard for education. Derek Bok, ethicist and president emeritus of Harvard University, notes, "[Socrates] argues that those who had not learned to reason about moral aims and questions would not be able to apply moral principles to the dilemmas they would face in life."[5]

More for-profit institutions (62 percent) require business ethics education than do not-for-profits (24 percent). The two groups are a little more similar regarding medical ethics education; however, for-profits again outpace not-for-profit institutions, 38 percent to 21 percent. As with codes of ethics, this statistic may be a product of the governmental scrutiny that has been focused on for-profit hospital organizations. This sector is anxious to install the mechanisms to assure a wary government and public that laws and basic values are being upheld.

With all the changes that have happened in their world, physicians have begun to develop a base of business and financial knowledge. The drive toward business education for physicians is evidenced in part by the great number of MBA programs for physicians that have sprouted all over the country.

Physicians lag significantly in training in business ethics and, ironically, even in medical ethics. (The irony might be explained by the paradox described above: Physicians feel they do not need ethics training because they already have the Hippocratic oath.) Only 15 percent of the responding physicians indicate that they are required to participate in business ethics training programs, and 17 percent said they are required to participate in medical ethics training programs. Whether the physician worked in a not-for-profit setting or a for-profit setting did not make a difference. In both settings, the survey findings indicate minimal expectations for ethics training.

Though few physicians are required to participate in ethics training programs, many more believe that such training is important. One recent survey of 300 physicians, (general practitioners, surgeons, other specialists), asked the participants to rate the importance of formal undergraduate training in each of 16 competencies. More than 75 percent thought it was "very important" to include ethics. Additionally, more than 40 percent acknowledged that they felt poorly prepared to "work in managed care settings or to accommodate increasing external scrutiny."[6]

The financing and delivery structures that have evolved under managed care turn the focus of attention from the individual to the population, and financial success derives from minimizing services delivered. The patient-focused Hippocratic oath no longer applies to all financial and strategic decisions. In this environment, then, do MCOs use ethics education to help their executives make values-based decisions? According to the *Hospitals & Health Networks* Leadership Survey, the answer is "minimally." MCOs are not ready to require that their senior managers receive education in either business or medical ethics. Thirty-two percent of MCOs require the former, and only 18 percent require the latter type of education.

IMPLICATIONS

With all that has challenged the ethical foundations of health care in the past decades, the demand for a solid core of ethical considerations in management decisions continues to grow. Developments in science and shifts of a sociological nature continually throw into relief the need for ethical standards. The Human Genome Project is developing astounding capabilities for genetic engineering. The influx of ethnic populations complicates the decision-making process as it enriches the demographic mix. The aging of society adds to the complexity of ethical decision making and significantly increases the number of decisions to be made. Challenges to and changes in financing mechanisms determine who does and does not receive medical treatment in this country; and for those who do receive treatment, the course of that treatment is determined against financial criteria that, too frequently, appear to take precedence over medical criteria.

Those who find themselves in roles of leadership, whether in hospitals, physician practices, or MCOs, must accept their responsibility to, first of all, act ethically in their day-to-day functions, in the deals they cut, in the policies they establish, and most of all in their relationships with individual patients. It is too easy to treat the faceless patient as a commodity while seeking to improve the health of whole population groups. The reality is that population groups are made and kept healthy one patient at a time.

With the concurrent factors of integration, managed care, risk shifting, and Medicare reform, many health care providers are joining the ranks of endangered species. In the race to survive, ethical considerations are too often ignored or compromised in the expediency of the moment. In today's climate of takeovers, downsizing, declining profits, shrinking market share, and insufficient cash flow, corporate and individual survival are seriously threatened. Survival depends on a willingness to take risks, to deal creatively with resource management and resource utilization issues, to recognize and avoid conflicts of interest, to recognize and build working relationships with a complex array of stakeholders, to come to see the patient as both a statistical life and as a *unique individual.* It means functioning outside comfortable boundaries. Yet the pressures to do "whatever it takes to win all too frequently lead to ethical shortcuts, at best, and major moral crises at worst."[7]

MCOs lag significantly behind in formal medical ethics activities, which may be a reflection of their role as payer organizations. While they bill themselves as experts in managing the delivery of care, many do not actually deliver care themselves and therefore may place little importance on medical ethics. MCOs assume a critical role in making patient care decisions, in approval or denial of the clinical decisions of physicians at the bedside. Managed care's push for population-based medicine may hamper not only physician autonomy, but also patient autonomy, giving rise to ethical dilemmas around fairness to the individual and to the population as a whole.

Codes of ethics, when they form the culture of an organization, do more than just guide behavior. They define leadership and ensure success. Dr. Kenneth Blanchard maintains that ethical leaders and effective leaders are one and the same: "To create an ethical institution the leader must be able to recognize and respond to ethical issues, foster appropriate policies, processes, and behavior based on ethical reasoning."[8]

Study after study has demonstrated a clear relationship between ethical conduct and success. In 1991, S. J. Harrington found that "63 percent of Fortune 500 CEOs maintain that strong ethics result in strategic advantage."[9]

Recent surveys have indicated that 90 percent of Fortune 500 companies and nearly 50 percent of all companies have instituted some form of corporate ethics code."[10] Are these codes indicative of financial success? Dr. Kenneth Blanchard thinks so. He studied 21 companies that had a written code of principles stating that serving the public was central to their being. He found that if an individual had invested $30,000 in the composite Dow Jones 30 years ago, it would be worth $134,000 today. If that individual had invested the same $30,000 in each of the companies in the survey, it would be worth over $1 million today.[11] J. Batten and J. Vanhorn built on this theme when they reported that "studies of corporations that have risen and fallen reveal that the viability and vitality of each was closely linked to the rise and decline of morality as practiced in the corporation."[12]

Based on all the research that says that ethical organizations are the most successful, it is not only morally right that codes of ethical conduct be established but it simply makes good business sense. Those codes will do little, though, if they are left just hanging on the wall. They will need to define the organizational culture, and the only way to make that happen is by example and education. A renewed emphasis and commitment of resources to ethics education, both in medical and business ethics, will be needed to make the code come alive in the organization.

It is clear that the code of ethics must be made "real," that is, translated into behavior. To make that happen the organization needs first to provide structural, systemic support for ethical behavior and, second, needs to provide the educational base to support ethical decision making. Yet this essential ingredient is markedly lacking in hospitals as is seen in the results of the *Hospitals & Health Networks* Leadership Survey. Just as Socrates endorsed moral education, in modern times repeated studies have shown consistently that education is a powerful influence on moral reasoning and decision making.

Nevertheless this field of study has its cynics, those who believe that ethical conduct is foretold in an individual's upbringing—in the values that are inculcated in the home and from the very early days of childhood—and that education in this subject serves no purpose. However, the role of ethics education is not to instill values (though it may well do that) but to give individuals the tools to recognize the ethical dimensions of the decisions they face and to apply an ethical reasoning process to those decisions. Ethics education enables individuals to work through complexity and to act with confidence within their value structure.

A recognition of the need for education is only the first step to improving the ethical decision-making skills. As Gauthier has said, "There are skills, attitudes, certain approaches to the patient and to the therapeutic relationship that can be taught in medical school and residency programs. But this education is going to take a long time: it's going to be generational."[13] It takes vision, foresight, and commitment.

References

1. Quoted in K. Lumsdon, "Talk Shows," *Hospitals & Health Networks* 70, no. 14 (July 20, 1996): 49–58.

2. M. Waymack (Conference on Medical Ethics sponsored by Chicago Clinical Ethics Programs, Aug. 7–8, 1997).

3. C. Appleby, "Managed Care's True Values," *Hospitals & Health Networks* (May 5, 1996): 20–26.

4. Tenet corporate profile, p. 33.

5. D. Bok, "Can Higher Education Foster Higher Morals?" *Business and Society Review* (1993): 4–12.

6. L. J. Pinocchio, P. J. Bailiff, R. W. Grant, and E. H. O'Neil, "Professional Competencies in the Changing Health Care System," *Academy of Medicine* 70, no. 11 (Nov. 1995): 1023–28.

7. H. E. Dolenga, "An Iconoclastic Look at Business Ethics," *Advanced Management Journal* 55 (Autumn 1990): 13–17.

8. K. Blanchard, "Ethical Management," *Executive Excellence* 4, no. 11 (Nov. 1987): 3–4.

9. S. J. Harrington, "What Corporate America Is Teaching about Ethics," *Academy of Management Executive* 5, no. 1 (Feb. 1991): 21–30.

10. J. W. Hill, M. B. Metzger, and D. R. Dalton, "How Ethical Is Your Company?" *Management Accounting* (July 1992): 59–61.

11. Blanchard, "Ethical Management."

12. J. Batten and J. VanHorn, "Total Quality Living," *Executive Excellence* (Dec. 1992): 17.

13. C. Appleby, "Managed Care's True Values."

Organizations with Formally Adopted Codes of Ethics--All Respondents

Business

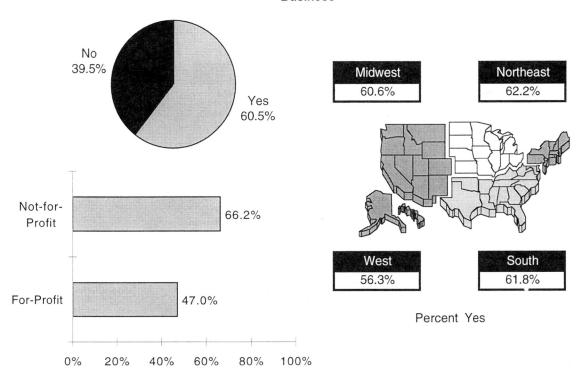

Medical

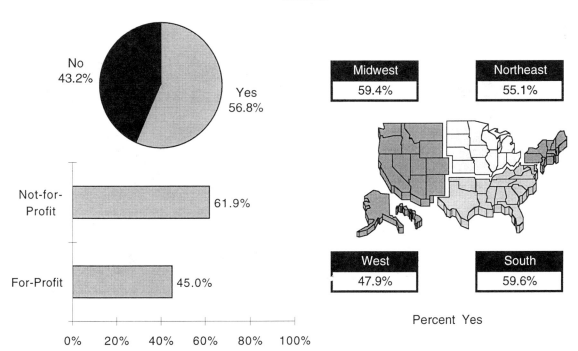

Organizations with Formally Adopted Codes of Ethics--Hospital Executives

Business

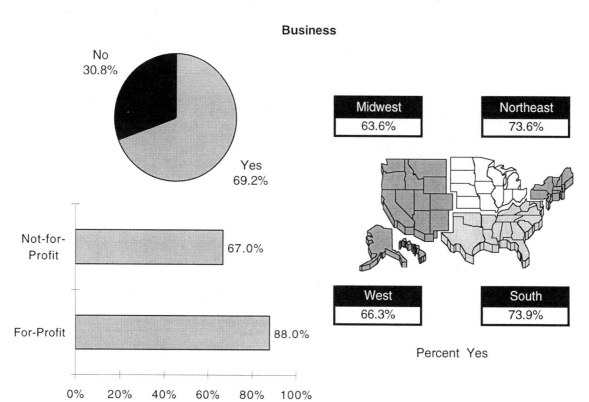

Medical

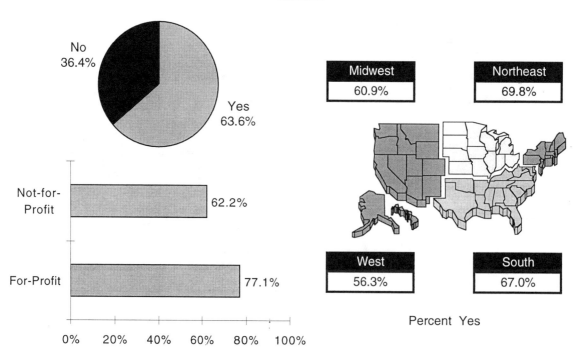

Ethics   **Codes of Ethics**

Organizations with Formally Adopted Codes of Ethics--Managed Care Executives

Business

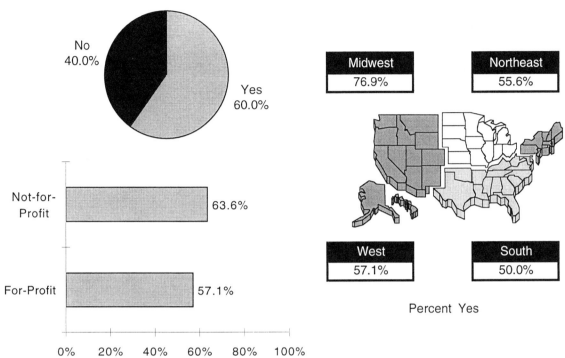

Medical

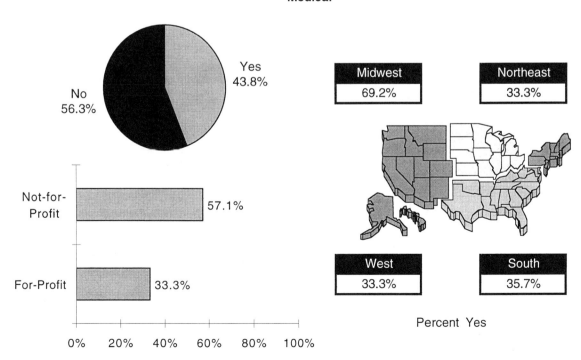

Organizations with Formally Adopted Codes of Ethics--Physician Group Executives

Business

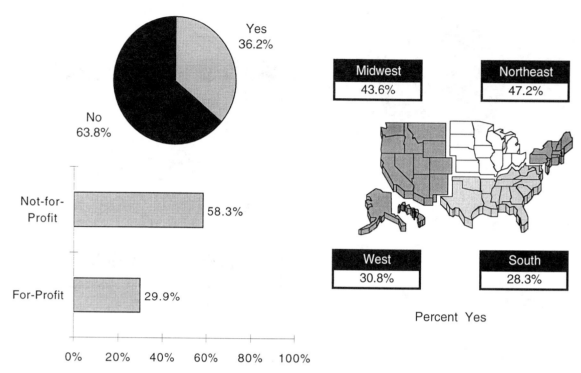

Yes 36.2%

No 63.8%

Not-for-Profit 58.3%

For-Profit 29.9%

0%   20%   40%   60%   80%   100%

Midwest 43.6%

Northeast 47.2%

West 30.8%

South 28.3%

Percent Yes

Medical

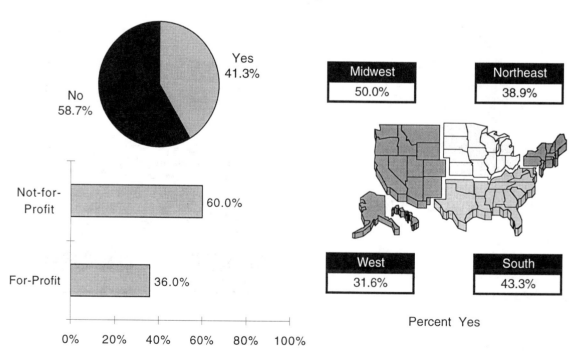

Yes 41.3%

No 58.7%

Not-for-Profit 60.0%

For-Profit 36.0%

0%   20%   40%   60%   80%   100%

Midwest 50.0%

Northeast 38.9%

West 31.6%

South 43.3%

Percent Yes

Organizations Require Ethics Training for Senior Staff--All Respondents

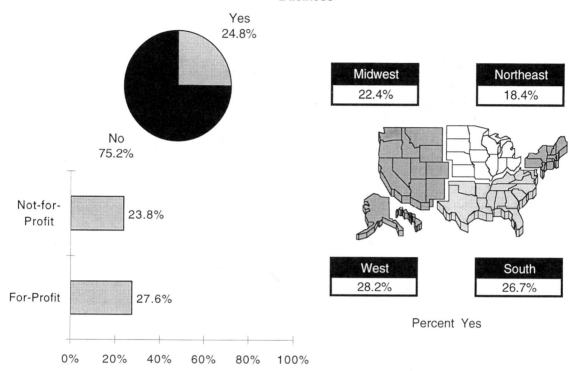

Business

Yes
24.8%

No
75.2%

Not-for-Profit 23.8%

For-Profit 27.6%

0%   20%   40%   60%   80%   100%

Midwest	Northeast
22.4%	18.4%

West	South
28.2%	26.7%

Percent Yes

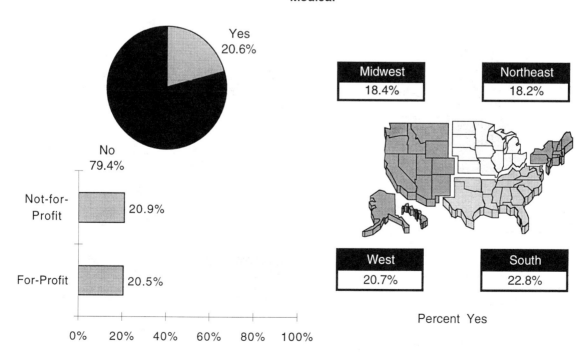

Medical

Yes
20.6%

No
79.4%

Not-for-Profit 20.9%

For-Profit 20.5%

0%   20%   40%   60%   80%   100%

Midwest	Northeast
18.4%	18.2%

West	South
20.7%	22.8%

Percent Yes

Organizations Require Ethics Training for Senior Staff--Hospital Executives

Business

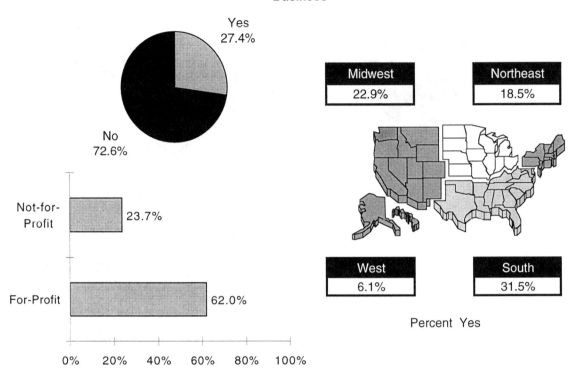

Medical

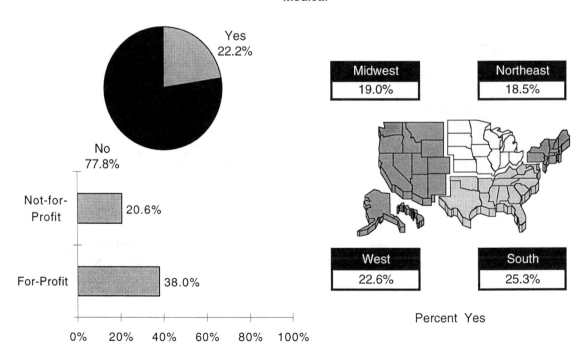

Ethics　　　　　　　　　　　　　　　　　　　**Ethics Training**

Organizations Require Ethics Training for Senior Staff--Managed Care Executives

Business

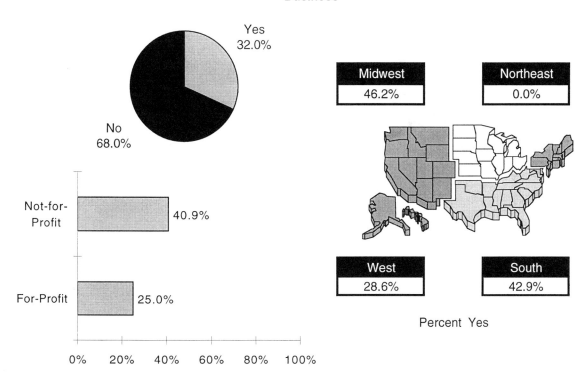

Midwest
46.2%

Northeast
0.0%

West
28.6%

South
42.9%

Percent Yes

Medical

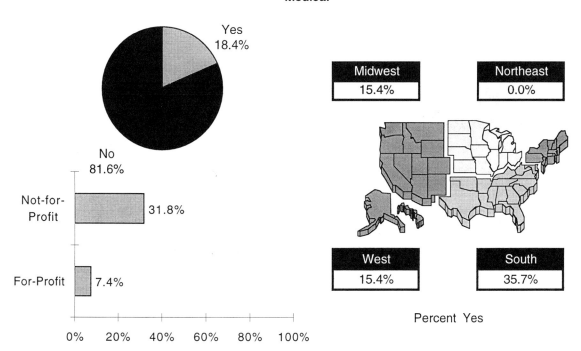

Midwest
15.4%

Northeast
0.0%

West
15.4%

South
35.7%

Percent Yes

Organizations Require Ethics Training for Senior Staff--Physician Group Executives

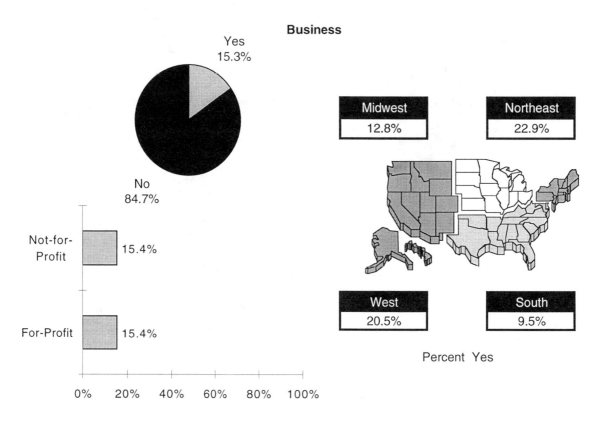

Business

Yes
15.3%

No
84.7%

Not-for-Profit 15.4%

For-Profit 15.4%

Midwest	Northeast
12.8%	22.9%

West	South
20.5%	9.5%

Percent Yes

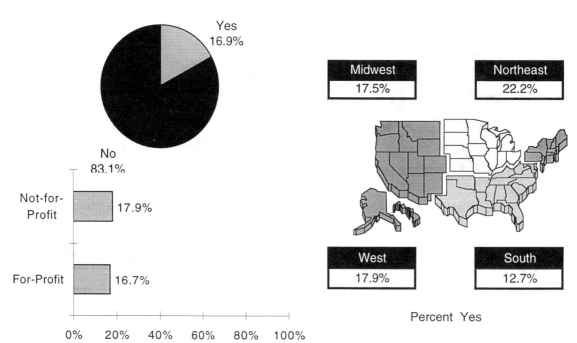

Medical

Yes
16.9%

No
83.1%

Not-for-Profit 17.9%

For-Profit 16.7%

Midwest	Northeast
17.5%	22.2%

West	South
17.9%	12.7%

Percent Yes

Should Health Care Executives Be Held to a Higher Standard Regarding . . .

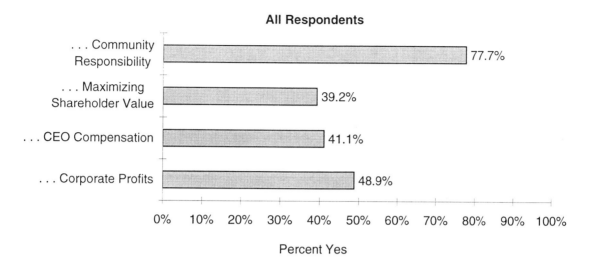

All Respondents

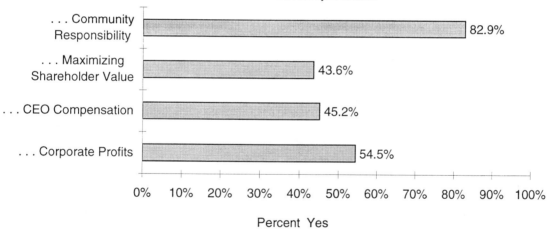

Not-For-Profit Respondents

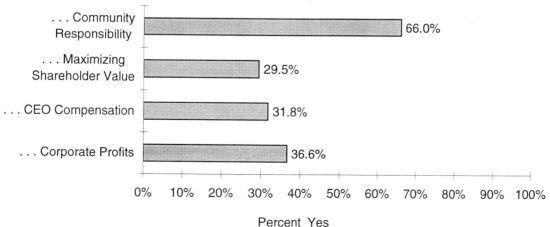

For-Profit Respondents

Ethics   **Ethical Standards**

Should Health Care Executives Be Held to a Higher Standard Regarding . . .

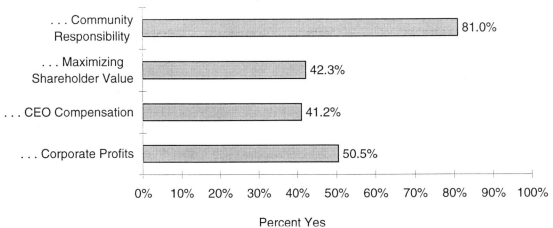

Hospital Executives

	Percent Yes
. . . Community Responsibility	81.0%
. . . Maximizing Shareholder Value	42.3%
. . . CEO Compensation	41.2%
. . . Corporate Profits	50.5%

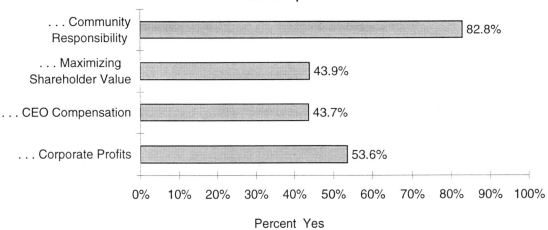

Not-For-Profit Hospital Executives

	Percent Yes
. . . Community Responsibility	82.8%
. . . Maximizing Shareholder Value	43.9%
. . . CEO Compensation	43.7%
. . . Corporate Profits	53.6%

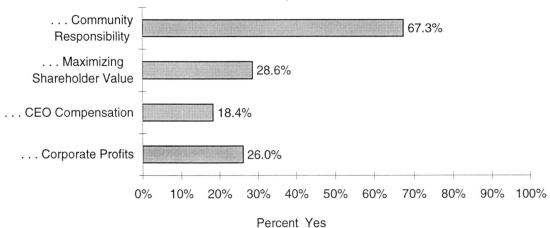

For-Profit Hospital Executives

	Percent Yes
. . . Community Responsibility	67.3%
. . . Maximizing Shareholder Value	28.6%
. . . CEO Compensation	18.4%
. . . Corporate Profits	26.0%

Ethics   Ethical Standards

Should Health Care Executives Be Held to a Higher Standard Regarding . . .

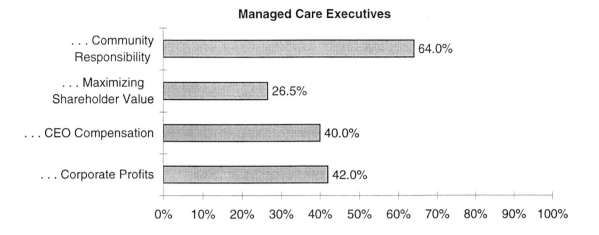

Managed Care Executives

. . . Community Responsibility — 64.0%
. . . Maximizing Shareholder Value — 26.5%
. . . CEO Compensation — 40.0%
. . . Corporate Profits — 42.0%

Percent Yes

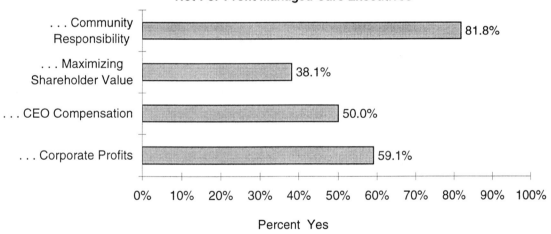

Not-For-Profit Managed Care Executives

. . . Community Responsibility — 81.8%
. . . Maximizing Shareholder Value — 38.1%
. . . CEO Compensation — 50.0%
. . . Corporate Profits — 59.1%

Percent Yes

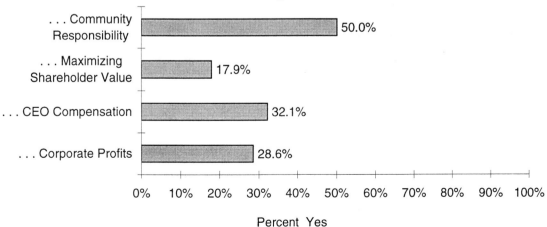

For-Profit Managed Care Executives

. . . Community Responsibility — 50.0%
. . . Maximizing Shareholder Value — 17.9%
. . . CEO Compensation — 32.1%
. . . Corporate Profits — 28.6%

Percent Yes

Should Health Care Executives Be Held to a Higher Standard Regarding . . .

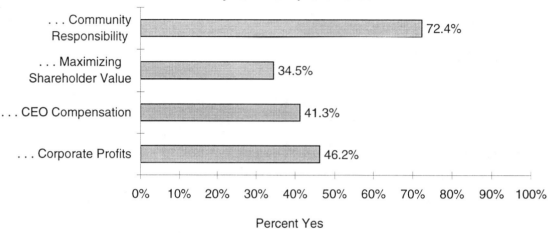

Physician Group Executives

. . . Community Responsibility	72.4%
. . . Maximizing Shareholder Value	34.5%
. . . CEO Compensation	41.3%
. . . Corporate Profits	46.2%

Percent Yes

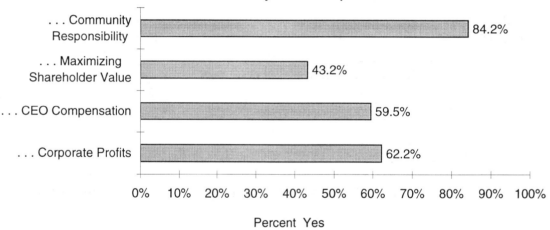

Not-For-Profit Physician Group Executives

. . . Community Responsibility	84.2%
. . . Maximizing Shareholder Value	43.2%
. . . CEO Compensation	59.5%
. . . Corporate Profits	62.2%

Percent Yes

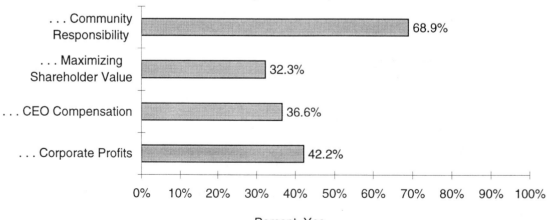

For-Profit Physician Group Executives

. . . Community Responsibility	68.9%
. . . Maximizing Shareholder Value	32.3%
. . . CEO Compensation	36.6%
. . . Corporate Profits	42.2%

Percent Yes